ESSENTIALS OF
LAW FOR MEDICAL
PRACTITIONERS

D1615564

ESSENTIALS OF LAW FOR MEDICAL PRACTITIONERS

Kim Forrester
RN, BA, LLB (Advanced), PhD,
Barrister at Law
Associate Professor, Faculty of Health Science and
Medicine, Bond University, Queensland

Debra Griffiths
RN (Mid), BA, LLB, LLM, PhD,
Legal Practitioner
Senior Lecturer, Faculty of Medicine, Nursing and Health
Sciences, Monash University, Victoria

CHURCHILL
LIVINGSTONE

ELSEVIER

Sydney Edinburgh London New York Philadelphia St Louis Toronto

Churchill Livingstone
is an imprint of Elsevier

Elsevier Australia. ACN 001 002 357
(a division of Reed International Books Australia Pty Ltd)
Tower 1, 475 Victoria Avenue, Chatswood, NSW 2067

National Library of Australia Cataloguing-in-Publication Data

---

Forrester, Kim.

Essentials of law for medical practitioners / Kim Forrester, Debra Griffiths.

ISBN: 9780729539142 (pbk.)

Includes index.

Medical laws and legislation--Australia.

Griffiths, Debra.

344.94041

Publisher: Sophie Kaliniecki
Developmental Editor: Neli Bryant
Publishing Services Manager: Helena Klijn
Project Coordinator: Natalie Hamad
Cover and internal design by Trina McDonald
Edited, proofread and indexed by Forsyth Publishing Services
Typeset by TNQ Books and Journals
Printed in China by China Translation and Printing Services

CONTENTS

FOREWORD

Contemporary medical education and practice in Australia traverses and incorporates a wide range of ideas, information, knowledge and practical experience. Increasingly the curriculum content of Australian Medical Schools includes the legal principles, legislative provisions and case law that direct, underpin and support the practice of medicine. This first edition of the text, *Essentials of Law for Medical Practitioners*, written by Dr Kim Forrester and Dr Debra Griffiths, not only meets an expanding need for discipline specific legal content within the medical degree program, it does so in a way that enhances and compliments existing medical curriculum content. This text is particularly useful in that it meets both the educational requirements of the medical students while simultaneously providing a valuable information resource for medical practitioners.

Dr Forrester and Dr Griffiths are registered nurses with many decades of clinical experience. They are both admitted as lawyers and hold academic positions at Bond University and Monash University, respectively. They are actively involved in the teaching of medical students and research in the area of medical law. As the authors of this text they therefore bring a unique perspective and understanding of the practical application of the law to clinical practice.

The text is written in a manner which aims to assist medical students and practitioners to identify and understand their legal responsibilities and obligations when providing patient or client care and treatment. Each chapter of the text includes learning objectives, scenario questions and answers, review questions and activities in addition to suggested further readings. This approach compliments the current problem-based learning pedagogy and interactive learning strategies adopted by many medical faculties. The content of this book includes an introduction to the Australian legal system, an overview of the quality and safety framework in health, the legal requirements in relation to documentation, privacy and confidentiality of patient information, the law of negligence and consent, the legal considerations relevant to end of life decisions, fertility and reproduction, medication handling and administration, professional regulation and clinical research.

The authors have provided a comprehensive explanation and overview of the most common areas of law impacting on daily clinical practice. The text makes an important and significant contribution to the ultimate aim of medical education; to produce competent medical practitioners.

Professor Steve Wesselingh, BMBS FRACP PhD
Dean, Faculty of Medicine, Nursing & Health Sciences
Monash University, Australia

PREFACE

This book has been written with the intention of providing medical students and medical practitioners with an overview of the legal principles and law that applies to, or influences, everyday clinical practice. Current medical practice requires a working knowledge of a broad range of legal areas ranging from patient consent, end of life issues and privacy, through to the more recent and emergent areas relating to quality and safety in patient care and research.

Medical practitioners and students of medicine are required to be sufficiently informed so as to ensure that their clinical practice reflects legal expectations. In a country with many states and territories, each with its own ability to make and shape the law, practitioners are faced with differing legal expectations or approaches to a number of practice areas. This book seeks to introduce and provide, for the practitioner and student alike, the basis for an initial understanding of many key areas of law as they relate to medical practice. Though the law is always evolving and changing, this book addresses the current legal position and attempts, where relevant, to provide some background in a number of areas, which highlight or explain the more recent changes and legal expectations.

The authors both have many years experience working as health professionals in various public and private environments and they are both lawyers with interest, research and teaching experience in the everyday practice of health professionals. It is with teaching experience in mind that this book has been formulated with objectives at the commencement of each chapter and review questions, scenarios (complete with answers at the end of the book) and further readings, located at the conclusion of each chapter. The authors acknowledge that the law is often imprecise, nevertheless they have highlighted and commented on those areas of the law that lack clarity. This book is not intended to provide legal advice, rather it is a starting point when medical practitioners and students are seeking to explore a medico–legal topic which may influence clinical decisions and practice.

Chapters 1–2 provide an introduction to the features of the Australian legal system and issues relating to adverse events, complaints mechanisms and government strategies designed to assist in the quality and safety of healthcare. Chapters 3–4 address the significance of maintaining accurate and contemporaneous patient records and the obligations and exceptions of medical practitioners in relation to privacy and confidentiality. Chapter 5 considers the law of negligence, outlining the elements of the action, highlighting the significant Australian cases and addressing expected standards of medical practice, while Chapter 6 discusses the important issue of consent. Chapter 7 considers end of life decisions, including processes for advance directives, withdrawal of treatment and guardianship requirements. Chapter 8 deals with key areas relating to infertility and reproductive technology, including the differing approaches to the law of abortion, the rights of the foetus and father, cloning and surrogacy. Chapter 9–10 contain pertinent practice features relating to medication prescription, administration and mental health legislation. Chapter 11 provides information relating to registration and the recent changes to move to a national framework of registration and regulation. Chapter 12 introduces readers to the legal issues relevant to clinical research, including the standards provided by the national funding bodies and the significance of maintaining research practices consistent with legal and ethical expectations.

Kim Forrester
Debra Griffiths

ACKNOWLEDGMENTS

The preparation of this manuscript has been both challenging and inspiring. There are individuals who have contributed to and supported the formulation of this text. The authors wish to express their thanks and dedicate this book to Dr Katya Goeneveld and Dr Edmond Kwan who, as medical students of Bond University, provided thoughtful and constructive feedback to the initial drafts of this text, Mrs Phyllis Newnham who has been an inspiration and mentor not only in relation to this book but also to a generation of Australian health professionals, and Mr George Conrad for his endless support and very valuable contribution in researching and checking resource materials. The legislation and commentary in this text is as current as possible at the time of going to press; however, no statement of the law should be relied on without verification.

REVIEWERS

David Adam
MBBS/BA student, University of Western Australia, Perth
Charles Austin-Woods, BSc (Hons), MBBS
Basic Psychiatry Trainee, Shellharbour Hospital, Shellharbour
Sarah Jensen, BMSc, MBBS
Intern, The Canberra Hospital, ACT
Tiffany Khoo, MBBS
Intern, Sir Charles Gairdner Hospital, Perth
Felicity Lee
6th year medical student (MBBS), University of Western Australia, Perth
Dinusha Subasinghe
Medical Student, University of Western Australia, Perth

1

Introduction to law

LEARNING OBJECTIVES

This chapter aims to introduce you to the features of the Australian legal system relevant to medical practice and the provision of healthcare services. While reading this chapter you should focus on:

- identifying the sources of the law
- understanding the different types of law
- identifying the features of the Australian legal system
- differentiating between criminal and civil law
- explaining the operation of the doctrine of precedent
- describing how to find and read a case citation
- understanding how to read an Act (also called a statute).

INTRODUCTION

Medical services are, to a significant extent, regulated and controlled by the law and the legal system. For example, a medical student is required by law to fulfil the educational and practical components of a medical degree before seeking registration to practice. Once registered as a medical practitioner it will be necessary to consider the relevant legal principles and issues prior to making clinical decisions about care and treatment of patients and clients. The provision of healthcare by medical practitioners, as with any other health professional, is therefore based on a framework of legal principles and legislative provisions which regulate and determine the standard of care to be delivered and the rights and obligations of both the providers and the recipients of the care. This area of law, which has come to be referred to as *health law* or *medical law*, operates to control not only what medical practitioners and healthcare institutions are expected to do, but also what they are to refrain from doing as part of their professional practice in the provision of their services.

An understanding of health law is fundamental to the provision of safe and competent medical care to a patient or client and, as such, exists as a resource for professional decision-making. Within the Australian context, health law refers to a wide variety of legal concepts. These include the common law, civil and criminal law, contract law, the regulation of industrial relations and agreements as well as the statutory arrangements between state and federal governments and Australia's commitment to international treaties.

As health law is one subject area of the law that governs the conduct of medical practitioners, it is important to have an understanding of the Australian legal system and the language and terminology relevant to legal processes and structures. The purpose of this chapter is therefore to provide you with a broad outline of the structure and features of the Australian legal system, including the hierarchy of the courts, the impact of the doctrine of precedent and the sources of the law, so as to assist in an understanding of the content of the following chapters.

WHERE DOES THE LAW COME FROM?

The Australian legal system, as it currently exists, developed from both the historical links with Britain as a colonial power and the federation of the colonies. Each colony had developed independently and came together as the Commonwealth of Australia in 1901. Initially the British imposed their laws and system of government on the individual colonies. Despite the fact that each of the colonies had developed its own constitution by the end of the 1890s, it was considered desirable that they federate under one constitution. The Commonwealth Constitution Act 1900 (UK), passed by the British Parliament, effectively transformed each of the colonies into separate states federated under the name of the Commonwealth of Australia.

In Australia, there are two *sources of the law*:

1 The first is *legislation* passed by the parliaments at both the state and federal levels. Each of the state parliaments, through their individual constitutions, may pass laws for the 'peace, welfare and good government' of the state.[1] In addition, the federal parliament may pass legislation as specifically determined by the Commonwealth Constitution.

2 The second source is the law which has developed from *decisions of judges handed down by the courts*. This is also referred to as 'common law'.

As the laws emanate from the state, territory and federal parliaments and the courts it is necessary that medical practitioners have an understanding of the laws that control and regulate the practice. Refer to Table 1.1.

> **Table 1.1** Where the law comes from
>
> **Judge-made or common law**
> - Judges decide on cases brought before the courts.
> - Court proceedings are initiated by litigants (the parties to the proceedings) who have a dispute needing a legal remedy.
> - Judges develop common law principle known as precedents.
> - Cases are decided on the evidence presented and also within the parameters of established precedent or prior judgments.
> - Judges apply legal remedies to actual disputes between people, or about points of law including equitable principles.
> - The *ratio decidendi* is the reason for deciding or the principle of law upon which the case was decided.
> - The judgment may contain comments that clarify a situation but do not make new law (*obiter dictum*). Comments made in *obiter* are not regarded as new law.
>
> **Legislation or statutory law (also referred to as an Act)**
> - Legislation passed by parliament on a matter is known as a statute or Act (primary legislation).
> - Statutory bodies and ministers have the power to make regulations and rules (delegated legislation).
> - Legislation can apply to specific groups, individuals or context, or to the whole population.
> - Judges may be asked to interpret the meaning of certain sections of legislation or regulations should a dispute arise in response to the application of the legislation.

Australia is often referred to as a common law country. This means that the system of government and courts are, in the main, similar to those of other common law countries, for example, the United Kingdom, Canada and New Zealand. These countries also have both common law (from the courts) and statutory law (from the parliament) embodied in their legal systems.

Parliamentary law

One of the functions of a parliament is to enact *legislation*, also known as *Acts* or *statutes*, which are designed to regulate certain aspects of society. An Act of Parliament is considered to be the primary source of the law. This means that the law contained in the Act has priority over the common law (judicial decisions from the courts). Some states or territories have Codes. Where a Code exists, it is intended to be a complete statement of law in that particular area; for example, the Criminal Code (WA) which is intended to operate independently of the case law. While parliament enacts the legislation, the role of the court is to interpret those sections of the legislation that are relevant to the cases before it.

The state and federal parliaments consist of a lower house of representatives and an upper house of review. The exceptions are Queensland and the territories where there are no upper houses of parliament. There is an established procedure for the passage of legislation through both the state and federal parliaments. An item of legislation will be known as a 'Bill' prior to it being finally passed into law when it then becomes an Act. Refer to Figure 1.1.

There are many Acts of Parliament at both the state and federal levels which regulate and control the practice of medical practitioners and the provision of medical services. To give some examples, at the state level, there are statutes that set the standard of practice against which the conduct of medical practitioners will be compared in making a decision as to whether there has been a breach of the duty of care, legislation identifying substitute decision-makers when a patient lacks capacity to make their own healthcare decisions, legislation controlling workplace health and safety and legislation providing avenues for complaints by healthcare consumers about the care they have received from a medical practitioner. At the federal level, the legislation may address issues such as funding and regulating Commonwealth healthcare agencies and services.

The law at the state and federal level is also impacted upon by Australia's international obligations. International law is a body of rules that regulate and control the conduct of nations in their dealings with one another in an international context. These general principles of international conduct are variously called treaties, protocols or declarations and are negotiated by members of the United Nations. When the Commonwealth government is a signatory to an international treaty, it must pass domestic legislation that is consistent with the obligations of that particular treaty. Therefore, the influence of international treaties and conventions on Australian domestic law is becoming increasingly significant. For example, the language of the mental health legislation in each of the states and territories draws heavily on the Universal Declaration of Human Rights and the laws in relation to children reflect the obligations imposed under the Declaration of the Rights of the Child (Article 4) and the United Nations Convention on the Rights of the Child (Article 24). Australia is a signatory to these documents.

The process of enacting an Act (statute)

While a law is progressing through parliament, it is referred to as a *Bill*. Once passed by parliament and assented to by the Governor-General, it becomes an *Act of Parliament*. The process involved in the passing of an Act entails the following of certain procedures in a prescribed sequence as shown in Figure 1.1.

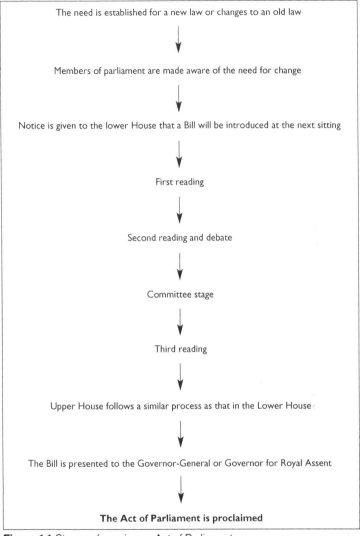

The need is established for a new law or changes to an old law

Members of parliament are made aware of the need for change

Notice is given to the lower House that a Bill will be introduced at the next sitting

First reading

Second reading and debate

Committee stage

Third reading

Upper House follows a similar process as that in the Lower House

The Bill is presented to the Governor-General or Governor for Royal Assent

The Act of Parliament is proclaimed

Figure 1.1 Stages of passing an Act of Parliament

The first stage is when members of parliament are given notice that at the next sitting of parliament a Bill will be introduced. Explanatory documents and a brief outline of the reasons for the Bill usually, but not always, accompany this announcement. The Bill is then placed on the agenda for the next parliamentary sitting. Unless the Bill pertains to a matter of urgency, it is not dealt with in detail at that sitting other than by way of a reading of the long title. This is known as the *first reading* and generally the whole Bill is not read. Ministers are given the documents to take away and read in preparation for the next stage. If the matter is urgent then standing orders will be suspended and the Bill will be debated and passed that day. Such a situation occurred in New South Wales in 1984 when the Minister for Health was given power to close public hospitals without prior consultation with the public or officers of the Department of Health. As a result, and despite public outcry, Crown Street Women's Hospital in Sydney was closed the following day.

Under ordinary circumstances, the Bill is debated at a later date. This is referred to as the *second reading*. At that time the matter is debated and the parties in opposition may propose amendments before the Bill is passed by the lower house.

At the committee stage, each of the provisions of the Bill will be debated with the full house of parliament sitting as a committee. This stage of the process is a procedural mechanism and does not require the members of the parliament to operate as an investigative committee. The purpose is to consider the details of a Bill after the second reading and examine any amendments proposed by the upper house if it is referred back. Basically this process is a way of determining whether any of the provisions in the Bill fail to meet the intention of the proposed law, or if there are any unintended consequences arising from any sections of the Bill. The Bill then moves on to a *third reading* and is passed by the lower house. In situations where the government has an overwhelming majority in the house, it is possible that the Bill can be forced through all of these processes and emerge without undergoing the scrutiny that would be insisted upon if the numbers of government and opposition were more balanced.

The Bill is then referred to the upper house where it is examined and debated in a manner and sequence similar to that of the lower house. Any amendments to the Bill recommended by the upper house are referred back to the lower house and if these are accepted, the Bill is presented to the Governor-General or Governor for Royal Assent. Once this occurs the Bill becomes an Act of Parliament. The Act may not become effective immediately as it must be proclaimed. Sometimes the proclamation date will be mentioned in the Act, but usually it will be at a date to be fixed. One reason for this delay is to enable the executive government or bureaucracy to establish the necessary mechanisms for implementing the Act. Rarely will an Act be set up to take effect retrospectively.

REGULATIONS

One of the last sections in an Act confers on the Governor-General the power to make regulations that may be necessary for the administration of the Act. Regulations provide the essential details of administration that may change more frequently than the Act can be amended by parliament. Regulations are necessary to enable the daily implementation of the Act. The regulations are called *delegated legislation*. Regulations are usually drafted in the Attorney-General's Department, advised by the department responsible for administering the Act. Though the regulations are tabled in parliament they do not progress through parliament in exactly the same manner as a Bill.

Statutory interpretation

Statutes and regulations determine much of the professional activity in the delivery of healthcare. For example, the respective civil liability legislation in each of the states and territories identifies the standard of care for health professionals; the legislation and regulations controlling drugs and poisons set out the requirements for the storage, possession and administration of drugs and poisons; and the guardianship legislation provides for a substitute decision-maker for those patients and clients who have no capacity to make healthcare decisions. Legislative provisions pertaining to the health industry are therefore regularly amended and updated.

When reading legislation and regulations the focus must be on the actual words used. Examples of words that compel include *will*, *must* or *shall* whereas words such as *may* are discretionary. The first step in interpreting the legislation is to read the statute as a whole so that the context of the words can be identified. Words that have a simple meaning can take on a technical or special meaning in legislation. Explanatory notes sometimes accompany the statute and associated regulations, to help resolve ambiguity or emphasise the intention of the law. The interpretation of statutes is now governed by various commonwealth, state and territory Interpretation Acts[2] that enshrine the common law rules regarding interpretation of legislation.

Legislation may be accessed via hard copy or 'online' via the world wide web (www) or other dedicated databases generated and maintained by Commonwealth, state and territory governments. In addition to the individual government websites,[3] all Australian legislation can be found at www.austlii.edu.au.[4] The format of the legislation in hard copy will differ from that available online however, the following aims to provide a general overview to assist in reading an Act.

The coat of arms of the particular jurisdiction usually appears at the top of the front page of an Act. All Acts are given a number; for example, the Health Quality and Complaints Commission Act 2006 (Qld) is Act No 25 of 2006. Numbering is strictly in the order in which the Acts are assented to by the Governor-General.[5] If the date of assent is included it usually appears in brackets under the long title (see Figure 1.2 Reading an Act); this is the date on which a Bill formally completes its passage through the parliament and meets the constitutional requirements for becoming an Act. It is not necessarily the date on which the Act comes into effect (see Commencement in Figure 1.2).

The layout of an Act depends on its subject matter. Many Acts are divided into chapters and/or parts, which are like chapters in a book. For example, the Health Quality and Complaints Commission Act 2006 (Qld) has 241 sections in 17 chapters. Within many of the chapters are parts, which are broken down further into divisions. For example, 'Chapter 1 — Preliminary' is comprised of sections 1 to 10 and contains items such as the short title, the commencement, main objectives, who is bound by the Act, the dictionary and meanings of 'health service', 'provider', and 'user'. Certain items and prescribed forms are more conveniently set out in a list appended to an Act. This is achieved in the form of a schedule. Sections in the Act will refer to a schedule and this has the effect of incorporating it into the law. The schedules in the Health Quality and Complaints Commission Act 2006 (Qld) identify facilities and institutions that are declared to be, or declared not to be, health services, relevant registration boards, amendments to other Acts consequential to the operation of this Act, and a dictionary of terms.

Delegated legislation

An Act as passed by parliament may provide that a particular person or body, for example a Minister of the Crown, the Governor-General or professional regulatory authority, is delegated the power to make rules, regulations, by-laws or ordinances in relation to specified matters. For example, section 101 of the Healthcare Complaints Act 1993 (NSW), empowers the Governor, under the Act to:

(1) …make regulations, not inconsistent with this Act, for or with respect to any matter that by this Act is required or permitted to be prescribed or that is necessary or convenient to be prescribed for carrying out or giving effect to this Act.

(2) The regulation may create an offence punishable by a penalty not exceeding 20 penalty units.

Although this delegated power is derived from the Act and does not exist in its own right, such rules, regulations, by-laws and ordinances are binding and are to be read as one with the Act. A regulation made

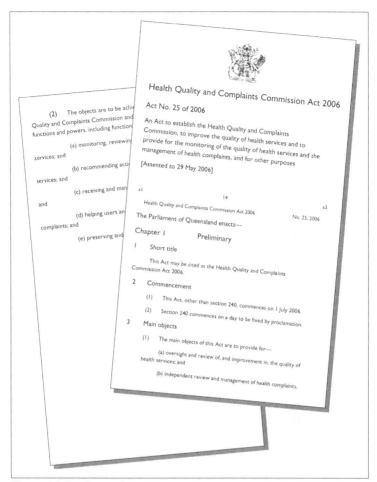

Figure 1.2 Reading an Act

under the delegated power is inherently more detailed and precise in its practical application than what is provided in the Act. It is of note that in relation to the management of drugs and poisons, it is often the regulations that state the individual practitioner's obligations in prescribing and administering the substances.

Common law

The common law is the accumulated body of law made by judges as a result of decisions in cases that come before the courts. Since the Norman Conquest in the 11th century the decisions handed down by judges have been applied in similar cases that came before them. The recording of cases and the principles established in the decisions provided a level of certainty in the operation of the law (refer to the doctrine of precedent below). These decisions can be located in the law reports of the jurisdiction where the case was decided.

Australia inherited the common law at the time of British settlement. However, since that time, both prior to and following federation, the Australian legal system has continued to develop a large body of judge-made law. *Generally, statute law overrides common law and common law prevails when no specific statute exists.* Both common law and statute law are applied in the courts. In Australia, there is a hierarchy of courts (refer to Figure 1.3) within the state and territory jurisdictions and the federal jurisdiction.

One feature of the common law is the development of *equitable principles*. These principles were developed by the English Court of Chancery. Equitable principles have evolved to address the issues of fairness and justice in those cases where common law remedies were considered to be inadequate. The rules of equity prevail over inconsistent common law rules. An example of an equitable maxim is 'He who comes to equity must come with clean hands'. That is, where parties are seeking an equitable remedy, they themselves must have behaved in an honest, fair and lawful manner.

THE COURT HIERARCHY

The Australian court system is structured hierarchically so as to delineate the extent of authority and the jurisdictional limits of each court (refer to Figure 1.3). The word *jurisdiction* refers to the authority, or power, vested in a court of law allowing it to adjudicate or decide on an action, suit, petition or application brought before it. Jurisdictional power varies according to the seriousness of the offence, the amount of compensation that can be awarded, the nationality or place of residence of the parties, whether the matters are criminal or civil in nature, or even when and where the offence or event occurred. For example, a charge of unsatisfactory professional conduct bought against a medical practitioner will be heard initially by a disciplinary tribunal such as the Queensland Civil and Administrative Tribunal. This tribunal has, under the relevant legislation, the jurisdiction, or power, to make a finding of guilt or innocence and, if necessary, make an order if the medical practitioner is found guilty. There is no such jurisdiction or power under the legislation for the District or Supreme Court to hear the charge or make an order. Another example is a claim by a patient alleging negligence against a medical practitioner which would be heard in a civil court. If a medical practitioner were charged with murder,

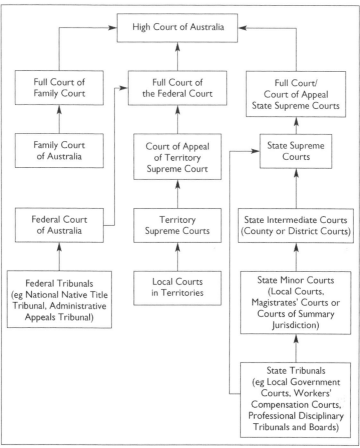

Figure 1.3 The court system[6]

manslaughter or criminal negligence in relation to the death of their patient this trial would be conducted in a criminal court. Clearly courts such as the Family, Maritime or Environmental Courts would have no power (jurisdiction) to hear such matters, award damages or pass sentence should the plaintiff or prosecution succeed.

Original and appellate jurisdiction

When a matter first appears, the court in which it is heard has what is known as *original jurisdiction*. Before a decision may be appealed in another court, the dissatisfied party must be able to establish appropriate grounds. In this case, the subsequent court will be exercising its *appellate jurisdiction*. A decision may be the subject of an appeal in certain circumstances, including when a judge has misdirected a jury, made an error in relation to admitting or refusing to admit evidence, or there is an issue as to the severity or leniency of the sentence. For example, the Supreme Court may hear a matter and if its decision is appealed, then the Court of Appeal of the Supreme Court will hear the following case using its appellate jurisdiction, where appropriate. Appellate jurisdiction is restricted to the superior courts including the District/County Court, Supreme Court, Federal Court, Family Court and High Court. In relation to the High Court, special leave (permission) must be sought before it will exercise its appellate jurisdiction. An overview of the court hierarchy follows, to illustrate the differences in both structure and jurisdiction of the courts in the hierarchy. Refer to Figure 1.3.

Overview of the courts/tribunals

Magistrates' Courts or *Local Courts* are presided over by magistrates who are addressed during the proceedings as 'Your Worship', or in some jurisdictions as 'Your Honour'. Magistrates sit alone as there are no juries at this level in the court structure. The jurisdiction of the Magistrates' Courts is determined by the relevant legislation in each of the states and territories. These courts are the lowest courts in the hierarchy and determine the greatest volume of cases. As a general principle, Magistrates' Courts deal with minor civil and criminal matters and with more serious criminal matters by way of committal proceedings. For example, a medical practitioner may appear before a magistrate in relation to practising without a licence or being in possession of property they have unlawfully removed from the premises of the employing institution. It is from this level of the hierarchy that magistrates are appointed as coroners or to preside over Children's Courts and Licensing Courts. These courts developed in response to the need to reduce the load from the Magistrates' Courts and in recognition of the requirement for specialist knowledge. Coroners' Courts are of particular relevance to medical practitioners. It is in the Coroners' Courts that an inquiry will be conducted to establish the identity, the time, circumstances and/or cause of a patient's death. The jurisdiction of a coroner to conduct an inquiry into the death of a person is determined by the legislation in each of the individual states and territories.

Coroners' Courts are presided over by a coroner who is, as indicated above, a magistrate. The significance of the coroner lies in their power, inherent in the relevant legislation, to hold public hearings on 'reportable' deaths' (referred to as a Coroner's Inquest) in which the public issues can be investigated and considered. In Australia a coroner will usually be assisted in the inquest by the expertise of specialist investigators such as police, scientists, forensic pathologists, aviation investigators, navigation investigators and medical specialists. The role and function of the Coroner's Court, and the coroner, is established by the legislation in each state and territory.[7] The principal role of the coroner is to investigate deaths that are unexpected, unnatural, accidental or violent. These are called 'reportable deaths' and must be reported to the coroner. The legislation in each of the states and territories identifies the meaning of a 'reportable death' and the jurisdiction of the coroner. Generally, a 'reportable death' will include not only as stated above, one that is unexpected, unnatural and/or violent, but also a suspicious death, a death that occurs following an operation, an anaesthetic, a medical, surgical, dental, diagnostic or health related procedure, or when a person dies in custody or in care. As the requirements differ between the individual jurisdictions, a medical student or medical practitioner must familiarise themselves with the legal provisions applicable in the state or territory in which they are practising. In addition, the role of the coroner is to determine whether there are public health or safety issues arising from the death and whether there is any action that is required in order to prevent deaths occurring in similar circumstances. A feature of this court is that it is designed to be inquisitorial rather than adversarial. The coroner is not bound by the rules of evidence and may conduct an inquiry in any manner which facilitates the inquisitorial nature of the proceedings.

District or *County Courts* are presided over by judges who sit with or without a jury. Their jurisdiction is both original and appellate. District Courts hear and determine civil and criminal matters that are governed by the relevant legislation in each of the states and territories. As a general statement, all criminal matters other than murder, manslaughter, serious drug matters and serious sexual assault will be heard in the District or County Court. The judges who preside in these courts and more senior courts are referred to as 'Your Honour'.

Supreme Courts are the most senior courts in the states and territories and are presided over by a judge, with or without a jury. Supreme Courts have an internal appeal mechanism referred to as the Full Court of the Supreme Court. When the court is sitting as the Full Court, there are three or more judges. While the jurisdictional limitations are determined by the relevant legislation in each of the states and territories, in civil matters the court may hear claims for unlimited damages and in the criminal jurisdiction for murder, manslaughter, serious drug matters and serious sexual assault. It is in the Supreme Court that most medical negligence cases involving medical practitioners will be conducted.

The *High Court* was established under the Constitution of the Commonwealth of Australia and is comprised of the Chief Justice and six other judges. The first High Court was appointed under the Judiciary Act 1903 (Cth). Historically, the Privy Council in England was the final Court of Appeal for State Supreme Courts and the High Court of Australia. The right to appeal to the Privy Council was abolished progressively between the 1960s and the 1980s. While the High Court is the most senior court in the Australian hierarchy, it is possible for a case to be heard by an international court or tribunal. This can occur if federal parliament has become a signatory under an international declaration or convention.

The original jurisdiction of the High Court concerns any matters that involve interpretation of the Constitution of the Commonwealth of Australia, or disputes between residents of different states, or between states and the Commonwealth government.

Provided permission (referred to as 'leave') has been obtained, appeals to the High Court of Australia can come from the Federal Court, the Family Court and the Supreme Court of any state or territory involving civil or criminal matters. The full bench of the High Court, comprising all seven justices, hears cases in which the principles are of major public importance, involve interpretation of the Constitution or invite departure from a previous decision of the High Court. Appeals from state and territory Supreme Court decisions, and from decisions of the Family Court, will be dealt with by the full court of not less than two justices. A single justice may hear and determine specified matters. You will note in the following chapters that a number of the cases in relation to actions taken against medical practitioners have progressed on appeal from the state or territory courts to the High Court of Australia for determination.

The *Federal Court of Australia* was established under the Federal Court of Australia Act 1976 (Cth). This court was set up to further reduce the load on the High Court. Constitutional cases involving such matters as trade practices, bankruptcy and federal industrial disputes are heard. Appeals on decisions can be made to the High Court or the Full Court of the Federal Court.

The *Federal Magistrates' Court* was established in 2000 to deal with less complex matters than would otherwise have been heard in the Federal or Family Courts. The range of cases coming before the Federal Magistrates' Court include matters relating to bankruptcy, discrimination, privacy and family law. This court does not hear appeals.

Specialist tribunals may be established under Commonwealth or state laws to exercise specific jurisdiction and perform functions similar to that of the courts. The number and type of tribunals are increasing as government regulation of society becomes more complicated. Tribunals are established by statutes for different purposes and therefore their powers and composition vary greatly. Examples of tribunals include administrative appeals tribunals, tenancy tribunals, small claims tribunals and professional regulatory tribunals. These tribunals perform 'quasi judicial' functions in that they make decisions within the ambit of their limited or specific roles. Decisions are made in a variety of ways and may involve a judge or, alternatively, a board of specialists who may, or may not, be qualified in law. Unlike the courts, the tribunals do not make laws that are applied by the courts. In a number of Australian states and territories the individual specialist tribunals have been amalgamated into multi jurisdictional tribunals. The ACT Civil and Administrative Tribunal (ACAT), Queensland Civil and Administrative Tribunal (QCAT), Victorian Civil and Administrative Tribunal (VCAT), and the Western Australian State Administrative Tribunal (SAT) include an extensive range of jurisdictions. In New South Wales the Administrative Decisions Tribunal (ADT) deals with administrative appeals and particular civil matters while the Consumer, Trade and Tenancy Tribunal deals with commercial, consumer and tenancy disputes. Although tribunals lie outside the court hierarchy, appeals may be made from their decisions into the court system, if permitted under legislation. Often the role of tribunals is limited and narrowly defined.

THE DOCTRINE OF PRECEDENT (*STARE DECISIS*)

In the discussion of common law, mention was made of the role of judges in making law. The word 'common' is used to denote the fact that judges have developed a process whereby courts are, to a certain extent, bound to follow decisions they have made previously as well as being bound by decisions made by other judges at the same level of the hierarchy or in senior courts. Judge–made law, or common law, began as a custom that valued the accumulation of judicial wisdom passed on through the ages. In this way, a common thread of judicial certainty was maintained despite different judges presiding. Early in the 19th century, this custom became enshrined as a doctrine known as *stare decisis* or the doctrine of precedent. It allows for some predictability when dealing with legal matters involving courts because one is able to determine the outcomes of similar cases that have occurred before, and estimate the probability of similar judgments being passed.

The doctrine of precedent originated in England and over time developed into a sophisticated and historically consistent system of justice. The underlying principle is that if a case is decided in a certain way today then a similar case should be decided in the same way tomorrow. The reason or ground of a judicial decision is called the *ratio decidendi*. It is the *ratio decidendi* of a case which makes the decision a precedent in future cases. When the courts hand down their decisions, they are to be found in the many law reports that emanate from the state, federal and international jurisdictions. It is important to remember that many cases are not included in the published law reports; however, unreported decisions should be equally regarded as establishing precedent.

All judgments do not bind all courts. Nor are all judges compelled to follow all that has been set down in previous decisions. Precedent can only bind if it comes from a higher court within the same hierarchy. For example, a decision in the Supreme Court of NSW is binding upon the District Court in NSW and Local Courts in NSW but it is not binding on the equivalent courts in other states and territories of Australia because they are not in the same court hierarchy. Even so, a lower court in one state or territory would be unlikely to depart from a decision taken in a higher court of another Australian state or territory where the issues are similar.

Australian laws apply only to Australian courts. Australian courts are not bound to follow decisions made in foreign courts; however, they can influence decisions taken in Australia. This is sometimes referred to as *persuasive precedent*. For example, decisions made in other common law countries such as Canada or the United Kingdom may be considered by the Australian courts. Judgments made in English courts are no longer binding on any Australian court.

Case references

It is important for medical practitioners to understand decisions from the courts as contained in the various law reports. The following will provide an overview of the elements of a case reference to assist you in reading and understanding cases. For example, in the case of *Harriton v Stephens* (2006) 226 CLR 52 means:

- *Harriton v Stephens* refers to the parties involved in the case. If it is the first time the case has come to court the first party named is *the plaintiff* and the second party is *the defendant*. If the case is on appeal then the first party will be *the appellant* and the second party *the respondent*. It is usual form to italicise the names of both litigants.
- (2006) 226 CLR 52 provides information on the case and the location of the full court report of the case. This refers only to published law reports of which there is a wide range available in higher court jurisdictions.

- (2006) refers to the year the case was reported. When the year is in round brackets it indicates that the volume number, and not the year, is the essential identifying feature of the citation. When the year is in square brackets it indicates that the year is the important identifying feature of the report and that the volume number is not essential, and may not even be present. An example is [1975] VR 1. When more than one volume is published in a particular year the volumes in that year will be numbered.
- 226 refers to the volume number of the law report.
- CLR is the abbreviation for the Commonwealth Law Reports series containing the report on the case of *Harriton v Stephens*.
- 52 refers to the page reference for the beginning of the case report. Commonly used law reports are listed in the abbreviations section of the appendices.

Law reports

For medical practitioners to understand the common law principles that apply to their practice, it is necessary to have the skills to read a reported case. The following will provide an overview of the features of the case of *Rosenberg v Percival* (2001) 74 ALJR 734 (refer to Figure 1.4).

As this is an appeal to the High Court, Rosenberg is the appellant and Percival is the respondent. The letter 'v' between the names of the parties is the abbreviation of the Latin word versus and signifies that the parties are against one another in the adversarial process of litigation. Directly beneath the names of the parties is the court in which the case was decided, in this instance the High Court of Australia. Below the court title are the names of the justices before whom the case was heard, being the Chief Justice, Mr Anthony Gleeson, and Justices McHugh, Gummow, Kirby and Callinan.

As this is an appeal, the last court that decided the case is referred to next; in this case it was the Supreme Court of Western Australia. Directly below are words or phrases that are written in italics. These are the catchwords considered to be the important aspects of the case. Catchwords in this case include:

… Negligence — Breach of duty — Whether failure to warn amounted to breach — Identification and meaning of material risk.

The next section is referred to as the 'headnote' which is a summary of the case. These are the facts of the case which the reporter, responsible for providing the 'headnote' to the publisher, considered important to that decision. It is essential therefore to

HIGH COURT OF AUSTRALIA (2001)

ROSENBERG v PERCIVAL
[2001] HCA 18

Before Gleeson CJ, McHugh, Gummow, Kirby and Callinan JJ

Perth, 24 October 2000
Hobart, 5 April 2001

Appeal — Powers of appellate court — Limits of appellate review in respect of credibility-based findings.

Negligence — Causation — Failure to warn of material risk — Whether patient would have proceeded with treatment in any event.

Negligence — Breach of duty — Whether failure to warn amounted to breach — Identification and meaning of material risk.

The respondent patient sued the appellant surgeon for negligence following complications resulting from an operation on the patient's jaw. The patient alleged that the surgeon failed to warn her of the risks inherent with the surgery. It was also alleged that had the patient been aware of the risks, she would have proceeded with the operation.

The action in the District Court was dismissed. The trial judge found that the surgeon had not been negligent in not warning the patient of any material problem that might develop. The trial judge also found that even if the patient had been warned of the slight possibility of complications, she would have proceeded with the surgery in any event. The patient's appeal to the Full Court of the Supreme Court was successful. The Full Court held that the surgeon had breached his duty by failing to warn of the risks involved in the surgery. The Full Court also overturned the trial judge's finding on the credibility of the patient and ordered a re-trial on the issue of causation.

Held (unanimously allowing the appeal): (1) There was sufficient evidence to justify the trial judge's finding that the patient would have proceeded with the surgery, even if she had been adequately warned of the risks involved. The Full Court was in error in overturning the trial judge's findings. [17], [23], [92], [165], [220]

(2) An appellate court has a limited scope for review where a trial judge's findings of facts are based on an assessment of the credibility of a witness. A case must be exceptional to justify an appellate court overturning a credibility-based assessment of a trial judge. [27], [37] [41], [162]

(3) (By Kirby J) The Full Court was correct in holding that the evidence established that the surgeon had failed in his duty to provide her with a significant warning of a material risk inherent in the proposed treatment. [147]

(4) (By Gummow J) In order to ascertain whether there has been a breech of a duty to warn, the first step is to define the relevant risk by reference to the circumstances in which the injury can occur, the likelihood of the injury occurring, and the extent or severity of the potential injury if it does occur. This approach directs attention to the *content* of any warning that *could* have been given at the time. The Full Court erred in failing to identify the content of the risk. [69], [72]

(5) (By Kirby J) Unless such risks may be classified as "immaterial", in the sense of being unimportant or so rare that they can be safely ignored, they should be drawn to the notice of the patient. [149]

(6) (By Gummow J) It is not necessary when determining materiality of risk to establish that the patient, reasonable or otherwise, would not have had the treatment had he or she been warned of the risk in question. However, it is necessary that the patient would have been likely to seriously consider and weigh up the risk before reaching a decision on whether to proceed with the treatment. It was open to the trial judge to conclude that a reasonable

Figure 1.4 Reading a case

have a comprehensive understanding of the case by reading the entire judgment. The actual decision of the court, indicated by the word 'Held' contains the *ratio decidendi*. A summary of the findings of each of the judges who heard and determined the case is also provided. This may appear as separate reasons as delivered by each of the justices or, where there is agreement (where they concur), two or more justices may hand down a joint decision. At the end of the written determination the 'orders' (the judges' final decision) handed down by the court will be reported.

Cases may also be found 'online' via the world wide web (www) or on CD-ROM or disc.[4] The increase in cases able to be accumulated through storage on the electronic databases has resulted in unreported cases (those not formally reported in the printed volumes of the law reports) now being available. As an example, though the unreported case of *Edwards v Kennedy* is not available in the reported cases it is able to be located via LexisNexis, AustLII or a number of other legal databases. It is to be noted that the format of case reports on web-based and online databases differs from that of the traditional paper-based law reports in that there are no volumes or page numbers in the report, and the paragraphs are individually numbered for reference. As an example, the unreported case *Edwards v Kennedy*, a case involving allegations of medical negligence, is reported on the LexisNexis data base as:

Edwards v Kennedy BC 200901404,

Supreme Court of Victoria – Common Law Division

Kaye J

5714 of 2007

26,27 February, 12 March 2009

Citation: Edwards v Kennedy [2009] VSC 74

There are various methods of classifying the different types of law, one method being to describe law as either substantive or procedural.

Substantive law is the law that regulates citizens in specific areas of their lives. This includes industrial law, contract law, criminal law, family law, tort law and even constitutional law. *Procedural law* governs the way in which laws are implemented and enforced. This would include rules of the courts, rules applied to civil and criminal procedures and rules of evidence. An understanding of the different types of law will assist with identification of the differences, similarities and effects of both the substantive and procedural law. Both common law (the decisions of judges in cases before the courts) and parliamentary law (Acts of state and Federal parliaments) combine to produce substantive law. The list below is not exhaustive but refers mainly to those areas of law that impact on the practice of medical practitioners.

Some examples of substantive law include the following.

- *Industrial law* where matters arising from the employer and employee relationship are identified and defined. Primarily industrial law involves agreements and awards that establish the obligations and rights of both parties in their working environment.

- *Contract law* which places agreements within a formal framework that enables promises made by the parties to be enforced. Medical practitioners come into contact with a range of contractual agreements, including contracts of employment, contracts between a specialist medical practitioner and their patients and contracts for the purchase and sale of goods and services.

- *Criminal law* identifies activities which the state considers unacceptable to a degree that warrants punishment. Criminal law may apply in the healthcare setting in relation to grossly unacceptable conduct or behaviour such as theft, criminal assault, manslaughter or murder.

- *Tort law* is concerned with civil wrongs. The word 'tort' essentially means 'twisted' and was interpreted as amounting to conduct which was 'wrong'. The primary purpose of tort law is to redress the wrongs suffered by a plaintiff. This is accomplished by the provision of compensation which seek to put the injured party in the position they would have been in, had they not suffered the damage. There is rarely an element of punishment; however, one of the functions of tort law is to act as a deterrent by regulating behaviour to an acceptable standard. In the healthcare context, examples of tort law include negligence, negligent misrepresentation and trespass to the person.

- *Constitutional law* sets out the legal framework within which the country's political and legal systems operate.

Procedural law involves the processes of litigation, controlling the actions of all parties involved prior to trial and then regulating the way the trial will proceed. This aspect of law is the machinery that allows substantive law to be processed and applied. For example, it will determine: the legal rules governing evidence that can be presented in court; how a case progresses through court; and the requirements of proof.

Another significant distinction of the law is that between civil and criminal law. Table 1.2 sets out the common distinguishing features that differentiate civil from criminal jurisdictions.

Table 1.2 Features of the civil and criminal jurisdictions

Features	Civil	Criminal
Who brings the legal action.	The legal action involves one citizen, for example a patient, bringing an action against another citizen (who could also be a corporation such as a hospital or healthcare facility).	The legal action is initiated by the state (represented by the public prosecutor or the police) against an individual or institution (the defendant) who has allegedly committed the crime.
The standard required to prove.	On the balance of probabilities.	Beyond reasonable doubt.
The outcome sought in a civil action.	Financial compensation.	Punishment through imprisonment or fine.

GENERAL FEATURES OF THE AUSTRALIAN LEGAL SYSTEM

Adversarial system

The function of the law is to resolve disputes when there are conflicts between individuals, companies or institutions. This takes place in a court when a case is brought before a magistrate, judge, or judge and jury, and the parties are adversaries to one another and only one of the parties will be declared the 'winner'. This competition between the parties takes place within the courts and is referred to as the *adversarial process*. The role of the judge during court proceedings is to remain impartial and to ensure that the procedural rules are adhered to. The judge or jury will determine the outcome where only one of the parties to the proceedings will be successful.

This adversarial process is different from the inquisitorial approach where the court is effectively inquiring into a set of circumstances and may thereby become a participant in the actual process. That is, the court is not confined to the evidence put before it by the police and lawyers, but may seek out information in its own right as part of the process of reaching a decision. Within the healthcare context, the operation of the Coroner's Court in investigating the cause, time, and location of a death as described earlier would be classified as inquisitorial. Cases involving negligent actions, for example a patient suing a medical practitioner in negligence, will progress in an adversarial manner.

Natural justice

In a general sense, the notion of natural justice ensures that the proceedings are conducted fairly, impartially and without prejudice. Natural justice is a fundamental principle that applies to all courts and tribunals. It means that the court or tribunal must give the person against whom the accusations are made a clear statement of the actual charge, adequate time to prepare an argument or submission, and the right to be heard on all allegations. It is described as making two demands:

> before a person's legal rights are adversely affected, or their 'legitimate expectations' disappointed: (1) an opportunity to show why adverse action should not be taken…; and (2) a decision-maker whose mind is open to persuasion, or free from bias.[8]

Presumption of innocence

The law regards all accused people as being innocent until proven guilty. This is a core principle of the Australian legal system. As an example, in a criminal matter the presumption is that the accused is innocent until proven guilty. In civil proceedings, the presumption operates so as not to allocate liability until all of the elements of the action are proven.

Mediation

In all Australian jurisdictions, Alternate Dispute Resolution (ADR) is used in the civil jurisdiction as a mechanism to assist the parties, either before or after the commencement of legal proceedings, to negotiate and resolve their dispute. Mediation has become one of the more popular methods of ADR and is defined as 'a process … under which the parties use a mediator to help them resolve their dispute by negotiated agreement without adjudication'.[9] Whether mediation is the appropriate mode for the attempted resolution of a dispute will be determined on a case-by-case basis, however, in many jurisdictions both the legislation or court may refer proceedings to mediation whether or not the parties object.[10] It has been suggested the objective of ADR in legal proceedings is 'to assist the parties to reach a negotiated and satisfactory resolution of their dispute, improve access to justice and reduce the cost of delay'.[11]

SCENARIO AND ACTIVITIES

A medical practitioner working in general practice fails to order appropriate tests for a patient they have been treating for the past year. The patient continues to attend the practice, complaining of the same signs and symptoms, however, the medical practitioner ignores the complaints and tells the patient to take Panadol and rest. The patient dies suddenly and it is discovered on autopsy that the patient had a large malignant tumour which caused a rupture of the aorta and sudden death. The patient's family is now commencing legal proceedings against the medical practitioner, seeking damages for their father upon whom they were all financially dependent.

- What action do you think the family would initiate against the medical practitioner?
- In what court would such an action be conducted?
- What other courts or tribunals may be involved given the facts of this scenario?

REVIEW QUESTIONS

To ensure you have identified and understood the key points of this chapter please answer the following questions.

1 What are the sources of law in the Australian legal system?

2 Identify some Acts of Parliament (state, territory and Commonwealth/federal) that will regulate and control your practice as a medical practitioner.

3 Describe how you would identify a professional obligation that was required on the basis of the delegation of power from an Act.

4 What is the significance of the doctrine of precedent to negligence cases involving a breach of the duty of care by a medical practitioner?

5 How does the legal concept of natural justice operate?

6 Describe the difference between an adversarial and an inquisitorial process. Identify the legal proceedings in which the parties are adversaries and a legal process in which an inquiry would be undertaken.

7 Describe the legal term 'jurisdiction'.

> **8** Identify the courts in the court hierarchy from the lower court to the most senior court. Where are tribunals located in relation to the court structures?
>
> **9** Please go onto the website www.austlii.edu.au or attend the law library in your university and locate one of the following health-related cases. Identify the court in which the proceedings are being conducted, the parties to the proceedings (the litigants), the health-related legal issues and the outcome.
>
> (a) *Harriton v Stephens* (2006) 226 CLR 52.
>
> (b) *Hunter Area Health Service & Anor v Presland* [2005] NSWCA 33.
>
> (c) *Gardner; re BWV* [2003] VSC 173.
>
> **10** What are the features that distinguish a civil from a criminal action?

Further reading

Butterworths Concise Australian Legal Dictionary, 3rd ed (P Butt, ed.), Butterworths, Sydney, 2004.

Carvan, J, *Understanding the Australian Legal System*, 5th ed, Law Book Co, Sydney, 2005.

Chisholm, R and Nettheim, G, *Understanding Law*, 6th ed, Butterworths, Sydney, 2002.

Cook, C, *Laying Down the Law*, 6th ed, LexisNexis, Sydney, 2009.

Hall, K, Macken, C, *Legislation and Statutory Interpretation*, 2nd ed, LexisNexis Butterworths, Sydney, 2009.

Hanks, P, *Australian Constitutional Law*, 5th ed, Butterworths, Sydney, 1997.

Heilbronn, GN (ed.), *Introducing the Law*, 7th ed, CCH Australia, Sydney 2008.

Hinchy, R, *The Australian Legal System: History, Institutions and Method*, Pearson Education, Sydney, 2008.

Wallace, M, *Healthcare and the Law*, 3rd ed, Law Book Co, Sydney, 2001.

Waller, L, *Derham, Maher and Waller: An Introduction to Law*, 8th ed, LBC Information Services, Sydney, 2000.

Zines, L, *The High Court and the Constitution*, 4th ed, Butterworths, Sydney, 1996.

Endnotes

1 For example, the Constitution Act 1867 (Qld) s 2, and the Constitution Act 1902 (NSW) s 5. The Victorian Constitution Act 1974 s 16 provides the parliament 'to make law in and for Victoria in all cases whatsoever'.

2 Acts Interpretation Act 1901 (Cth); Interpretation Act 1987 (NSW); Interpretation of Legislation Act 1984 (Vic); Acts Interpretation Act 1915 (SA); Interpretation Act 1984 (WA); and Interpretation Act 1967 (ACT).

3 Cth: www.comlaw.gov.au, ACT: www.legislation.act.gov.au; NSW: www.legislation.nsw.gov.au; NT: www.nt.gov.au/dcm/legislation; Qld: www.legislation.qld.gov.au; SA: www.parliament.sa.gov.au/dbsearch/legsearch; Tas: www.thelaw.tas.gov.au; Vic: www.dms.dpc.vic.gov.au; WA: www.slp.wa.gov.au/statutes

4 Case law can be located on www.austlii.edu.au for all Australian jurisdictions and on individual court websites in each of the individual states and territories.

5 *Acts of Parliament: A reader's guide*, Parliament House, Canberra, 1992 (brochure).

6 Morris, G, Cook, C, Creyke, R and Geddes, R, *Laying Down the Law*, 5th ed, Butterworths, Sydney, 2001.

7 Coroners Act 1997 (ACT); Coroners Act 2009 (NSW); Coroners Act (NT); Coroners Act 2003 (Qld); Coroners Act 2003 (SA); Coroners Act 1995 (Tas); Coroners Act 2008 (Vic); Coroners Act 1996 (WA).

8 Forbes, JRS, *Justice in Tribunals*, 2nd ed, Federation Press Sydney, 2006 at 100.

9 Supreme Court of Queensland Act 1991 s 96.

10 Supreme Court of Queensland Act 1991 s 102; District Court Act 1967 (Qld) s 97; Magistrates Court Act 1921 (Qld) s 29.

11 Cairns, BC, 'A review of some innovations in Queensland Civil Procedure' (2005) 26 *Aust Bar Rev* 158 at 161.

25

2

Safety and quality in health

LEARNING OBJECTIVES

This chapter aims to introduce you to the key areas relating to safety and quality in health. While reading this chapter you should focus on:

- identifying what is meant by the terms 'adverse' or 'sentinel' events and their frequency in clinical practice
- outlining the approach adopted at the federal level to improve patient safety and quality of healthcare
- identifying the state and territory mechanisms, including their roles and powers established to deal with patient complaints
- outlining the broad process adopted to deal with a patient complaint
- explaining whether human rights or patients' rights exist in the Australian context.

INTRODUCTION

It has been estimated that on an average day in Queensland 7456 inpatients and 25 093 outpatients are cared for in the public health system.[1] If these figures are extrapolated across the public and private sectors of all Australian states and territories it becomes clear that there are many hundreds of thousands of patient–health professional contacts per year within Australia. While the vast majority of these contacts are carried out by competent, skilled professionals who deliver safe and high quality healthcare, there are mistakes made that result in patient injury and death. These mistakes occur for a wide variety of reasons, which include incidents arising from system failure through to incidents resulting from professional incompetence. Recent media coverage of high-profile litigation and community concern in relation to unacceptable medical practices in Bundaberg and Bega serve to illustrate the need for constant monitoring and analysis of the safety and quality of healthcare services. This chapter will address the attempts by government at Commonwealth, state and territory levels, with the involvement of professional bodies, to address and improve the safety and quality of healthcare in Australia, and will distinguish between human rights and patient rights.

ADVERSE PATIENT OUTCOMES

The incidence of patient injuries occurring in a healthcare context has more recently become a significant issue in considering malpractice claims against health professionals. It is important, therefore, to have an understanding of the rate at which these injuries, referred to as adverse events, adverse patient outcomes, or iatrogenic injuries, are estimated to occur.

Adverse events or *adverse patient outcomes* have been defined by Tito as:

> an unintended injury to a patient which resulted in a temporary or permanent disability, prolonged length of stay or death and which was caused by healthcare management and not by the patient's underlying disease.[2]

In Australia, there is limited information on the nature and number of adverse patient outcomes or events that occur in the healthcare system. However, the types of injuries included in these incidents could be categorised as: damage resulting from the administration of incorrect medications or incorrect dosages of medication; failure to notice significant test results or understand their significance; injuries such as infection or perforation occurring during surgical interventions; and incorrect or missed diagnosis of disease or injury. In 1994, the Australian Institute of Health and Welfare (AIHW) conducted a study that involved the examination of hospital records of patients admitted in 1992 to 28 acute and public hospitals in South Australia and New South Wales.[3] In total, 14 179 admissions were reviewed. The findings of the study were that 16.6% or 2353 of the admissions had suffered an adverse event. This percentage equated to 11% of the total admissions. Though the causes of the individual events were not examined in detail, a preliminary analysis indicated that preventability was considered to be in the vicinity of 8.2% or 1157 of the admissions.[4] Tito reported that:

> 50% of all adverse events were associated with operations, 15% related to system errors, 13% related to diagnostic errors and 2% related to anaesthesia. In the case of system error, over 50% of these were attributed to an absence of, or failure to follow, a protocol or plan.[5]

NATIONAL APPROACH TO QUALITY AND SAFETY

The Commission on Quality and Safety in Healthcare[6] was established by the Australian, state and territory governments to develop a *national* strategic framework and associated work program that will guide their efforts in improving safety and quality across the healthcare system in Australia. The Commission commenced on 1 January 2006, and its key roles are to:

- lead and coordinate improvements in safety and quality in healthcare in Australia by identifying issues and policy directions, and recommending priorities for action
- disseminate knowledge and advocate for safety and quality
- report publicly on the state of safety and quality, including performance against national standards
- recommend national data sets for safety and quality, working within current multilateral governmental arrangements for data development, standards, collection and reporting
- provide strategic advice to Health Ministers on best practice thinking to drive quality improvement, including implementation strategies
- recommend nationally agreed standards for safety and quality improvement.

The AIHW[7] is a statutory authority, established by the Australian government operating under the provisions of the Australian Institute of Health and Welfare Act 1987 (Cth). The AIHW is a national agency set up to provide information on Australia's health and welfare, through statistics and data development, that inform discussion and decisions on policy and services. The AIHW works closely with all state, territory and Australian government health, housing and community services agencies in collecting, analysing and disseminating data.

The AIHW has established and is involved in a large number of national committees and supports health and welfare investment by providing statistical expertise in a range of health, housing and community services areas. Some committees are concerned with developing standards or performance indicators, whilst others are internal committees supporting projects to influence public debate and policy. For example, the Cancer and Screening Unit at the AIHW provides the secretariat for the Australian Association of Cancer Registries (AACR) executive. Cancer registration is an important and fundamental tool in cancer monitoring. Australian states and territories are required by legislation to maintain a cancer registry of new cases of malignant cancer and the cancer statistics collected are coordinated on a national basis.

In 2007 the AIHW and the Australian Commission on Safety and Quality in Healthcare[8] published the first national report of sentinel events in Australian public hospitals.[9] *Sentinel events* have been variously defined as:

> Events that lead to serious patient harm ... Events in which death or serious harm to a patient has occurred ... An unexpected occurrence involving death or serious physical or psychological injury, or the risk thereof ... An accident with actual or potential serious harm, or death ...[10]

The report reveals that in 2004–05 there were 4.3 million admissions into 759 Australian public hospitals. These hospitals also recorded 42.6 million non-admission services to patients over the same period.[11] During this time there were 130 sentinel events reported. The most commonly reported 'event type' was procedures involving the wrong patient or body part, and the most common contributing factor was the lack of, problems with, or breakdown in, the rules, policies or procedures.

More recently the AIHW released its fifth report in the Safety and Quality of Healthcare Series, *Medical Indemnity National Data Collection Public Sector 2006–07*.[12] The report contains information on the allegations of harm that give rise to claims against medical practitioners, the people affected by such claims and the amounts, lengths of time and modes of finalisation of medical indemnity claims. In the 2006–07 reporting year, 4100 claims against medical practitioners were current. In 27% of the finalised claims no payment was made and no defence or claimant legal costs were incurred. Fifty-five per cent of claims (1218) resulted in a claim of under $10 000 and in 83% the total claim (including legal costs) was less than $100 000. Approximately 4% of claims had a total claim of over $500 000. In relation to the mode of finalisation, almost half the claims were 'discontinued', two-thirds recorded as 'settled other' and one-fifth settled through 'state and territory complaints processes'. Fewer than 5% of the claims were resolved through the 'Courts'.[13] The data indicated:

> *General surgery* was the most frequently recorded 'Clinical Service Context' ... overtaking O*bstetrics* for the first time. Three recorded clinical service contexts (*General surgery, Obstetrics,* and *Accident and emergency*) were associated with roughly half of all claims. The pattern was similar for new claims arising during the year. Medical and surgical procedures (36%) were the most commonly recorded 'Primary incident/ allegation type' in medical indemnity claims, followed by *Diagnosis* (23%) and T*reatment* (16%).[14]

As litigation has historically involved medical practitioners and the provision of medical services, it is not surprising that much of the research into the incidence of adverse events has focused on this sector of healthcare services. However, this is not to suggest that the incidence of such injuries is purely a medical issue. The fact that patients are injured as a result of treatments and procedures, or lack thereof, within the healthcare system is an issue of concern for all health professionals. As members of a healthcare team, all health professionals are potentially liable for the damage or injury sustained by a patient while under their care.

When a patient or client sustains damage or suffers an adverse event while under the care of a health institution or provider, he or she may wish to have the issues addressed without resorting to the legal system. While recognising that tort law aims to maintain the quality of healthcare through the threat of litigation, it must also be considered that it is often ineffective in the pursuit of this goal. A high proportion of negligent conduct never becomes the subject of a claim and, of those that reach the courts, the costs — financial, professional and emotional — are often high for all the parties involved.

National accreditation and the establishment of consistent standards

An additional role of the Commission on Quality and Safety in Healthcare has entailed the initiation of a review of health services accreditation arrangements in 2006; the aim being to propose a package of reforms, including a national set of standards by which health services could be assessed. The review and implementation of the new model of national safety and quality accreditation for health service organisations has focused on the following key areas:

- review of National Safety and Quality Accreditation Arrangements
- development of an Alternative Model for Safety and Quality Accreditation
- development of the draft National Safety and Quality Healthcare Standards
- consultation on the draft National Safety and Quality Standards
- piloting the draft National Safety and Quality Standards
- national coordination of accreditation
- legislation and regulation review
- accreditation research projects.

Since the initial review, National Safety and Quality Healthcare (NSQH) Standards have been formulated. The first stage of implementing the accreditation reforms has commenced and focused on the development of a preliminary set of NSQH Standards. The draft NSQH Standards focus on areas that are essential to improving the safety and quality of care for patients. The NSQH Standards provide an explicit statement of the expected level of safety and quality of care to be provided to patients by health services organisations and provide a means for assessing an organisation's performance. The draft NSQH Standards address the following areas:

- governance for safety and quality in health service organisations
- healthcare associated infection
- medication safety
- patient identification and procedure matching
- clinical handover.

A pilot study of the refined draft NSQH Standards will commence in 2010. The aim of the pilot study will be to test the NSQH Standards, supporting tools and guidelines, and to identify issues for implementation of the standards. The pilot will involve representative organisations from a range of private and public health service providers where the NSQH Standards apply.[15]

STATE AND TERRITORY COMPLAINTS MECHANISMS

The national Medicare funding arrangements prescribed the establishment of independent statutory bodies in every Australian state and territory in response to the increasing numbers of complaints lodged in relation to the care received by healthcare consumers in both the public and private sectors of the Australian health system. These bodies, initially established *as independent complaints bodies* have, in a number of jurisdictions, extended their roles to include a focus on the improvement of safety and quality in health. The relevant legislation is listed in Table 2.1.

In all jurisdictions, *alternative dispute mechanisms* have been created as a means by which consumers can have their complaints answered and resolved. And, with the exception of New South Wales, *conciliation* is the predominant mode of complaints resolution in all states and territories. In relation to the provision of some Complementary and Alternative Medicines (CAMs), consumer complaints may be directed to the Federation of Natural and Traditional Therapists. This peak body represents CAM professionals' associations and provides an avenue for the resolution of complaints against practitioners in this area of health service delivery (refer also to Chapter 11, professional regulation and discipline).

The discussion below, while focusing on the Queensland Health Quality and Complaints Commission and the Western Australian Office of Health Review, provides an overview of the operation of a process which offers an alternative to the adversarial system.

Table 2.1 Health complaints legislation

State/territory	Legislation
Australian Capital Territory	Human Rights Commission Act 2005
New South Wales	Healthcare Complaints Act 1993
Victoria	Health Services (Conciliation and Review) Act 1987
Western Australia	Health Services (Conciliation and Review) Act 1995
Tasmania	Health Complaints Act 1995
Northern Territory	Health and Community Services Complaints Act 1998
Queensland	Health Quality and Complaints Commission Act 2006
South Australia	Health and Community Services Complaints Act 2004

These authorities seek to resolve disputes between healthcare consumers and providers through investigation and conciliation. As the New South Wales Healthcare Complaints Commission is legislatively empowered to prosecute in relation to healthcare complaints it will also be discussed. Though the legislative requirements and processes for dealing with complaints, quality, safety and monitoring of health services differ between the jurisdictions, the legislation is consistent in establishing state and territory based independent statutory bodies to receive and act on complaints made about health professionals and healthcare institutions.

Queensland

The Health Quality and Complaints Commission is an independent statutory body established under the Health Quality and Complaint Commission Act 2006 (Qld) (hereafter referred to as the Act).[16] The Commission, which absorbed the Health Rights Commission, was established by the Queensland government in response to the recommendations of the Queensland Health System Review (Foster Review). The role of the Health Quality and Complaints Commission is to improve the quality and safety of health services in Queensland through the development of healthcare standards, monitoring health service quality and providing for the independent review of complaints.[17] The main objects of the Act are set out in s 3 and provide for:

• oversight and review of, and improvement in, the quality of health services
• independent review and management of health complaints.

The objects are to be achieved mainly by establishing the Health Quality and Complaints Commission and conferring on the Commission functions and powers, including functions and powers relating to:

• monitoring, reviewing and reporting on the quality of health services
• recommending action to improve the quality of health services
• receiving and managing complaints about health services
• helping users and providers to resolve health service complaints
• preserving and promoting health rights.

The terms 'health service', 'provider' and 'user' within the Act are defined quite broadly and expand the power of the Commission to deal with the quality of health services and the management of complaints well beyond that of the previous Health Rights Commission. For example, under s 8 of the Act a 'health service' is defined as:

(a) a service provided to an individual for, or purportedly for, the benefit of human health (i) including a service stated in schedule 1, part 1 ... or (b) an administrative process or service related to a health service under paragraph (a).

A 'provider' means 'a person who provides a health service or a registered provider'[18] and a 'user' is defined as 'an individual who uses or receives a health service'.[19] It can be seen therefore that the power of the Commission in relation to quality and complaints extends to, and includes, all public and private health services, incorporating hospitals, day surgery facilities, alternate health providers, registered and unregistered health professionals and workers.

The Act imposes a mandatory duty on the providers of health services under s 20 to:

(1) ...establish, maintain and implement reasonable processes to improve the quality of health services provided by or for the provider, including processes to monitor the quality of health services; and to protect the health and wellbeing of users of the health services.
(2) If a commission standard applying to a provider states a way of complying with subsection (1), the provider complies with the subsection if the provider complies with the standard.

Subsection (2) does not limit the way the provider may comply with subsection (1).

2 Safety and quality in health

Health service complaints

The functions of the Commission in relation to health service complaints include the receipt, assessment and management of health service complaints, *encouraging users and providers to resolve complaints*, assisting providers to develop procedures to effectively resolve complaints and, if resolution is not possible, to conciliate or investigate the health service complaint.[20]

A significant issue pertaining to the Queensland legislation is the requirement for the complaint to be lodged within 12 months of the incident,[21] unless the complaint relates to a matter that the Commission reasonably believes may warrant suspension or cancellation of a provider's registration, enrolment or authorisation. While the complaint may be made in writing or orally, the Commissioner will require that the person substantiate the complaint in writing within a reasonable time of making the original contact. In accordance with the obligation of procedural fairness it is also a requirement that where there is not a public interest the Commissioner has the discretion, in 'special circumstances', to elect to keep the identity of a complainant confidential. For example, where an employee of a hospital or other healthcare facility lodges a complaint and is fearful that in having done so he or she runs the risk of unpleasant treatment at the hands of his or her colleagues or employer, the Commissioner will recognise the need for anonymity.

The stages of processing a complaint

As a statutory body, the powers of the Health Quality and Complaints Commission and the Health Quality and Complaints Commissioner in responding to, and managing, complaints are determined by the Act. The Act provides for the early resolution of health service complaints where there is a reasonable likelihood that the Commission can facilitate an early resolution and the complainant agrees to proceed in this way.[22] Most frequently, early resolution will involve the Commission arranging mediation between the complainant and the provider. Where a complaint is not suitable for an attempted early resolution it must be assessed immediately by the Commissioner.[23] As soon as practicable, and within 14 days, the Commissioner must give notice to the complainant, the provider and the registered provider's regulatory authority that the complaint is being assessed. In making an assessment of the complaint the Commissioner may invite submissions from the complainant and provider, seek information from a third person and consult with the relevant registration authority.

Upon assessment of the complaint, the Commissioner has a number of options. The Commissioner may decide not to accept the complaint for action,[24] or to take no action on the basis that the complaint is vexatious, frivolous, trivial, misconceived, lacking in substance or has been adequately dealt with by another authority or the Health Quality and Complaints Commission.[25] The Commissioner may refer the matter to conciliation,[26] or initiate an investigation into the complaint.[27] The Commissioner is also empowered to refer the matter for investigation by the relevant health practitioner registration boards.[28] It is noteworthy that a high proportion of the complaints are resolved without an assessment. This is achieved through the provision of information, advice and referrals that enable the complainant and provider to address the issues raised in the complaint directly. There are prescribed time limits and notifying procedures that control the process and ensure that the complainant and the provider are aware of the progress of the matter through the stages.

As previously discussed, the healthcare provider and complainant may be invited to make a submission once the Commissioner has determined to accept the complaint for assessment. Health professionals and providers must be aware that privilege does not attach to the response and is separate from the communication between the parties that may occur as part of the conciliation process.

Conciliation under Chapter 6 of the Act is performed by one or more conciliators assigned by the Commissioner. Under s 74(2), the conciliator, in encouraging the settlement of a complaint, may arrange negotiations between the provider and the complainant, assist in the conduct of the negotiations, assist the provider and complainant to reach an agreement, or assist in the resolution of the complaint in any other way. Participation in the conciliation process is voluntary and attracts statutory privilege under s 82. This section precludes the use of anything said or admitted during conciliation as admissible evidence in proceedings before courts or tribunals. The documents gathered in the course of the conciliation are not accessible through the Right to Information Act 2009 (Qld). The Commissioner is also precluded from using the information as grounds for an inquiry or an investigation. *The conciliation, therefore, provides the parties with the opportunity to discuss their particular incident without the threat of litigation, thus enabling progress towards a mutually agreeable resolution.*

The conciliation process can potentially result in a number of outcomes depending on the nature of the particular grievance and the goals of the actual participants.

1   The consumer and health professional may benefit equally from
    an exchange of information and the offer of an explanation
    as to how the injury or event occurred. In this era of high
    technological advancement and increasing medical knowledge,
    the expectations of the consumer often go well beyond that
    which is possible as a medical reality.

2 Through the conciliation process, the institution or health professional is made aware of any need to change their practices, update existing policies and procedures or draft new policies and procedures aimed at ensuring that there is not a recurrence of the incident which has resulted in the complaint.

3 Where it is considered appropriate and acceptable to the parties, the complainant may be happy to accept an offer by the health professional, or the institution, of remedial medical treatment. In many circumstances, once the grievance has been acknowledged, the primary aim of the complainants is to have their injury or damage treated so that they may return to their normal lifestyle.

4 Where the complaint relates to the standard of practice of a health professional, there may be a recommendation to the professional regulating authority on the particular practice issue.

5 The parties have the right to negotiate their own financial compensation arrangements.

The Commissioner has wide powers in relation to the initiation and progress of an *investigation* including the power to appoint an authorised person to conduct the investigation. The authorised person investigating a complaint may compel a person to provide information, produce documents or appear before the authorised person to answer questions or produce stated things[29] and, in prescribed circumstances, to enter onto and search of premises. The power extends to the seizure and retention of documents discovered in the process of the search. However, at the completion of the investigation the Commissioner is limited to the recourse of preparing a report with comments and recommendations. The Commissioner does not have the power to bring an action against an individual health professional.

Quality of health services

The statutory obligation of the Commission in relation to the quality of health services in Queensland includes: monitoring and reporting of provider compliance under s 20(1) of the Act; making standards and assessing the quality of health services; responding to health quality complaints; promoting quality improvement and effective coordination of health service reviews; making recommendations for the improvements of health quality; identifying and reviewing issues arising from health complaints; and receiving, analysing and disseminating information about the quality of health services.[30] If the Commission believes a provider has contravened s 20(1) it may, under s 24(1):

a) advise the provider of the contravention and recommend ways for the provider to comply with the subsection;

b) prepare a report about the contravention for the purpose of giving it to an entity mentioned in subsection (2);

c) if the Commission considers the contravention should be
    investigated or otherwise dealt with by an entity that has a
    function or power under another Act or a Commonwealth Act
    to investigate or otherwise deal with the contravention or a
    matter related to the contravention — refer it to the entity.

In 2007–08 the Health Quality and Complaints Commission
released seven standards as prescribed under the Act. The standards
were aimed at encouraging providers to adopt measurable best
practice processes to improve the quality to health services. The
initial seven standards were as follows:

1   review of hospital related deaths;
2   management of acute myocardial infarction following
    discharge;
3   surgical safety;
4   hand hygiene;
5   credentialing and scope of clinical practice;
6   complaints management;
7   providers' duty to improve the quality of health services.

Western Australia

The Office for Health Review was established as an independent
state government agency under the Health Services (Conciliation
and Review) Act 1995 (WA). The director of the office is appointed
by the Governor and is delegated the legislative responsibility for
receiving, investigating and conciliating complaints lodged against
health professionals, and or institutions in relation to healthcare
or the provision of healthcare services. In addition, since 1999 the
director has also had the responsibility of accepting and managing
complaints about disability services in Western Australia. The director
is also responsible for assessing the cause of complaints and educating
consumers and healthcare providers in relation to complaint
procedures. This includes referral of complaints to health professional
registration boards. In addition, the director may extend an inquiry
initiated by an original complaint to include broader health issues.
The mission of the Office of Health Review is 'to contribute to the
improvement of health and disability services through the impartial
resolution of complaints'.

Lodging a complaint about a health service

A complaint can be lodged orally or in writing with the Office of Health
Service Review. However, where the initial complaint is received
verbally it must be confirmed in writing prior to the commencement
of the process. Complainants must lodge their complaint with the

Office within 12 months of the incident which gave rise to the complaint. However, where the director is of the opinion that there is good reason for the delay, an extension of the limitation period may be granted. A complaint may be made by a user of a healthcare service (or their representative), a provider of a healthcare service in relation to the conduct of another healthcare provider or a carer, in relation to a failure by a provider to comply with Carers Charter as set out in the Carers Recognition Act 2004 (WA).

A complaint must, as with the Queensland jurisdiction, denote some reference to the 'unreasonable conduct'. In the Western Australian context, the 'unreasonable conduct' must have occurred in: relation to the provision of, or failure to provide, a health service; the failure to appropriately attend to complaints based on the healthcare or the healthcare service; the charging of excessive fees in relation to the health service provided; the failure to provide the consumer with access to their health records or disclose the information contained therein; or that a provider (as defined under s 4 of the Carers Recognition Act 2004 (WA) has failed to comply with the Carers Charter (as defined in the section). Once the director has made an assessment of the complaint, it may be rejected, or referred to conciliation, or investigation. The latter two options are only available to complainants who can demonstrate that they have made a prior reasonable attempt to resolve the matter with the healthcare provider.

Conciliation and investigation

Conciliation is available to complainants and providers. Unlike the Queensland conciliation process, neither party is able to be represented (legally or otherwise) unless the director of the Office of Health Review is of the opinion that the effectiveness of the process is dependent on the representation of a participant by a third party. Once a referral for conciliation is made, the parties concerned must be informed in writing within 14 days of the arrangements for the conciliation.[31] This notification will include, in relation to the health provider, the opportunity to provide a written submission to the conciliator. Written reports on the conciliation process are forwarded to the director. Evidence of anything said or admitted during the conciliation process is not admissible before a court or tribunal and cannot be used by the director as a ground upon which to investigate the complaint.[32]

A complaint considered to be too serious for conciliation, maybe forwarded by the director to investigation. In addition, where a complaint is initially forwarded to conciliation but discovered during the process to be too serious for conciliation a recommendation may be made that it is forwarded for investigation. This may occur during or after the conciliation. The investigation process is directed to making an assessment as to whether 'unreasonable conduct' has occurred. Under the legislation, the director must forward to the health provider within 14 days of the commencement of an investigation a written notice of the initiation of the investigation and the details of the complaint. As part of the investigation, the director is not bound by the rules of evidence and must proceed with as little formality and technicality as possible while adhering to the requirements of natural justice. While the director may make recommendations following an investigation there is no power to enforce compliance.

Referral to health professional registration boards

The director, on receipt of a complaint, may refer allegations made in relation to the conduct of a health professional to the appropriate health professional registration authority. The registration authority must then investigate the complaint to assess whether it is a matter suitable for an inquiry. If the registering authority and the director of the office form the view that the complaint is suitable for the conciliation process and the respective parties agree to consent to participate in the conciliation, the matter may be dealt with under the Health Services (Conciliation and Review) Act 1995 (WA).

New South Wales

The New South Wales Healthcare Complaints Commission was established under the Healthcare Complaints Commission Act 1993 to deal with healthcare complaints. The role of the Commission includes the investigation and prosecution of healthcare complaints and the provision of advice to the Minister on the trends in healthcare complaints in New South Wales.[33] The New South Wales Commission is the only health service complaints authority that has, as part of its response to complaints, the power to prosecute.

Any person can make a complaint to the Commission about healthcare, or a healthcare service, provided in New South Wales. A complaint may be made by the person who experienced the problem while receiving a healthcare service, a parent or guardian of that person or a relative, friend or representative of that person. A complaint must be in writing and may be made to the Commission and/or to the particular regulatory authority such as the Nurses and Midwives Board or the Medical Board. Regardless of whether the complaint is made to the professional board or the Commission, it is for the Commission to notify the health professional or healthcare facility that a complaint has been lodged against them.

Upon receipt of a complaint, the Commission must undertake an assessment so as to determine how the complaint will be managed. In most circumstances the health practitioner, healthcare institution or facility (being the subject of the complaint, the respondent) will be notified and requested to provide a response. This will be part of the fact-finding process necessary for the Commission to make a decision as to the most appropriate next step. The Commission may, based on the information available, decide not to deal with the complaint on the grounds that it is trivial, frivolous or vexatious. As in other jurisdictions, the Commission may encourage the complainant to attempt to discuss and resolve their concerns with the particular health service provider or institution. The legislation also provides for the Commission to refer the complaint to conciliation or investigation. Where the complaint involves the conduct of a registered health professional, the Commission must consult the relevant regulatory authority.

An investigation of a complaint by the Commission will involve the collection of information from a wide variety of sources. This would include interviews and written reports from other health professionals and healthcare workers, and opinions from peer reviewers or peer review panels. A written report of the investigation findings is forwarded to both the complainant and respondent at the completion of the investigation. The options available to the Commission at this point are to:

- prosecute the health practitioner by lodging a complaint alleging unsatisfactory professional conduct or professional misconduct
- intervene in proceedings before a disciplinary body
- refer the complaint to the regulatory authority with recommendations for disciplinary action
- make adverse comments to the health practitioner or healthcare facility
- refer the matter to the Department of Public Prosecutions.

Amendments to the Healthcare and Complaints Commission Act came into force in May 2009. Under these amendments the Commission can request information to assist in the assessment of a complaint from any person,[34] compel any person to provide relevant information as part of an investigation,[35] provide the results of an investigation to any relevant person or body,[36] and disclose complaint-related information to law enforcement agencies and other appropriate bodies.[37]

Victoria

The Office of the Health Services Commissioner was established by the Health Services (Conciliation and Review) Act 1987, making it the forerunner to complaint mechanisms in all other Australian jurisdictions. At the time the legislation was enacted it was considered pioneering as the aim was to establish an independent and accessible review mechanism and to provide a means for reviewing and improving health service provision. The incorporation of conciliation as a means to address complaints between patients and health professionals was also unique. As with the other state and territory legislation, the Victorian Act defines 'users' and 'providers' of 'health services'[38] and establishes the powers and functions of the Health Services Commissioner. Generally, a complaint must be lodged with the Commissioner within 12 months of the incident and the Commissioner in Victoria does not have the power to prosecute health professionals. Table 2.2 provides a summary of the complaints process and the scenarios below highlight some examples of actual complaints received and addressed by the Health Services Commissioner.

Table 2.2 Summary of the complaints process utilised by the Victorian Health Services Commissioner

Key features of the HSC process	• It is impartial and confidential. • HSC does not charge fees. • Participation in the complaints process is voluntary. • Complaints are resolved through co-operation. • HSC encourages open discussion, with all parties asked to give their point of view. • It can be an alternative to legal proceedings.
Who can be complained about	A complaint can be made against any health service provider, for example: • doctors, pharmacists, alternative therapists, dentists, hospitals, physiotherapists, ambulance services, nurses, psychiatric services, optometrists, chiropractors, counsellors. A complaint can also be made against: • any person or organisation that collects, holds or discloses health information.

continued

What happens when a complaint is made	• Send complaint to the health service provider to give them the opportunity to respond. With the provider's consent, a copy of the response will be sent to the complainant. • Many complaints are resolved through the provision of an explanation, detailed information or an apology where needed. This can be achieved at an early stage without the need for direct intervention by the HSC. • Most people who complain to the HSC want to know what went wrong and why, and they want to know that there have been improvements made to prevent similar incidents in the future.
If the complainant is not satisfied with the response	• If the response does not satisfy the complainant's concerns, the HSC will identify the unresolved issues. • The complainant may be asked to provide information to support their complaint. This can include reports from current treating doctors, copies of hospital records etc.
Possible options	If the complaint is unresolved there are three options: 1 no further action – the HSC decides 2 referral to a registration authority – where there is unprofessional conduct or the issue is not suitable for conciliation 3 referral to conciliation.
Outcomes	There are a number of outcomes, including: • an explanation of what happened or more detailed information about the treatment or medical condition • an opportunity for the complainant and provider to discuss what happened in a face-to-face meeting • an apology • a change to systems or procedures so a similar incident does not happen again • provision of remedial treatment • payment of compensation.

Scenarios addressed by the Health Services Commissioner

The following case examples have been identified from the Victorian Health Services Commissioner's 2009 Annual Report[39] and provide some insight into the types of complaints and the resultant outcomes.

Scenario 1

A man was admitted to a private hospital for surgery to his middle finger. The man identified to nursing staff which finger was to be operated on as their documentation was incorrect. The nurse then changed the documentation to reflect this. However, the surgeon proceeded to operate on the incorrect finger. When the fault was recognised the man was taken back to theatre and a second operation was undertaken on the correct finger. The hospital reviewed their policies and procedures and implemented a 'Marking of the Limb Policy' to ensure the correct surgery site is marked by the surgeon prior to surgery commencing. The man received a financial settlement from the hospital and the surgeon.

Scenario 2

A man attended the emergency department of a hospital after falling from a ladder. X-rays showed he had fractured his wrist and ankle and these were treated. He complained of pain in his arm and shoulder but no further investigations were done at the time. One month later he returned to the hospital as he was still in pain and further X-rays showed he had dislocated his shoulder in the fall. The surgeon told him the injury would be more complex to treat after the delay. He had been unable to work for an extended period of time and so the complaint was referred to conciliation in order for him to discuss his claim for loss of income arising from the delay.

Scenario 3

A woman who is the primary carer of her adult son who is being treated for a mental illness complained that the hospital psychiatrist refused to communicate with her, even though the patient had consented to the sharing of his health information. The hospital explained the patient was willing for only some aspects of the information to be disclosed to his mother. A meeting was organised between the doctor, the patient and the complainant, and agreement was reached about how the information would be shared in the future.

HUMAN AND PATIENT RIGHTS

One issue related to the quality of healthcare provided relates to the 'rights' individuals have as citizens and as patients. However, unlike a number of countries Australia does not have a distinct Bill of Rights establishing individual human or civil rights or privileges. The *Commonwealth Constitution refers to only a few human rights including voting rights, the right to freedom of religion, the right not to be discriminated against, and the right to trial by jury for serious criminal offences.* Although, there are a number of statutes enacted at both federal and state level prohibiting discrimination on the grounds of marital status, sex, race, age and disability and legislation relating to privacy. There is also the *Human Rights and Equal Opportunity Commission*, established by the federal government, which is charged with the function of promoting, and inquiring into alleged breaches of human rights.

In recent years two jurisdictions, the Australian Capital Territory (ACT) and Victoria, have enacted legislation to specifically identify certain human rights, incorporating individual civil and political rights.[40] The rights identified in the statutes include a broad array of concepts; for example, the recognition of the right to life, the right to privacy, and freedom of expression and movement. In relation to healthcare, the right to life in both statutes identifies that no individual may be arbitrarily deprived of life. The ACT legislation specifically states that this right applies from the time of birth.[41] The courts are to interpret any legislation passed by the ACT and Victorian governments in accordance with the human rights legislation. Should a court find that any legislation is inconsistent with the human rights legislation then it is to be reviewed by parliament.

In terms of 'patient rights', the Australian government has required states and territories to provide a patient charter of rights for public hospital patients since the 1993–98 Australian Healthcare Agreement. *These 'rights' are not enshrined in legislation*; they arise as an agreement between the ministers of the federal, state and territory governments. Despite the fact that all state and territory governments adopted patient charters, they were not consistent in content or implementation. In July 2008 Australian Health Ministers endorsed the *Charter of Healthcare Rights* (the Charter) for use in all Australian healthcare settings. The Charter identifies seven patient rights, including the right to access, safety, respect, communication, participation, privacy, and comment. The rights are expressed as statements; for example, the right to communication states that individuals 'have the right to be informed about services and treatment', and the right to participation states that individuals 'have the right to be included in decisions and choices regarding care'.[42] It is important to note that while the Charter is not legislation, it expresses and incorporates a number of obligations health professionals owe patients under existing law, professional codes and employer policies.

REVIEW QUESTIONS AND ACTIVITIES

To ensure you have identified and understood the key points of this chapter please answer the following questions.

1 What moves are currently afoot at the federal level to improve quality and safety in healthcare?
2 Do you think that employers and practitioners should be encouraged to collect and report adverse events more widely? Should consumers have access to detailed information related to adverse events and should specific health facilities be identified?
3 Discuss the rates of adverse patient outcomes and consider the particular areas of clinical practice identified. What factors contribute to making these areas of practice problematic? Select a specific practice domain and consider how the rules and procedures can be ameliorated so as to be followed by practitioners.
4 Compare the processes involved in litigation and those established by the complaints authorities, highlighting the advantages and disadvantages of each process.
5 Discuss the varying 'rights' patients have, distinguishing between those enshrined in law and those emanating from your professional codes of ethics and conduct.

Further reading

Australian Commission on Safety and Quality in Healthcare — Reports & Publications. Online. Available: www.safetyandqu ality.gov.au/internet/safety/publishing.nsf/Content/pubs-1lp (accessed 9 April 2010).

Australian Institute of Health and Welfare (AIHW) and Australian Commission on Safety and Quality in Healthcare, Sentinel Events in Australian Public Hospitals 2004–2005, AIHW, Canberra, 2007.

Australian Institute of Health and Welfare site for organisational structure, committees, publications and reports. Online. Available: www.aihw.gov.au/index.cfm (accessed 12 April 2010).

Australian Institute of Health and Welfare, Medical Indemnity National Data Collection Public Sector 2006–07, AIHW, Canberra, 2009.

Health Services Review Council 2005. *Guide to Complainant Handling in Healthcare Services*. Online. Available: www.health. vic.gov.au/hsc/downloads/complaints_handling.pdf (accessed 4 May 2010).

Review of Professional Indemnity Arrangements for Healthcare Professionals. Compensation and Professional Indemnity in Healthcare: Final Report, Australian Government Printing Service, Canberra, 1995.

Wakefield, J, 'Patient safety: From learning to action', First Queensland Health Report on Clinical Incidents and Sentinel Events, Queensland Health, Queensland Government, 2007.

Endnotes

1 Wakefield, J, 'Patient safety: From learning to action', First Queensland Health Report on Clinical Incidents and Sentinel Events, Queensland Health, Queensland Government, 2007 at 3.

2 Review of Professional Indemnity Arrangements for Healthcare Professionals. Compensation and Professional Indemnity in Healthcare: Final Report, Australian Government Printing Service, Canberra, 1995 at 20.

3 Ibid.

4 Ibid.

5 Ibid.

6 The Commission's details and reports can be accessed online. Available: www.safetyandquality.gov.au/internet/safety/publish ing.nsf/Content/home (accessed 10 April 2010).

7 See the Australian Institute of Health and Welfare website for organisational structure, committees, publications and reports. Available: www.aihw.gov.au/index.cfm (accessed 12 April 2010).

8 Previously named the Australian Council of Safety and Quality in Healthcare.

9 Australian Institute of Health and Welfare (AIHW) and Australian Commission on Safety and Quality in Healthcare, Sentinel Events in Australian Public Hospitals 2004–2005, AIHW, Canberra, 2007.

10 Ibid at 33.

11 Ibid at 3.

12 Australian Institute of Health and Welfare (AIHW), Medical Indemnity National Data Collection Public Sector 2006–07, AIHW, Canberra, 2009.

13 Ibid at viii.

14 Ibid.

15 Australian Quality and Safety Commission. Online. Available: www.safetyandquality.gov.au/internet/safety/publishing.nsf/Co ntent/PriorityProgram-07#acc-ProgUp (accessed 10 April 2010).

16 'In performing its functions the Commission must act independently, impartially and in the public interest': s 12.

17 Health Quality and Complaints Commission Annual Report 2007–2008.
18 Health Quality and Complaints Commission Act 2006 (Qld), s 9.
19 Health Quality and Complaints Commission Act 2006 (Qld), s 10.
20 Health Quality and Complaints Commission Act 2006 (Qld), s 13.
21 Health Quality and Complaints Commission Act 2006 (Qld), s 63(3)(b).
22 Health Quality and Complaints Commission Act 2006 (Qld), s 52.
23 Health Quality and Complaints Commission Act 2006 (Qld), s 53.
24 Health Quality and Complaints Commission Act 2006 (Qld), s 59(1)(a).
25 Health Quality and Complaints Commission Act 2006 (Qld), s 59(1)(b), s 63(1).
26 Health Quality and Complaints Commission Act 2006 (Qld), s 61 (2)(a) and Chapter 6.
27 Health Quality and Complaints Commission Act 2006 (Qld), s 61 (2)(b) and Chapter 7.
28 Health Quality and Complaints Commission Act 2006 (Qld), s 61(2)(c).
29 Health Quality and Complaints Commission Act 2006 (Qld), s123(1).
30 Health Quality and Complaints Commission Act 2006 (Qld), s 14.
31 Health Services (Conciliation and Review) Act 1995 (WA), s 37.
32 Health Services (Conciliation and Review) Act 1995 (WA), s 42.
33 For more information relating to the complaints process see: www.hccc.nsw.gov.au/Complaints/Complaint-Process/default.aspx.
34 Section 21A.
35 Section 34A.
36 Section 45.
37 Section 99B.
38 Health Services (Conciliation and Review) Act 1987 (Vic), s 3.
39 Health Services Commissioner Annual Report 2009. Online. Available: http://www.health.vic.gov.au/hsc/downloads/hsc_report_2009_3.pdf (accessed 4 May 2010).
40 Human Right Act 2004 (ACT); Charter of Human Rights and Responsibilities Act 2006 (Vic).
41 Human Right Act 2004 (ACT), s 9.
42 Australian Commission on Safety and Quality in Healthcare, *Australian Charter of Healthcare Rights* 2008. Online. Available: www.health.gov.au/internet/safety/publishing.nsf/Content/PriorityProgram-01 (accessed 9 April 2010).

3

Documentation

LEARNING OBJECTIVES

This chapter aims to introduce you to the legal issues relevant to medical record documentation. While you are reading this chapter you should focus on:

- the legal and medical significance of maintaining accurate, objective and contemporaneous patient records
- identifying the factors that you must consider when recording information pertaining to a patient's care and treatment
- identifying your professional responsibility in retaining and disposing of medical records
- identifying your legal obligations in relation to notification of births and deaths.

INTRODUCTION

Documentation of the care and treatment of a patient is fundamental to the practice of all healthcare professionals. This is particularly so for medical practitioners who, in the main, are directing the care and treatment of the patient via the medical records which serve as a vehicle by which to communicate with the other members of the healthcare team. A patient's records (variously referred to as the 'medical records', the patient's 'health information',[1] or the patient's 'health records'[2]) may include not only the medical, nursing and research notes held by hospitals and other healthcare institutions or facilities but also those notes written at the pre-admission or post-discharge phases of care delivery. *The purpose of the medical records is to facilitate an optimal patient outcome through the accurate, objective and contemporaneous description of the ongoing care.* In addition to providing an account of the relevant patient information, the records serve as a method of communication from one health professional, or group of health professionals, to another. Patient records may also be used for research purposes, as educational tools and as documentary evidence in legal proceedings. For these reasons, it is imperative that medical practitioners understand the significance of the content of any patient's medical records and the potential for the use of such documents. Entry of patient information into the medical records by a medical student must be consistent with their level of competency and the policies and guidelines of the institution in which they are undertaking their clinical practicum. Entries into a patient's medical records by medical students must also be consistent with, and in response to, the delegation of this activity by the supervising clinician.

The content of a patient's medical records depends not only on the particular care and treatment the patient received, but also on the particular institution or healthcare facility which has created and maintained the documents. As stated by Queensland Health and quoted in Field:[3]

> A health record provides a vehicle for recording a consumer's health status, particular conditions and illnesses, results of examinations and tests, diagnosis of conditions, assessments of the need for treatment, treatment prescribed, information provided, and the results of treatment. Its value rests in the content of the records, its historical basis, and its potential as a tool for accountability purposes.

Medical practitioners have both professional and ethical responsibilities to create and maintain accurate records in relation to the treatment and care given to patients. For example, the Australian Medical Association Code of Ethics requires that doctors '[m]aintain accurate contemporaneous clinical records'.[4]

EFFECTIVE DOCUMENTATION

There is no Commonwealth legislation mandating the recording of patient or client information by health professionals or facilities. At the state level the recently repealed Medical Practice Regulations 2008 (NSW) mandate that a medical practitioner or medical corporation must 'make and keep' a medical record,[5] and the Health Services (Private Hospitals and Day Procedures Centres) Regulations 2002 (Vic) regulations 21 and 22 provide that a proprietor of a private hospital or day procedure centre must commence a clinical record 'as soon as practicable after the admission' and maintain that record over the period of the patient's stay in the facility. Regulation 22 identifies information, such as the patient's name, address, date of birth, sex and unit record number, details of relatives or friends nominated as contact persons and the relevant clinical details which are to be included in the clinical records. While there are no specific legal requirements as to the formatting of medical records, the policy provisions of the employing healthcare institution, and the case law, provide guidelines as to the particular information which should be included in the patient records. Dix et al suggest that while the 'form and content' of medical records created by private practitioners continues to be at the discretion of the particular provider, there is a trend towards a more uniform approach to record-keeping.[6]

The following are factors to be considered when recording information in relation to the care and treatment of a patient.

1 Medical practitioners *must ensure that the information recorded is clear, concise and accurate.* Their documentation must be 'objective, devoid of pejorative comment and worthy of independent scrutiny'.[7] This requirement is significant not only in relation to the accurate transfer of information between health professionals of all disciplines but also where the documents may be relevant to potential legal proceedings. The comments written by a medical practitioner as to the care given, the condition of a particular patient and their demeanour or state of mind may be used at a later time to provide evidence of an allegation of negligence, malpractice, or the degree of damage and disability sustained by the patient. The medical practitioner must exercise extreme care in the use of language or opinion which, when recorded in the clinical records, is open to interpretation by all those members of the healthcare team who are involved in this patient's care.

In the case of *McCabe v Auburn District Hospital*,[8] the deceased was admitted for an emergency appendicectomy. Post-operatively, his condition was poor and deteriorating. He was spiking a temperature, sweating, complaining of severe abdominal pain, unable to keep fluids down and suffering with diarrhoea. On the fifth day post-operatively, the medical practitioner ordered a full blood count. This was undertaken and the results, which showed a high white cell count and other abnormalities indicative of a severe infection, were forwarded to the ward the same day. As it was the weekend, the medical practitioner, though 'on call', had left the hospital. The registered nurse receiving the results proceeded to file them in the incorrect section of the medical records and neither notified the medical practitioner nor raised the findings with the nurses on the next shift. The pathology results were not discovered until two days after they had been received in the ward. The patient later died from peritonitis.

The deceased's mother brought an action against the hospital and the hospital staff alleging negligence. In upholding her claim, his Honour made the following comments:[9]

I am of the view that the hospital notes were not, in the current case, reliable. In particular there is unreliability in recording the manifest and observable continuing deterioration of the deceased's condition. I am satisfied that the routine temperature checks even if accurate as to scale were accompanied by a failure to note what was there to be seen, namely that the deceased was perspirant and 'hot'. This was evident even to non-medical appreciation ... I do conclude ... that there were things significant in assessing the patient's deterioration which were overlooked and the written record simply does not truly reflect the currency of the events.

His Honour went on to conclude:[10]

It would be apparent from my earlier findings and remarks ... that the clinical and nursing notes were deficient. Their inadequacy must have been a major factor in bringing about a situation which allowed the patient's condition to deteriorate fatally without timely remedial treatment.

2   The *timing of the documentation* of patient information is often dependent on a number of factors. The institution or healthcare facility may have guidelines or protocols stipulating when the patient's records are to be updated or the timing of documentation may be left to the discretion of the particular professional. It is important that the documentation of patient information is considered as a valuable part of the total patient care and therefore adequate time should be set aside to undertake the task. If a patient's condition becomes unstable or deteriorates it would be necessary to carry out and document the observations more frequently. The documentation of patient information should be contemporaneous with the event and recorded in chronological order. A contemporaneous recording of an event ensures greater accuracy on the part of the writer and is more likely to be interpreted by the court as the true version.

It is not acceptable to go back and add information to the medical records once the medical practitioner becomes aware that litigation has been initiated. Often such an addition may be inaccurate due to the passage of time or, where accurate, is not considered as a contemporaneous record of what actually occurred at the time of the patient contact. In institutions or practices where the patient records are computerised, there is often an 'audit trail' which will identify when the entry was made. The inclusion of handwriting experts in the pre-trial stage has also increased the possibility of additions and alterations to the patient notes being detected. A finding that

a medical record has been altered will obviously have
a detrimental impact on the testimony of a medical
practitioner who has given sworn evidence that the
documentation was contemporaneous. Where the medical
practitioner wishes to make an addition to the records it
is acceptable to do so by clearly indicating, through the
inclusion of the date and time of the entry, that the addition
or amendment was made. For example, giving the date and
time of the actual entry and then commencing with the prior
date and approximate time the medical practitioner became
aware of the information or made the actual observation.
The issue of taking and maintaining thorough and complete
medical records was raised in *Locher v Turner*[11] and *Vale v Ho*.[12]
In *Locher's* case, the medical practitioner had failed to order
or carry out investigative procedures on a female patient
who presented with rectal bleeding. Over the 12 months
between the initial consultation and a diagnosis of carcinoma
of the sigmoid colon with metastases in the liver, the plaintiff
had consulted the doctor on a number of occasions. The
parties were in dispute as to whether, on these occasions,
the patient had referred to the continuation of the rectal
bleeding. The medical records did not thoroughly outline
or detail the progress of the patient's condition. The Court
of Appeal therefore held that as there were no adequate
contemporaneous notes recorded then neither the evidence
of the doctor nor the patient could be taken as correct. In
contrast, *Vale's* case involved a doctor who had recorded
extensive and detailed notes regarding his patient. The patient
had undergone plastic and reconstructive surgery to his nose.
His Honour, Judge Sinclair, when confronted with different
versions of the events by the parties, preferred the medical
evidence as it was consistent with the contemporaneous notes
which had detailed the care that the patient had received.

3   Where there is no entry to record a change in the condition of
a patient, the court may infer that no observations have been
undertaken. Even the routine observations and assessments
undertaken on the patient must be recorded. In the American
case of *Javis v St Charles Medical Centre* (1996),[13] the medical
practitioner had ordered hourly observations on the fractured
leg of the patient to assess for the development of compartment
syndrome. The medical practitioner requested that he be
notified immediately of any change in the circulation to the
leg. The initial observations were undertaken and recorded;
however, the entries on the observation chart after that time

were sporadic. When the medical practitioner saw the patient the following day, the foot was pulseless, white and the patient was complaining of pain. The last recorded observation was taken some four hours previously. The jury concluded that 'as there were no records, there were likewise no observations and decided against the nursing staff and the hospital'.[14]

In the New South Wales case of *Strelec v Nelson*[15] the Supreme Court found the obstetrician had been negligent in the delivery of a child. This finding was influenced, by the fact the doctor did not document the events. Smart J stated:

He [Dr Nelson] acknowledged that his failure to make any note of what he had done and what had happened was a serious departure from proper practice. It was his usual practice to write what happened at the delivery. He denied that he had failed to make notes because he did not know why the delivery had gone wrong or to prevent anyone from reviewing what he had done and discovering the mistake … He had no satisfactory explanation for what had happened. He probably asked himself whether he should have pursued a different course … He was worried that he had made a mistake. It was a subject that he found disturbing. It was a combination of such reasons that led him not to make the notes.

4   *All entries must be prefaced with the complete date and time of the entry* and the writer of the report clearly identified by his or her signature and designated position. This information is significant when there is a query at a later time as to the care given or the condition of the patient at a particular time on a particular day. The use of military time is most effective as a means of distinguishing whether the entry is recording the 'am' or the 'pm'.

5   The recording of information by all health professionals *must be legible*. There is little value in maintaining records that can not be read or understood by others. The case of *Prendergast v Sam and Dee Ltd, Kozary and Miller*[16] illustrates the fact that the failure to write legibly may result in liability in negligence. In this case, the medical practitioner wrote a prescription for Ventolin inhaler, Phyllocontin and Amoxil. However, the pharmacist read the Amoxil as Daonil, a drug used in the treatment of diabetes. The patient, Mr Prendergast, who did not suffer from diabetes, took the drug and sustained irreversible brain damage. It was not in dispute that the manner of the writing of the drug could have been read by the pharmacist as Daonil. However, counsel for the doctor argued that there was no causal link

between the illegible writing and the injury, as the features of the prescription should have alerted the pharmacist to the fact that he had not correctly read what he thought was written. The court held that it was reasonably foreseeable that the drug Daonil could have been prescribed, and therefore the medical practitioner was held liable. The requirement of legibility of healthcare records is not only fundamental to good patient care, it is also necessary for the purposes of maintaining the quality of health services through quality assurance monitoring and audits. In legal proceedings it is imperative that the documentation of patient and client care in the medical records is legible and able to be read by the court. In addition, as noted by McSherry, for the purpose of the private health funds and the national health insurer the writing on the documentation must be legible for reimbursement of fees for service. It is suggested that 'legibility as a requirement for reimbursement from third party payers has been the major reason why healthcare professionals now prefer to dictate their records, which are then transcribed by third parties as an electronic file'.[17] With the ever increasing introduction of databases for the recording of patient and client information the issue of legibility of entries into the medical records is decreasing.

6   *Health professionals should write only what they themselves have witnessed or assessed* and avoid documenting information which is passed on to them by others. Where the event has not been witnessed, the information is hearsay evidence. If the patient relates an incident that has occurred without a witness, then the records should clearly reflect that it is the patient's version of the event that has been recorded. As an example, the report would state that 'Mr Black said that he fell in the shower ...' or 'Mrs Smith is complaining that her pain is becoming more severe ...'. This principle also applies to charting or signing for work done or observations made by other health professionals. Each report should be an accurate record of what the person signing the entry knows to be true. At the Coroner's Inquest into the death of Tracey Baxter (1979), the registered nurse working on the morning shift admitted making entries on the fluid balance chart based on information given to her by the night duty nurse at the handover of the shift. The registered nurse, when questioned by the coroner as to why she had made the entries when she obviously was not on the ward at the time, said that she had intended to do the night duty nurse a 'favour'. The obvious implication is that the credibility in recording accurate information must be seriously questioned.

7 *Each page of a patient's medical records must identify him or her by name and numerical identifier.* This may take the form of a computer printout a computer generated patient identification sticker or writing the information by hand.

8 The use of abbreviations and popular terms must conform to the particular institution's policy or protocol. *There is a great danger in using abbreviations* that are not commonly known and understood by other health professionals. On the other hand, medical terminology, being a very precise language conveying precise meaning to other health professionals, should be used whenever appropriate.

9 When documenting the care or treatment of a patient, words such as 'appears' and 'apparently' should be avoided. As an example, the description of a patient as 'appears to be drunk' does not provide objective or factual information of the patient's status. It would be appropriate and preferable to *write an accurate, specific and factual description of the physical* condition of the patient such as 'the patient's speech was slurred and he was walking with an irregular gait'. The patient may have sustained a head injury.

10 The medical practitioner must *never chart or write a report on a patient in advance.*

11 *Reports should not be rewritten at a later time and entries must be sequential,* following directly on from the previous report. This avoids the possibility of tampering with, adding to or backdating entries with information that may be detrimental and expose the health professional to legal liability.

12 Where an error is made in the recording of information, the policy or protocol of the hospital should be followed. Where the medical records are paper-based the usual procedure will require that the medical practitioner draw a line through the erroneous material, identify it as having been written in error, date and initial it. Errors should never be torn out, removed, erased or covered over with correction fluid. The reason for this is the possibility of inferring that the medical practitioner has made an error in the treatment of the patient which he or she now wishes to conceal. Medical records maintained on an electronic database will permit the contemporaneous deletion and correction of content but do not allow for the correction of errors once the user has exited the database.

13 Documentation in the medical records is to be *written in ink.*

Medical practitioners must always read the patient's medical records. While most hospital and healthcare facilities provide for a verbal handover (either in person or via recordings) at the change of the shift, this is, by its very nature, only a summary of the events that have taken place over the preceding shift and should be treated as complementary to the written report. There is always the possibility that the professional giving the verbal handover has forgotten information or failed to recognise the significance of information which became available during the shift. As a result, information which may be critical to the patient's care and treatment will be missed.

COMPUTERISED RECORDS

Hospital and healthcare facilities are increasingly adopting computerised charting and record-keeping. The use of information systems to create and maintain patients' medical files has resulted in more accurate, easily accessed and up-to-date information on each individual patient. When a patient's records are available to all healthcare providers and institutions through technology, there are obvious advantages to the medical practitioner in being able to efficiently access accurate information which may be essential to the speed with which a patient is able to be treated. As an example, where a patient has sustained significant injuries in a road trauma, the ability to access information as to their cardiovascular and respiratory status and the presence or absence of underlying diseases and disorders will significantly impact on the initial treatment.

However, there are issues of concern when using computer technology for the documentation of patient information. The most obvious of the concerns is the potential threat to the privacy of the patient. If the information contained on the database is available to authorised users, then it may also be accessed by unauthorised individuals or entities. Hospital and healthcare facilities implementing electronic databases for the recording and storage of patient information need to have policies and protocols for the protection of the patients' right to privacy and confidentiality in relation to their health information.

Australia's proposed national health information network, Health*Connect*, has the highest Electronic Health Record profile[18] and has been described as follows:

[A] person's health-related information would be collected in a standard, electronic format at the point of care (such as at a hospital or a GP's clinic). This would take the form of health summaries, rather than all the notes that a healthcare provider may choose to keep about a consultation.

With the consumer's consent, these summaries would then be able to be retrieved at any time they were needed and exchanged via a secure network between those particular healthcare providers authorised by the consumer to access this information.[19]

In addition to the documentation required for the patient's medical record a medical practitioner is also required to complete other documents inherent to their role.

Birth certificates

Each state and territory requires notification and registration of births that occur within the particular jurisdiction with the Registrar of Births, Deaths and Marriages. Table 3.1 identifies the legislation for reporting births. The responsibility for notification is set out in the legislation and will usually fall to the parents of the child, however, the medical practitioner or midwife who assumed the professional care of the mother at the time of the birth or the Chief Executive Officer of the hospital in which the birth occurred may also have a responsibility to notify the Registrar. It is the legal responsibility of the institution or hospital in which the child is born to ensure the Registrar has been notified of a birth. Notification will include the name of the child and information about the parents. Each state or territory will have requirements in relation to a still-born child. A still-born child is a child who is at least 20 weeks gestation or, if gestation cannot be confirmed, weighs at least 400 grams and exhibits no sign of life after birth. Still-births are registered in the same manner as a live birth. It is an offence to provide false information to the Registrar or to fail to give notice of a birth or still-birth.

Death certificates

A cause of death certificate, also referred to as the death certificate,[20] will be completed by a medical practitioner once they have examined the patient or client and confirmed the person is deceased. The medical

Table 3.1 Notification of births and deaths	
ACT	Births, Deaths and Marriages Registration Act 1997
NSW	Births, Deaths and Marriages Registration Act 1995
NT	Births, Deaths and Marriages Registration Act 1996
Qld	Births, Deaths and Marriages Registration Act 2003
SA	Births, Deaths and Marriages Registration Act 1996
Tas	Births, Deaths and Marriages Registration Act 1999
Vic	Births, Deaths and Marriages Registration Act 1996
WA	Births, Deaths and Marriages Registration Act 1998

practitioner responsible for completing the certificate may be the patient's treating medical practitioner or a medical practitioner who examines the body after the death. In Queensland, a cause of death certificate may also be provided by a medical practitioner who is familiar with the deceased's medical history and can make an assessment of the probable cause of death. The medical practitioner can only complete this certificate where the cause of the death is ascertainable and the death does not give rise to any cause for further investigation by the coroner.

All medical practitioners must familiarise themselves with the legislative definition of a 'reportable death' under Coroners' legislation in the jurisdiction in which they practice (refer to Chapter 1, Introduction to law). In circumstances in which there is a 'reportable death' a medical practitioner must not provide a cause of death certificate. Certificates are forwarded to the Registrar of Births, Deaths and Marriages in all jurisdictions other than Queensland, where the certificate may be given to the Registrar or individual assuming responsibility for disposal of the body, and Western Australia, where the certificate is given to the individual arranging for disposal of the body of the deceased. Table 3.1 identifies the legislation requiring the registration of a death. Although the actual format of the document will vary from jurisdiction to jurisdiction it must be completed within 48 hours of a death and contain a clear statement of the medical practitioner's assessment of the cause of the death. In Queensland and Western Australia a still-born child is required to be registered on both the birth and death registers. However, in the other jurisdictions a still-born infant is not required to be registered as a death.

STORAGE, RETENTION AND DISPOSAL OF MEDICAL RECORDS

Medical records should be stored in a secure area that protects the records from unauthorised access, loss and damage. That is, the records must be stored in an area that is readily accessible for the purpose of retrieval and recording of patient information but also away from public access. The Privacy Act 1988 (Cth) does not impose an obligation on medical practitioners in relation to the length of time medical records are to be retained or the methods by which such records are to be destroyed or disposed of. *The length of time that a patient or client's medical records are to be retained is therefore found in the legislation in each of the states and territories and the individual policies and defence requirements of medical indemnity providers.* As a general principle, the medical records of patients and clients should not be destroyed but rather retained in secure storage. A medical practitioner should be particularly mindful of retaining records which give health information that may be of particular assistance to the patient's family (as an example, if a patient has a genetic disorder), where there has been an adverse outcome or the patient has expressed dissatisfaction with the care and treatment they have received from the medical practitioner, where there are threats of legal action or delays in diagnosis or treatment.

In the *Australian Capital Territory* there is no legislation specifying the length of time that a medical record should be retained, however, it is recommended that the records are kept by the medical practitioner for at least 7 years after the last health service was provided. That is, the records are retained to a time after the expiration of the limitation period for the commencement of a personal injuries claim.

In *New South Wales* and *Victoria* a medical practitioner may delete medical information as permitted by law or regulations. If the patient or client is a child their records should be kept until the child reaches the age of 25 years. For adults, the situation is similar to that in the ACT in that it is recommended the records are retained for 7 years from the time of the last health service. When medical records are destroyed it is recommended that the medical practitioner maintain a schedule of destruction which includes the name of the patient or client, the period for which the patient was under the care of the medical practitioner and the date on which the records were destroyed.

In *Tasmania* and *Queensland* there is no privacy legislation applicable to medical practitioners in relation to retention and storage of medical records. As described for other jurisdictions it is recommended that medical practitioners in Queensland retain medical records until after the expiration of the limitation period.

The *Western Australia* Department of Health, *Patient Information Retention and Disposal Schedule Version 3, 2008*, identifies the retention and disposal requirements for major categories of patient records created or received by Western Australia's Department of Health or healthcare facilities. The schedule is authorised under the State Records Act 2000 and is operative from June 2008 to May 2012. The retention periods for particular documents, such as obstetric records, Aboriginal and Torres Strait Islander health records and in-patient records are calculated from the 'date of last access' and can be accessed online.[21]

Medical indemnity providers, while having individual policies in relation to the safe and secure handling of medical documentation will require the medical practitioner produce the clinical records of a patient who is making a claim for compensation. The provision of indemnity cover will, in most situations, impose on the medical practitioner an obligation to fully cooperate and assist in the defence of a claim. Where the medical practitioner has disposed of or destroyed a patient's medical records it may provide the basis for denial of the indemnity cover.

ACTIVITIES

- What is the purpose of the medical records?
- What factors should be considered when recording a patient's information into the medical records?
- Locate and identify the legislation providing for the registration of births, including still-births, and deaths in the state or territory in which you are studying as a medical student.

REVIEW QUESTIONS

To ensure that you have identified and understood the key points of this chapter please answer the following:

1 In addition to providing information to other health professionals what other purposes do the medical records serve?

2 What are the possible legal implications of failing to appropriately record patient information?

3 List the factors to be considered when documenting patient care.

4 Identify the importance of documenting contemporaneously with a patient event. From an evidential perspective, why is this type of evidence significant?

5 Describe what you would do after making an error in writing up the patient's information in their medical records.

6 In your state or territory what are the requirements of a medical practitioner for notifying the Registrar of a birth, still-birth and death?

7 In your state of territory how long are you required to retain medical records?

Further reading

Elkin, K, Kerr, A, 'The importance of keeping comprehensive documentation in ensuring quality and continuity of care: Lessons from the New Zealand Health and Disability Commissioner', May (2009) *Australian Health Law Bulletin* 106.

Freckelton, I, 'Medical Records in Negligence Litigation' (1998) 5 *Journal of Law and Medicine* 305.

Nisselle, P, 'Answers to Some Common Questions about Medical Records' (1997) *Modern Medicine in Australia.*

Royal Australian College of General Practitioners (RACGP), *Handbook for the Management of Health Information in Private Medical Practice*, RACGP, 2002.

Endnotes

1 Health Information and Privacy Act 2002 (NSW); Information Act 2002 (NT); Personal Information Protection Act 2004 (Tas); Health Records Act 2001 (Vic).

2 Health Records (Privacy and Access) Act 1997 (ACT).

3 S Field, 'Documentation in Healthcare', *Healthcare Law and Ethics*, L Shotton (ed.), Social Science Publications, Katoomba, 1997, p 95.

4 Australian Medical Association, Code of Ethics, 2004 (editorially revised 2006).

5 reg 4.

6 A Dix, M Errington, K Nicholson and R Powe, *Law for the Medical Profession in Australia*, Butterworth Heinemann, Port Melbourne, 1996, p 161.

7 Ibid.

8 Unreported, Supreme Court (NSW), Grove J, No 11551 of 1982, 12 May 1989.

9 Ibid at 17.

10 Ibid at 31.

11 Unreported, Court of Appeal, Queensland, 21 April 1995.

12 Unreported, District Court of New South Wales, Sinclair DCJ, 11 May 1995.

13 G Guido Walker, *Legal Issues in Nursing*, Appleton and Lange, Stanford Connecticut, 1997, p 152.

14 Ibid.

15 (unreported) 12401/90 13 December 1996.

16 *The Times*, London, 14 March 1989; (1989) 63 ALJ 506.

17 McSherry, M, 'Electronic Medical Records: Perils of outsourcing and the Privacy Act 1988 (Cth), (2004) 12 JLM 8 at 9.

18 Terry, N P, 'Electronic health records: International, structural and legal perspectives', (2004)12 JLM 26 at 32.

19 Health*Connect* — An introduction: in Terry, N P, 'Electronic health records: International, structural and legal perspectives', (2004)12 JLM 26 at 32 (www.healthconnect.gov.au/pdf_docs/fshci.pdf).

20 Though the cause of death certificate is often referred to as the death certificate. A death certificate however is a document produced by the Registrar of Births, Deaths and Marriages and is the basis upon the information contained in the cause of death certificate.

21 www.health.wa.gov.au/circularsnew/attachemnet/342/pdf(accessed 21 July 2010).

Privacy and confidentiality
of patient information

This chapter aims to introduce you to the legal issues relevant to the privacy and confidentiality of patient and client information. While you are reading this chapter you should focus on:

- understanding the legal and professional obligation of confidentiality in relation to patient and client information
- identifying the legal and professional consequences when the obligation to keep information confidential is breached
- identifying the professional codes of ethics and conduct that protect patient and client confidentiality
- describing the practical effect of exceptions to the obligation of client confidentiality
- locating and understanding the Privacy Act (Cth) and/or National Privacy Principles (NPPs) and/or Information Privacy Principles (IPPs) and legislation relevant to the state or territory in which you will practise medicine
- discussing legislation that facilitates access to information contained in patient and client health records.

INTRODUCTION

The nature of medical practice, whether conducted in the private or public sectors, whether provided by a general practitioner practising alone in a rural area, or by medical practitioners working as members of an institutional healthcare team, will almost always include access to patient and client information. This access, to patient and client private and confidential information, is based on the therapeutic relationship which exists between a medical practitioner and their patient or client. Indeed, it is a combination of the legal, professional and ethical obligations imposed on medical practitioners to keep the patient's and client's information confidential — and the patient's and client's perception that such information will be kept confidential — that underpins the therapeutic relationship. That is, a medical practitioner needs the patient or client to disclose all their relevant health information to be able to make informed decisions regarding which medical treatment options may be most suitable and appropriate. The patient is only likely to disclose such information, however, if it is understood that their information will be kept confidential and used only for the purpose of clinical decision-making. It is therefore important that medical practitioners have an understanding of the legal, professional and ethical obligations that maintain the confidentiality of patient information and the mechanisms by which privacy of, and access to, patient information is secured.

Various situations in medical practice require the medical practitioner to follow and adhere to the strict provisions of privacy and confidentiality legislation, policies and guidelines. The *Good Medical Practice: Code of Conduct for Doctors in Australia*[1] and the Australian Medical Association (AMA) *Code of Ethics*[2] both expressly refer to the obligation and responsibility of a medical practitioner to keep patient information confidential. Flowing from the application of legislation, policies, guidelines and codes are the principles laid down in case law which have direct application to the day-to-day practice of any medical practitioner involved in the care and treatment of their patients and clients.

Skene[3] notes that privacy and confidentiality are different issues in that privacy is focused on the collection of information, whereas confidentiality is focused on communication of that information. Although the duties imposed on a medical practitioner in relation to these two issues differ conceptually, they are complimentary to one another in their application and there is a considerable overlap within a healthcare context.

THE OBLIGATION TO KEEP INFORMATION CONFIDENTIAL

The modern day notion of confidentiality, within the context of healthcare delivery by any health professional, originates in the provisions of the Hippocratic Oath. Under this oath a medical practitioner agreed to be bound by the ethical obligation to ensure:

> All that may come to my knowledge in the exercise of my profession or outside of my profession or in daily commerce with men, which ought not be spread abroad, I will keep secret and never reveal.[4]

The confidentiality of patient and client information is therefore one of the fundamental presumptions founding the relationship between medical practitioners and their patients or clients. Indeed, medical practice takes place in an environment in which the client expects their information will be kept confidential and the medical practitioner appreciates and respects the obligations imposed by that expectation. As stated in the case of *Seager v Copydex:*[5]

> [A person who] has received information in confidence shall not take unfair advantage of it. He must not make use of it to the prejudice of he who gave it without obtaining consent.

It could be argued that for any medical practitioner to provide optimum care to a patient or client they must have full and frank disclosure of all relevant information by that individual. In the case of *X v Y*, involving a medical practitioner, the court observed:

> If people felt that there was any chance of information given to their doctor, or the doctor's diagnosis, being passed on, people would be reluctant to seek advice and the disease would go underground. Confidentiality must be absolute or almost absolute … In the long run, preservation of confidentiality is the only way of securing public health; otherwise doctors will be discredited as a source of education, for future individual patients will not come forward if doctors are going to squeal on them. Consequently, confidentiality is vital to secure public as well as private health, for unless those infected come forward they cannot be counselled and self-treatment does not provide the best care.[6]

The obligation to keep information confidential has both a legal and ethical basis and includes information such as the patient's current and previous medical details, family history, social and financial circumstances and any facts in relation to the patient's or client's current or previous treatment or medication history. In fact the disclosure by a medical practitioner of information such as the person attended a hospital or a GP may constitute a breach of the duty of confidentiality.

Professional and ethical obligations

Professional codes of conduct and ethics protect the rights of patients and clients to have their information kept confidential. *The Good Medical Practice: A Code of Conduct for Doctors in Australia*[7] expressly recognises the obligation imposed upon medical practitioners to keep patient information confidential. Principle 3 of the Code, 'Working with patients' states at 3.2 under 'Doctor–patient partnership':

> A good doctor–patient partnership requires high standards of professional conduct. This involves …
>
> 3.2.3 Protecting patients' privacy and rights to confidentiality, unless release of information is required by law or by public interest considerations.

And under 3.4 'Privacy and Confidentiality':

> Patients have a right to expect that doctors and their staff
> will hold all information about them in confidence, unless
> release of information is required by law or public interest
> considerations. Good medical practice involves:
>
> 3.4.1 Treating information about patients as confidential.
> 3.4.2 Appropriately sharing information about patients
> for their healthcare, consistent with privacy law and
> professional guideline about confidentiality.
> 3.4.3 Being aware that there are complex issues related to
> genetic information and seeking appropriate advice
> about disclosure of such information.

Consistent with these provisions, the AMA *Code of Ethics* states
under the section 'The Doctor and the patient' at 1.1 'Patient care':
that the medical practitioner is to –

> 1. Maintain … patient's confidentiality. Exceptions to this
> must be taken seriously — may include where there is
> a serious risk to the patient or another person, where
> required by law, where part of approved research or where
> there are overwhelming societal interests.

The professional codes of conduct and ethics therefore impose
clear obligations on members of the medical profession to respect the
confidentiality of information acquired in the course of professional
practice relating to their patients. Such information must not be
disclosed to anyone without the consent of the patient or client.
Exceptions may arise where the health of the client or others is at
risk, where information is sought under legislation or common law,
where a court order requires the release of confidential information,
or the information is released to those assuming legal responsibility for
the patient; for example, when a patient looses capacity and requires
a substitute decision-maker for the purpose of healthcare decisions
(refer to Chapter 6, consent).

Statutory obligations

Legislation exists at state, territory and federal levels directed
specifically to the maintenance of confidentiality in relation to
patient and client information. The legislation generally provides
that patients and clients of healthcare services have a legally based
expectation that the health services are being provided in a way that
respects their right to the confidentiality of their information. That is,
there is a legislatively imposed obligation on all health professionals
(and others who come into contact with the patient's information as

part of their work in the delivery of healthcare services) to protect the patient's information from disclosure, unauthorised access and/or use. The legislation can be divided into two categories: first, that which protects the identity of the patient;[8] and second, that which protects information about the patient's medical condition.[9] In legislation protecting the confidentiality of patient information, health professionals, often referred to as the 'designated person' or 'relevant person', must not disclose patient information either directly or indirectly to others and there is usually a statutory penalty in circumstances in which information is disclosed inappropriately. As an example, the Queensland Health Services Act 1991, ss 60–62, imposes on public health sector employees a duty of confidentiality and a penalty for breach of that statutory duty. Section 62A states:

Confidentiality

(1) A designated person, or former designated person must not disclose to another person, whether directly or indirectly, any information (confidential information) acquired because of being a designated person if a person who is receiving or has received a public sector health service could be identified from the confidential information.

Maximum penalty — 50 penalty units.

Common law obligations

In addition to the legislative obligations there are obligations imposed on medical practitioners to keep patient information confidential which are imposed and maintained through the various common law decisions. The following is an overview of the legal basis upon which a client may initiate an action at common law in circumstances in which they consider there has been a breach of this obligation.

Negligence

The duty to keep information confidential is part of the duty of care owed by a medical practitioner to their clients. In circumstances in which this duty is breached through the medical practitioner divulging patient information, the medical practitioner may be sued in negligence for the damage caused by the breach.[10] In the case of *Furniss v Fitchett*[11] the medical practitioner disclosed the medical information about his patient to the patient's husband. The husband then used that information in legal proceedings. In this case Barrowclough CJ stated:[12]

[A] doctor's duty to care for his patients includes a duty not to give a third party a certificate as to his patient's condition, if he can reasonably foresee that the certificate might come to the patient's knowledge, and if he can reasonably foresee that that would be likely to cause his patient physical harm.

The decision suggests that where a medical practitioner causes injury, by carelessly revealing confidential information about the condition of the patient, it would amount to a breach of the duty of care. The duty however is not only 'to avoid telling unauthorised persons things that are confidential. It also covers taking proper precautions to ensure that confidential information does not fall into the wrong hands'.[13]

Contract

It is an implied term of a contract involving the provision of healthcare that all information disclosed in relation to that care will be kept confidential. In the public sector there are no contracts between individual health professionals such as medical practitioners and their patients and clients. Contracts in this context are most frequently between the healthcare institution and the government under the Medicare arrangements. However, in the private sector, where the patient receives a service for the fee paid directly to the medical practitioner, a contract will exist which may provide the ground for an action in breach of contract where a client's information is inappropriately disclosed.

Defamation

An action in defamation is founded on an allegation that the medical practitioner made a statement about a person, which though untrue, is published and thereby lowers the reputation of the person in the eyes of their peers. The subject of the defamatory statement can be any person, incorporated body or government department or agency, however, in a healthcare context it is most likely to arise in circumstances in which the medical practitioner makes a statement about a patient, a colleague or their employer. It is not necessary for the medical practitioner to actually name the person who is the subject of the comment. It is sufficient if the person is identifiable by their peers through the content of the statement. For example, it is not necessary to prove in an action in defamation that the medical practitioner used the actual name, Mr Smith. If the medical practitioner referred to 'the only 85 year old patient I have', and everyone in town knows that to be Mr Smith, that would suffice. The law of defamation is not uniform across Australia, with certain jurisdictions such as New South Wales,[14] Queensland[15] and Victoria[16] having enacted legislation.

Equity

The law recognises the power imbalance between the providers of healthcare services and their patients and clients. Where a medical practitioner discloses information about a patient or client, that person may claim a breach of the fiduciary duty owed to them by the medical practitioner that resulted in a loss. In *Coco v A N Clark (Engineers) Ltd*[17] Megarry J held:

In my judgement, three elements are normally required if, apart from contract, a case of breach of confidence is to succeed. First, the information itself … must have the necessary quality of confidence about it. Secondly, that information must have been imparted in circumstances importing an obligation of confidence. Thirdly, there must be an unauthorised use of that information to the detriment of the party.

The patient or client information must therefore have 'the necessary quality of confidence about it',[18] and 'must have been imparted in circumstances importing an obligation of confidence'. There has been discussion as to whether the requirement of a 'detriment' would be met in circumstances where the patient has not sustained an 'economic loss' as a result of the breach of the obligation to keep the information confidential. It has been suggested that, in cases involving medical confidentiality, the detriment in the use of the confidential information is not necessary and that the 'mere disclosure and its immediate consequences' is sufficient to warrant injunctive relief.[19] Australian courts have declined to interpret the medical practitioner–patient relationship as fiduciary in nature and therefore it is unlikely that disclosure of information by any medical practitioner will give rise to an action for breach of fiduciary duty.[20]

Disciplinary action

The Health Practitioner Regulation National Law Act 2009 (the National Law) states as one of the objects of the National Scheme; 'to provide for the protection of the public by ensuring that only health practitioners who are suitably trained and qualified to practise in a competent and ethical manner are recognised'.[21] One of the mechanisms through which this objective is met is the disciplinary process. Health practitioners who conduct themselves in a manner that amounts to 'professional misconduct' may be charged by the national regulatory authority and bought before a disciplinary tribunal (refer Chapter 11, professional regulation and discipline). The definition of 'professional misconduct' for a registered health practitioner includes 'unprofessional conduct … that is substantially below a standard reasonably expected …'[22] and 'unprofessional conduct' includes 'professional conduct that is of a lesser standard than that which might reasonably be expected of the health practitioner by the public of the practitioner's professional peers'.[23] The inappropriate disclosure of confidential information about a patient by a medical practitioner would, when benchmarked against these standards, provide the grounds for allegations of professional misconduct. In addition, the inappropriate disclosure of patient or client information may provide the basis for a mandatory[24] and voluntary[25] notification to the National Agency under the National Law.

Exceptions to the duty to confidentiality

It is clear from the foregoing that patients have the right to confidentiality of their information, however, this right is not absolute and may be overridden in particular circumstances.

Express consent

The disclosure of patient or client information is authorised where the medical practitioner has the express consent of the patient. It is suggested that the issue of with whom, if anyone, the patient's information may be discussed is clarified as soon as possible. There may be circumstances in which the patient or client consents to a spouse, parent, child or other health professional being given information about the client's health concerns or particular medication regime. Clearly, where a range of healthcare professionals and workers are caring for a patient or client there is an implied consent to the communication of information necessary for the patient's ongoing healthcare and wellbeing between those involved in the care.

Legal duty of disclosure

In all Australian states and territories there is legislation requiring the disclosure of patient and client information. Though the specific requirements of each jurisdiction are set out in the respective Acts, it is mandatory in all jurisdictions other than Western Australia for nominated professionals to report suspected child abuse.[26] In most jurisdictions the diagnosis of a communicable disease and/or the presentation of a client with suspicious injuries are also reportable. There are also legislative provisions in the respective jurisdictions to provide information, or produce documents or other materials, as part of the court process. Though in a number of the states or territories there is no legal protection inherent in the health professional–patient relationship, in Victoria,[27] Tasmania[28] and the Northern Territory,[29] doctor–patient privilege is permitted in civil proceedings. In both Victoria[30] and New South Wales[31] there is privilege in the communication between victims of sexual assault and their counsellors.

There may be situations in medical practice that would require a medical practitioner to weigh up the legal and ethical requirements regarding patient confidentiality against legislation that permits a breach of confidentiality.

Public interest disclosure

The obligation imposed on a medical practitioner to keep a patient or client's information confidential may be overridden in circumstances in which the disclosure of the information is necessary in the public interest. This public interest exception is not clearly defined and arises only where there is a real and significant threat of harm, or the possibility of death. For example, where a medical practitioner is told by the patient or client that they intended to kill or harm another person.[32] In the American case of *Tarasoff v Regents of the University of California*,[33] the patient told his treating psychotherapist during a consultation that he intended to kill a named individual. The patient carried out his threat and the family of the victim successfully sued the psychotherapist, alleging a negligent failure to warn their daughter of the threat that had been made against her. In this decision, which has not been applied by the Australian courts, the majority of the Supreme Court of California confirmed that the relationship between a psychotherapist or a medical practitioner and their patient was one which 'may support affirmative duties for the benefit of third persons'. Tobriner J stated:[34]

> We conclude that the public policy favouring protection of the confidential character of patient–psychotherapist communications must yield to the extent to which disclosure is essential to avert danger to others. The protective privilege ends where the public peril begins.

In the case of *W v Edgell and Others*[35] the doctor was employed to provide an assessment of W, a forensic prisoner, for the purpose of his release to a less secure mental health facility. The psychiatric assessment carried out by Dr Edgell was unfavourable to the prisoner and his legal representative withdrew the application. Dr Edgell, believing W still presented a considerable danger, forwarded his report to the Secretary of State. The court dismissed W's application based on a breach of doctor–patient confidentiality and held that the public interest in disclosing the information to the authorities outweighed W's right to have his information kept confidentiality. Bingham LJ of the Court of Appeal concluded:[36]

> The decided cases clearly establish that the law recognises an important public interest in maintaining professional duties of

confidence but the law treats such duties not as absolute but as liable to be overridden when there is held to be a stronger public interest in disclosure.

PRIVACY LAW

While there is an overlap between the concept of confidentiality and the privacy of patient or client information as discussed previously, they are recognised as two different concepts and therefore the requirements in relation to privacy need to be addressed separately. The privacy of a patient's or client's personal information is secured under the provisions of the Commonwealth Privacy Act 1988. The Act regulates how personal information is handled with 'health information' being classified as 'sensitive information'. The Privacy Act 1988 (Cth) as amended,[37] covers individuals and the private and public sectors establishing the ten *National Privacy Principles* (NPPs)[38] (which apply to parts of the private sector and to all health service providers) and eleven *Information Privacy Principles*[39] (IPPs) (which apply to the Commonwealth and Australian Capital Territory government agencies). These principles provide for the collection, storage, security, use and disclosure of personal information and, in addition, deal with the right of access to information and correction of information that is collected about an individual. The legislation creates the position of the Federal Privacy Commissioner to whom complaints may be directed when there is an alleged breach of the provisions.

Section 62A(2) of the Privacy Act 1988 (Cth) states that:

[An] organisation must not do an act, or engage in a practice, that breaches a National Privacy Principle.

An 'organisation' is defined under the legislation to include an individual, a body corporate and a partnership, but not a government agency. While small businesses are generally excluded, those that provide a health service are not.[40]

The NPPs, which apply to private sector organisations and individuals and all health service providers in the private sector, are summarised as follows:[41]

NPP 1: *Collection* and **NPP 10**: *Sensitive Information* and **NPP 8**:
Anonymity — identify the provider's obligations when collecting a patient or client's health information. This includes an obligation on a medical practitioner to collect fairly and lawfully only that health information that is necessary to provide a service. The information must be collected directly from the individual (if practicable) and only with the consent of the individual unless an exemption applies. If lawful and practicable, the individual has a right to remain anonymous during the interaction.[42]

NPP 2: *Use and Disclosure* — identifies how health information, once collected by the medical practitioner, can be used within the ambit of medical practise, the healthcare institution or disclosed to third parties outside the practice or the institution. As a general proposition the information can only be used for the purpose for which it was collected.

NPP 3: *Data Quality* and **NPP 4**: *Data Security* — identify the standards required for keeping information up-to-date, accurate and complete. The principles also address the obligation to protect information from misuse, loss, unauthorised access, modification or disclosure. When information is no longer required to be kept it has to be permanently de-identified or destroyed.

NPP 5: *Openness* — requires the medical practitioner to be open about how the client or patient's health information is managed and made available. This includes developing a policy document (privacy policy) explaining how the information is handled.

NPP 6: *Access and Correction* — provides patients and clients with a general right to access and correct information about themselves that a medical practitioner or healthcare institution may hold.

NPP 7: *Identifiers* — imposes an obligation to limit the use of commonwealth identifiers to the purpose for which they were intended.

NPP 9: *Transborder Data Flow* — identifies the obligations on a provider when transferring health information overseas.

A private organisation or provider may withhold information and refuse access, by third parties and, in some circumstances, the patient themselves, where disclosure would 'pose a serious threat to the life or health of an individual', ' have an unreasonable impact upon the privacy of other individuals', where the 'information relates to existing or anticipated legal proceedings between the organisation and the individual, and the information would not be accessible by the process of discovery',[43] provision of the information 'would be unlawful',[44] and 'providing access would be likely to prejudice an investigation of possible unlawful activity'.[45]

State legislation and government schemes

In relation to health records, a number of states and territories have enacted their own privacy legislation which operates in addition to the federal provisions.[46] Medical students and practitioners therefore need to be aware of any additional obligations imposed by privacy legislation in the particular jurisdiction in which they practise.

Australian Capital Territory

The amended version of the Commonwealth Privacy Act applies to government agencies and is administered by the Privacy Commissioner. In relation to health records, the Health Records (Privacy and Access) Act 1997 applies to those records held in public and private sectors. This legislation is based on the IPPs and provides patients and clients with access to their own health information. In the ACT, the Human Rights Commission handles health record privacy complaints.[47]

New South Wales

The Health Records and Information Privacy Act 2002 establishes fifteen Health Privacy Principles (HPPs), provides for the creation of 'Statutory Guidelines' to assist in the application of the principles and establishes a framework for managing complaints about the handling of health information. There are four statutory guidelines which are legally binding and apply to the use or disclosure of health information for the management of health services, for training purposes, for research purposes and the notification when collecting health information about a person from someone else. While the Health Records and Information Privacy Act 2002 applies to both the public and the private sectors (to every health service provider or health sector organisation that collects, holds or uses health information), the Privacy and Personal Information Act 1998 applies only to the information held within the public sector.

Northern Territory

The Northern Territory Information Act 2002 applies to the public sector and protects personal information, regulates record-keeping and archival management of information. The Act also incorporates the Privacy Principles and establishes the office of the Information Commissioner in the Northern Territory.

Queensland

Previously under a government privacy scheme, the Information Privacy Act 2009 now regulates the handling of personal information in Queensland. The Act contains eleven IPPs that provide for the handling of personal information by Queensland Government agencies (other than Queensland Health) and nine NPPs that set out how personal information is to be handled by Queensland Health.

South Australia

The South Australian government established a Privacy Committee and issued administrative instructions which require government agencies to comply with IPPs. The Code of Fair Information

Practice, which is based on the NPPs, applies to the handling of personal information by the South Australian Health Department.

Victoria

In Victoria the Information Privacy Act 2000 applies to the handling of personal information (except health information) across the public sector. The Health Records Act 2001 covers all personal information held by the health service providers in the public sector and governs the practices of handling health information in the private sector. The Act creates eleven Health Privacy Principles (HPPs) adapted from the NPPs and provides an individual with the right of access to health information collected and held by a health service provider (including a sole practitioner) or organisation. Under the Act an 'Organisation' as pertaining to the private sector is defined to include a 'natural person, body corporate, partnership, trust, unincorporated association or body that is a health service provider or collects, holds or uses health information': Health Records Act ss3(1), 11(1), (2). The Charter of Human Rights and Responsibilities 2006 also provides a general right to privacy for an individual in Victoria.

Western Australia

The Western Australian public sector does not have a legislative privacy scheme. At the time of writing the Information Privacy Bill 2007 is moving through the parliamentary process. If enacted, it will establish a set of IPPs and regulate the handing of health information in the public sector and private sectors.

ACCESS TO PATIENT AND CLIENT INFORMATION

At common law the physical property in the patient's file or records is with the person who made that file or record.[48] If the medical practitioner establishes and maintains a patient file, that file is the property of the medical practitioner who made it. This means that a patient has no legal right at common law to access their file and must therefore gain access under the relevant legislative provisions. Some of the legislation discussed above (in the section, state legislation and government schemes) facilitates access in the private and public sectors to health information. Additionally, there are also the freedom of information legislation at state, territory and federal levels that provide access to, and facilitate production of, personal records specifically in the public sector. The Freedom of Information Act 1982 (Cth) applies to the federal sector and provides any individual, subject to express exclusions, with a legally enforceable right to obtain access to their records in

Table 4.1 State and territory freedom of information legislation	
Cth	Freedom of Information Act 1982
ACT	Freedom of Information Act 1989
NSW	Freedom of Information Act 1989
NT	Information Act 2002
Qld	Right to Information Act 2009
SA	Freedom of Information Act 1991
Tas	Freedom of Information Act 1991
Vic	Freedom of Information Act 1982
WA	Freedom of Information Act 1992

accordance with the Act. Similar legislation is in place in the states and territories and is contained in Table 4.1. The provisions of this legislation may assist the medical practitioner in making a decision as to whether a patient is given access to their medical information and, in some jurisdictions, whether that information is to be made available to others after the patient is deceased. This legislation is accessible through the government websites in each of the states and territories.

Children

Whether a child has the right to have their information kept confidential is inextricably connected to both the child's capacity to make decisions on their own behalf and an assessment as to what is in the best interest of the child in the particular circumstances. Generally, there is an obligation on all health professionals to keep information about their patients and clients confidential unless there is express consent by the patient or client to disclosure. It could be suggested that similar obligations are imposed in relation to the information and data collected by medical practitioners about those of their patients or clients who are children. This obligation, to keep information confidential, is based on the legislation at Commonwealth and state levels, common law decisions and professional codes of ethics and conduct.

It stands to reason that if the child is considered as competent, referred to as Gillick competent, for the purpose of giving a legally valid consent to treatment they also have the right to expect that their information, in relation to that treatment, is confidential (refer to Chapter 6, Consent). The rationale for this proposition is that:

if the parents do not have the power to consent to the medical treatment their child seeks, they do not have the power to obtain medical information about that treatment.

(Law Reform Commission 2004)[49]

In circumstances in which a child confirms they want the information kept confidential, or the information is clearly confidential in nature, or given in a situation where confidentiality is implicit, there is a strong argument that there is an obligation of confidentiality attached to their information. However, there are situations in which the law permits, and in some circumstances compels, the disclosure of information pertaining to a child's health. This includes circumstances in which the child consents to such disclosure, particular situations in which a person with sufficient personal interest (usually a parent) seeks information in the child's best interests, and when disclosure is mandated by legislation or it is in the public interest to disclose.

As with adults at common law, there is no right of access by a child to their medical records, and any person seeking such access must make an application under the existing legislative provisions. The Commonwealth, state and territory freedom of information legislation operates in the public sector and gives an individual a legally enforceable right to seek access to their records. While it is acceptable in most jurisdictions for a parent to make an application under this legislation on behalf of their child, they may be denied access where the information is potentially prejudicial or where it would be otherwise unreasonable for the parent to be given the access requested. The Privacy Act 1988 (Cth), in its application to healthcare delivery in the private sector, is silent as to the exact age at which the right to access information is acquired. A child's right to access their own information would therefore appear to be dependent on similar criteria to that which determines their ability to give a legally valid consent; that is, their level of competence or capacity to understand the nature and effect of their decisions and their level of maturity and intelligence.

SCENARIO AND ACTIVITY

During a weekly consultation the patient confides in his psychiatrist that he has sexually assaulted one of his children.

- What are the legal obligations of the psychiatrist?

REVIEW QUESTIONS

1 Identify and describe the legal and professional obligation of confidentiality in relation to patient and client information.

2 What legal action may be taken by a patient against a health professional who breaches the obligation of confidentiality?

3 What are the professional disciplinary grounds available where a medical student or medical practitioner breaches the obligation not to disclose patient information?

4 Upon what ground may a health professional disclose patient information?

5 Identify the privacy legislation, principles or scheme in your jurisdiction. How do the provisions or principle apply to medical practice?

6 Identify the legislation in your jurisdiction which facilitates patient access to the content of their medical records.

Further reading

Aberdee A, 'The medical duty of confidentiality and the duty to disclose: can they co-exist?' (1995) *Journal of Law and Medicine* 75.

Attorney-General's Department. *Freedom of Information.* Online. Available:www.ag.gov.au/www/agd/agd.nsf/Page/Freedom-of-information (accessed 22 July 2010).

Carter M, 'Patient privacy in the electronic era: Legal and privacy considerations' (2000) *Australian Health Law Bulletin*, 117.

Commonwealth Attorney-General's Department (Privacy Division). Online.Available:www.ag.gov.au/www/agd/a...epartmentPrivacy_Statement/Privacy (accessed 22 July 2010).

Kloczko A, Payne K, 'Major changes to health privacy proposed' (2009) *Australian Health Law Bulletin* Vol. 17, No. 6–7 at 123–6.

Office of Federal Privacy Commissioner. Online. Available: Online. Available: www.ag.gov.au/www/agd/a...epartment Privacy_Statement/Privacy (accessed on 22 July 2010).

Patterson M, 'Shared electronic health records systems: The significance of the privacy dimension' (2008) *Australian Health Law Bulletin* Vol. 16, (No. 7).

Privacy Act 1988 and Privacy Amendment (Private Sector) Act 2000 (Cth). Online. Available: www.comlaw.gov.au (accessed on 22 July 2010).

Ruschena D, 'The virtues of fighting: The Commonwealth Privacy Act and regulation on privacy' (2009) *Australian Health Law Bulletin* Vol.17 No.5 at 85–8.

Endnotes

1 Developed by a working party of the Australian Medical Council on behalf of the medical boards of the Australian states and territories, July 2009. Note that this Code has been adopted by the Medical Board of Australia with amendments to reflect the National Law.

2 (2004) Editorially revised 2006.

3 Skene, L, *Law and Medical Practice-Rights, Duties, Claims and Defences*, 2nd edn, Lexis Nexis Butterworths, Sydney, 2004, paras 9.1 and 9.8.

4 Reproduction of the Hippocratic Oath, in Mason, J, McCall Smith, P, (1994) *Law and Medical Ethics*, 4th edn, Butterworths, London.

5 [1967] WLR 923.

6 [1988] 2All ER 648.

7 Developed by a working party of the Australian Medical Council on behalf of the medical boards of the Australian states and territories, July 2009.

8 Health Services Act 1988 (Vic), s 141; Mental Health Act 1986 (Vic), s 120A.

9 Guardianship Act 1987 (NSW) s 101; Mental Health Act 1990 (NSW) s 289; Mental Health Act 1993 (SA) s 48; Mental Health Act 1986 (Vic) ss 63, 117, 120A; Medical Practice Act 1992 (NSW) s 190; Health Administration Act 1982 (NSW) s 22; Health Act 1937 (Qld) s 100E; Health Services Act 1991 (Qld) s 5.1; Health Services Act 1988 (Vic) ss 126, 141; South Australian Health Commission Act 1976 (SA) s 64; The Privacy Act 1998 (Cth).

10 *Furniss v Fitchett* [1958] NZLR 396 at 404.

11 [1958] NZLR 396.

12 [1958] NZLR 396 at 405.

13 H v Home Office, *The Guardian*, 6 May 1992.

14 Defamation Act 2005.

15 Defamation Act 2005.

16 Defamation Act 2005.

17 [1969] RPC 41.

18 The necessary quality of confidence may include consideration of the following: What is the content of the information? Is it such that a reasonable person would understand it was confidential?

What is the situation in which the information is being disclosed? For example, is the conversation occurring in a public corridor or in the privacy of a consulting room? What is the medical student/ medical practitioner's understanding of the patient's intention of disclosing the information? That is, did the patient expressly ask that the information be kept confidential? Did the patient say they did not want the information communicated to others?

19 *X v Y* [1988] 2 All ER 648 at 658 per Rose J.

20 The Laws of Australia 'Confidentiality', Ch 20.7, para 5; *Breen v Williams* (1996) CLR 71; *McInerney v MacDonald* (1996) 93 DLR (4th) 415.

21 s 3(2).

22 Health Practitioner Regulation National Law Act 2009 s 5.

23 Ibid.

24 Health Practitioner Regulation National Law Act 2009 s 140: 'Definition of notifiable conduct … notifiable conduct in relation to a registered health practitioner, means the practitioner has — …(d) placed the public at risk of harm because the practitioner has practised the profession in a way that constitutes a significant departure from accepted professional standards'.

25 Health Practitioner Regulation National Law Act 2009 s 144: 'Grounds for voluntary notification (1) A voluntary notification about a registered health practitioner may be made to the National Agency on any of the following grounds — (a) that the practitioner's professional conduct is, or may be, of a lesser standard than that which might reasonably be expected of the practitioner by the public or the practitioner's peers;(b) that the knowledge, skill or judgement possessed, or care exercised by, the practitioner in the practice of the practitioner's health profession is, or may be, below the standard reasonably expected …'.

26 Children and Young People Act 1999 (ACT); Public Health Act 2005 (Qld); Children and Young Persons (Care and Protection) Act 1998 (NSW); Community Welfare Act (NT); Children's Protection Act 1993 (SA), Children; Young Persons and their Families Act 1997 (Tas); Children and Young Persons Act 1989 (Vic).

27 Evidence Act 1958.

28 Evidence Act 2001.

29 Evidence Act.

30 Evidence Act 1958.

31 Evidence Act 1995.

32 *Tarasoff v Regents of the University of California* 551 P 2d 334 (1976).
33 Ibid, 551 P2d 334 (1976) Supreme Court of California.
34 Ibid at 347.
35 [1990] 1All ER 855.
36 Ibid at 848.
37 Privacy Amendment (Private Sector) Act 2000.
38 Schedule 3 Privacy Act 1988 (Cth).
39 Schedule 14 Privacy Act 1988 (Cth).
40 Privacy Act s 16A(2) 6D(4)(b).
41 Australian Government. Office of the Privacy Commissioner. National Privacy Principles (NPP). Online. Available: http:// privacy.gov.au/materials/types/infosheets/view/6583 (accessed 11 June 2010).
42 Summary of Obligations for pharmacists, Guidelines on Privacy in the Private Health Sector, Office of the Federal Privacy Commissioner October 2001.
43 Privacy Act Schedule 3 NPP 6.1(b),(c), (e).
44 Privacy Act Schedule 3 NPP 6.1 (g) (h).
45 Privacy Act Schedule 3 NPP 6.1 (i), (k).
46 Australian Government. Office of the Privacy Commissioner. Online. Available: www.privacy.gov.au/privacy_rights/law/index.html#5 (accessed 11 June 2010).
47 Human Rights Act 2004.
48 *Breen v Williams* (1995) 186 CLR 71.
49 New South wales Law Reform Commision (2004) Issues paper 24. 'Minors consert to medical treatment: Disclosure and access to young people's health information':3.

5

Negligence

LEARNING OBJECTIVES

This chapter aims to introduce you to the civil action of negligence. This is the action which is most frequently referred to when discussions are had about medical or health law. It is important for you to recognise that by comparison to the actual number of medical practitioner–patient contacts the occurrence of an adverse event is *very* low and even lower is the initiation of legal proceedings against a medical practitioner. The basis of an action in negligence is that the medical practitioner has conducted themselves in a manner that is below an accepted standard. It is therefore important that you are vigilant in providing a standard of medical practice that is consistent with the professional expectations of your peers and the public. While reading this chapter you should focus on:

- describing the elements necessary for a plaintiff to succeed in an action in negligence against a medical practitioner
- identifying and understanding the standard of practice required of a medical practitioner
- explaining the legal requirements in disclosing risk, or warning a patient of risks prior to obtaining a consent
- understanding the issues of causation
- identifying and recognising the types of damages
- identifying the possible defence to a negligence action
- discussing the effect of the doctrine of vicarious liability
- identifying and understanding alternative actions to negligence in a healthcare context.

INTRODUCTION

Medical negligence litigation is considered as one of the means by which the quality of healthcare services is improved and maintained. That is, the threat of litigation effectively deters poor behaviour by healthcare professionals, including medical practitioners, and, through the publicity of cases, educates the public and professionals about what is an appropriate standard of care.[1]

In the 1960s, law suits brought against health professionals were exceptionally rare and considered by the medical and legal professions as aberrations. Patients who attempted to initiate actions were thought of as ungrateful and would find it almost impossible to engage expert witnesses to support their case.[2] As a consequence, not only were medical defence insurance contributions minimal, but the effect of such litigation was considered trivial and was virtually ignored in relation to public and private healthcare costs and general standards of patient care.

Since the 1970s, however, there have been assertions of a worldwide 'crisis' in medical malpractice litigation. Commentators speak of medical malpractice litigation and the financial and social costs associated with it as in the grips of 'crisis'.[3] A combination of the community perception of a medical malpractice 'crisis', the perceived lack of clarity and predictability in personal injury litigation, the amounts in damages awarded to successful litigants and the public liability insurance collapse necessitated intervention and response by the federal government. In 2002, the ministers from the Commonwealth, state and territory governments negotiated to undertake a national review of the law of negligence in Australia: *Review of the Law of Negligence* (the Ipp Report). As a result of the recommendations arising out of this review, civil liability legislation was introduced in all Australian jurisdictions.[4] As the civil liability legislation is not uniform across the individual Australian states and territories, medical practitioners must familiarise themselves with the legislative provisions in the individual states or territories in which they go to work.

Notwithstanding that within the Australian context negligence law is now an amalgam of case law and legislation, medical negligence litigation has been, and continues to be, credited with bringing about safer practices in the provision of healthcare services. All health professionals involved in the provision of healthcare services are becoming increasingly aware of their legal obligations to their patients and clients. This chapter examines the elements necessary to establish an action in negligence against a medical practitioner.

NEGLIGENCE

Negligence is the civil action initiated under the law of torts in which medical practitioners and healthcare institutions may become liable if a patient, or client, sustains an injury while in their care. *A claim in negligence alleges conduct that may include not only an act, but also an omission to act, which is causally linked to the injury. In relation to civil liability, negligence has been defined in legislation as the 'failure to exercise reasonable care and skill',*[5] *which may include 'a breach of a tortious, contractual or statutory duty of care'.*[6] For example, in a healthcare context, a patient who is injured or suffers a loss as a result of the acts or omissions of a medical practitioner may bring an action in negligence against the professional and/or their employer, seeking compensation. The basis of the claim is that the conduct of the medical practitioner fell below the standard of care appropriate to the particular circumstances and that this action resulted in damage, which the patient now seeks to have compensated in money. Unlike criminal proceedings, the action seeks to place the injured person (the plaintiff) in the position they would have been in had they not sustained the damage. The consequences of a finding of liability against a medical practitioner and/or the healthcare institution (the defendant) is therefore not considered as a punishment but rather as compensation to the injured party or their relatives. The principle underpinning this form of *legal redress is to shift the loss, as far as money is able to do so, from the individual who has sustained the injury or damage to the individual or institution who is held to have caused the loss.*

Proof

The person, usually a patient (the plaintiff), bringing the action in negligence must prove every element of the action according to the *civil standard of proof, which is on the balance of probabilities* to succeed in their claim. To do this, the plaintiff must adduce evidence in the form of documents, testimony from witnesses, or other relevant materials sufficient to satisfy this standard. If the plaintiff is not able to prove any one of the elements necessary to succeed in the negligence action on the balance of probabilities, the action will fail completely. That is, the *court must be satisfied that every element of the action has been proven on the balance of probabilities* for the plaintiff to succeed in their claim.

Though applied in *only exceptional circumstances,* the fact that an accident has occurred at all may raise the inference of negligence on the part of the defendant. This is the doctrine of *res ipsa loquitur,* 'the thing speaks for itself', which will only apply when:

- there is no evidence as to how or why the accident occurred;
- the accident is such that it would not occur without negligence; and
- the defendant is proved to have been in control of, or linked to, the situation either personally or vicariously.[7]

In *Cassidy v Ministry of Health,*[8] Lord Denning stated:

If the plaintiff had to prove that some particular doctor or nurse was negligent, he would not be able to do it. But he was not put to that impossible task: he says, 'I went into the hospital to be cured of two stiff fingers. I have come out with four stiff fingers, and my hand is useless. That should not have happened if due care had been used. Explain it, if you can'. I am quite clearly of the opinion that that raises a prima facie case against the hospital authorities ... They have nowhere explained how it could happen without negligence. They have busied themselves in saying this or that member of their staff was not negligent. But they have called not a single person to say that the injuries were consistent with due care on the part of all members of their staff. They called some of the people who actually treated the man, namely Dr Fahrni, Dr Ronaldson, and Sister Hall, each of whom protested that he was careful in his part; but they did not call any expert at all, to say that this might happen despite all care. They have not therefore displaced the prima facie case against them and are liable in damages to the plaintiff.

Kennedy and Grubb propose that there are two reasons as to why the *res ipsa loquitur* doctrine will not usually be available to a plaintiff in a medical case. The first is that there are no certainties in medical treatment. The second is based on significant changes in both medical and legal practices. These changes include an improvement in the way health professionals, including medical practitioners, document patient information and changes to rules of evidence and court rules which facilitate the nature and amount of evidence available to parties involved in litigation. The cumulative effect of both of these factors is that it is more likely that the plaintiff will know, or be able to find out, what happened during his or her period of care or treatment.[9]

ELEMENTS OF A NEGLIGENCE ACTION

Negligence has been defined by the courts as:

[T]he omission to do something which a reasonable man, guided upon those considerations which ordinarily regulate the conduct of human affairs, would do, or doing something which a prudent and reasonable man would not do.[10]

However, not every injury that occurs while a patient is under the care of a medical practitioner will result from negligence, and not all acts or omissions that result in an injury will be held to be negligent. The courts have acknowledged that where a medical practitioner makes a 'mere' error in clinical judgment[11] or embarks on procedures which, with hindsight, are recognised as a 'misadventure',[12] it will not, in all circumstances, constitute negligence. In such circumstances, the law confronts the practical reality of healthcare delivery in accepting that some injuries are the result of unforeseen circumstances that do not involve fault on the part of the medical practitioner or the institution.

To succeed in a claim in negligence against a medical practitioner therefore, the patient (plaintiff) must be able to establish, on the balance of probabilities all the elements:

- the patient was owed a duty of care by the medical practitioner (defendant)
- that there was a breach of that duty in that the medical practitioner's conduct fell below the required standard of care
- this conduct caused the damages suffered by the patient
- the loss or damage suffered was reasonably foreseeable.[13]

Duty of care

The first element that the plaintiff must prove is that the defendant owed the plaintiff a duty of care. In all but the most unusual circumstances where there is a medical practitioner–patient relationship, there will also be the legally recognised relationship upon which the courts impose a duty of care.[14] This is so, based on the 'neighbour principle' enunciated by Lord Atkin in what is now considered the landmark case of *Donoghue v Stevenson*.[15] In this case, the plaintiff sought compensation for the consequences flowing from drinking the contents of a bottle of ginger beer that contained a decomposing snail. Lord Atkin stated:

> You must take reasonable care to avoid acts or omissions which you could reasonably foresee would be likely to injure your neighbour. Who, then, in law, is my neighbour? The answer seems to be — persons who are so closely and directly affected by my acts that I ought reasonably to have them in contemplation as being so affected when I am directing my mind to the acts or omissions which are called in question.[16]

Though the facts of this case were specifically concerned with consumer law, it can be seen that the medical practitioner–patient relationship is one which gives rise to a duty of care. The patient is clearly a person whom the medical practitioner can reasonably foresee as likely to be injured if reasonable care is not exercised. In the case involving a medical practitioner, the majority judgment of the High Court of Australia in *Rogers v Whitaker* held:

> The law imposes on a medical practitioner a duty to exercise reasonable care and skill in the provision of professional advice and treatment. That duty is a single comprehensive duty covering all the ways in which a doctor is called upon to exercise his skill and judgment, it extends to the examination,

diagnosis and treatment of the patient and the provision of information in an appropriate case.[17]

The obligation to take 'reasonable care' against the risk of harm that is 'reasonably foreseeable' has long been considered by the courts. In *Swain v Waverley Municipal Council*, Gleeson CJ held that:

> People do not expect, and are not entitled to expect, to live in a risk free environment. The measure of careful behaviour is reasonableness, not elimination of risk.[18]

Reasonable foreseeability

As stated above, there is a requirement that the plaintiff is reasonably foreseeable to the defendant and that there is a reasonable foreseeability of harm. These are questions of fact and remain the basis for a determination of duty of care. The test is objective: was the plaintiff foreseeable as an individual, or member of a class to whom the duty was owed? In the particular circumstances, was the risk that eventuated to the particular plaintiff, or a class of people to which the plaintiff is a member, foreseeable?[19] The question for consideration is: '*What, in all the circumstances and having given the matter close attention, would the reasonable person have foreseen?*' In a case where a patient sues their medical practitioner, to succeed in establishing the existence of the duty of care the patient (plaintiff) must prove that the medical practitioner (defendant) ought to have foreseen that negligence on the part of the medical practitioner could lead to the patient being injured. It is not necessary that the patient establish that the medical practitioner foresaw the damage to the patient as an individual. The element will be satisfied if the patient was a 'member of a class' to whom the damage was foreseeable.[20] That is, the medical practitioner–patient relationship is such that the medical practitioner would know the patient was likely to be affected by their actions.

The people to whom medical practitioners, and all health professionals may owe a duty of care as part of their work can often be quite extensive. Not only is there a duty owed by medical practitioners, nurses and allied health professionals to their patients and clients but the New South Wales Court of Appeal, in the case of *Alexander v Heise*,[21] held that a medical practitioner's receptionist had a duty of care to make an assessment of a patient's condition, determine the urgency of the condition based on that assessment and schedule an appointment with the medical practitioner accordingly. A duty is owed not only to the patients and clients but also to third parties. The third parties could include the relatives of patients or people whom the patient may injure while under the care of the health professional.[22] The following are some specific examples of circumstances in which a health professional, particularly medical practitioners, may owe a duty of care.

DUTY TO THIRD PARTIES

As stated above, *a medical practitioner may owe a duty of care not only to their patients but also to others (third parties) who may be injured through the failure of the medical practitioner to take reasonable care of the patient.* That is, in failing to give a reasonable, appropriate, competent standard of care to a patient another person sustains an injury. In the case of *BT (as Administratix of the Estate of the Late AT) v Oei*,[23] the court held that the medical practitioner Dr Oei, owed the plaintiff, BT, a duty of care which he had breached in failing to advise the patient AT (who was the partner of BT) that he should undergo a HIV test. The patient, AT, had consulted Dr Oei over a number of years and had been diagnosed as suffering from hepatitis, cirrhosis of the liver, kidney stones and recurrent infections, which included a urinary tract infection. AT also informed Dr Oei that he had been participating in sexual activity with a prostitute. The patient AT and his partner BT (who was not a patient of Dr Oei) both tested positive for HIV and shortly thereafter AT died of renal failure. As BT had contracted HIV from AT, she sued Dr Oei in negligence, alleging that if Dr Oei exercised ordinary skill and care, he would have identified that AT was at risk of having contracted HIV (in light of his symptoms) and therefore Dr Oei had a duty to advise AT to undergo testing for HIV. A duty which he had breached. The case is of interest as it is indicative of the duty owed by medical practitioners to third parties such as BT. Of particular significance are the circumstances of the case. Not only was there no pre-existing medical practitioner–patient relationship between BT and the defendant Dr Oei, but also there was no evidence to suggest that he knew of the sexual relationship between his patient AT and BT. The court held that the medical practitioner ought to have known the patient had exposed himself to the risk of contracting HIV. As AT's condition was latent, neither he nor his partner were able to protect themselves from the risk of BT contracting HIV. Therefore, the medical practitioner owed a duty of care to advise AT to undergo HIV testing. It is important to note that, even though a duty of care has been established and breached, these elements alone will not sustain an action in negligence. It is also necessary for the plaintiff to prove that, once AT was armed with the knowledge that a test for HIV was advisable, he would have undergone that test (refer to the section in this chapter entitled 'Causation').

In the case of *McDonald v Sydney South West Area Health Service*,[24] the New South Wales Supreme Court was to determine whether the father of a child born, after the mother had a sterilisation procedure performed, was entitled to recover the costs of raising the healthy child. The statement of claim alleged negligence first in the failure of the medical practitioner to advise and warn in relation to the sterilisation procedure, and secondly that the tubal ligation procedure was not properly performed in that the Filshie clip on the left fallopian tube was not applied so as to completely occlude the tube. The court held that the medical practitioner knew, or ought to have known, that if he did not properly occluded the fallopian tube the mother and her partner (the plaintiff) would suffer a financial detriment from having to incur the cost of raising the child. The relationship between the mother and the plaintiff (her husband) was determined by the court to be so close as to give rise to a duty of care between the medical practitioner and the husband.

In *PD v Dr Harvey and Dr Chen*,[25] the Supreme Court of New South Wales also found the medical practitioner owed a duty of care to the patient's sexual partner who was herself a patient. In this case, the plaintiff and her then boyfriend together attended a medical practice, seeking to be tested for HIV and other sexually transmitted diseases. Though the couple attended the consultation together, the medical practitioner did not discuss with them whether they wished to be informed of the test results together or what should happen if one of their results returned positive. Some days later, the medical practitioner received the plaintiff's results, which were negative for HIV. The results for her boyfriend, however, were positive for both HIV and hepatitis B. The plaintiff, though given her own results, was told she could not access her boyfriend's results, as the information contained therein was confidential. The boyfriend was informed of his results and given a referral to a specialist. He neither attended the appointment nor disclosed the results to the plaintiff, but rather told her he was negative and produced a forged pathology report confirming that to be the case. Although the plaintiff attended the same medical practice twice over the next 6 months, neither of the medical practitioners (who had had access to the results of the boyfriend) sought to confirm whether the boyfriend had disclosed his HIV status to her. Neither was there any entry in her medical records identifying that she was in a sexual relationship with a person who had been identified as being HIV positive. The couple married and the plaintiff became pregnant. Shortly thereafter the plaintiff was diagnosed as being HIV positive. The plaintiff successfully sued in negligence with Cripps J finding that the defendants (the medical practitioners) owed the plaintiff a duty of care and had, through their conduct, breached that duty.

The defendants were held to be in breach of their duty in that, in the circumstances:

- they had failed to identify the potential conflict of interest should the plaintiff or her boyfriend (who were both patients of the medical practice) return a positive test result
- had failed to obtain instructions from either the plaintiff or her boyfriend as to how the information should be communicated were this to be the case
- had failed to ensure that the test results were provided personally
- failed to make provision for the cross-referencing of the medical records
- failed to provide adequate and appropriate advice, treatment and follow-up to the plaintiff's boyfriend in relation to counselling and post-diagnosis specialist treatment.

The existence of a duty of care owed by the medical centre to the plaintiff is evident in the decision. His Honour stated:

> [T]he obligation to look after [the plaintiff's] interests, insofar that could lawfully be done, continued while she was a patient of the practice … It may be argued that it has not been established that the doctor who vaccinated her for the trip to Ghana or the doctor who prescribed contraceptive pills were aware of the [boyfriend's] positive result and that he was the person that she was proposing to marry. But the … medical centre had that information and I do not think that the duty owed to the patient can be avoided by what appears to be an inadequate cross-referencing of patients' cards.[26]

Duty to the unborn

A person may owe a duty of care to a child who has sustained injury prior to birth. In the case of *Watt v Rama*[27] the negligent driver of a motor vehicle was held to owe a duty of care to other road users including any unborn child they may be carrying. The right to claim in negligence does not arise until the child is born alive and 'has a separate existence from its mother'.[28] *The medical practitioner who is caring for a pregnant woman therefore owes a duty of care not only to the mother (the patient), but also to her unborn foetus.* It may also be the case that a duty is owed for medical intervention and treatment before an infant is conceived. In the case of *Kosky v Trustees of the Sisters of Charity*[29] the female patient was negligently given incorrect blood. Though she did not suffer any adverse effects from the transfusion at the time, some 8 years later she gave birth to a child who suffered complications from Rh iso-immunisation and a premature induction made necessary by the transfusion of the incorrect blood. The court held that the healthcare institution in which she received a transfusion of the incorrect blood group owed a duty of care to the child who suffered damage as a result of the negligent conduct that occurred some 8 years prior to the birth. In addition to an action in negligence as described in this paragraph, are claims in negligence bought by children and/or their parents and/or the legal representatives of the children for 'wrongful life' or 'wrongful birth' (which includes claims for 'wrongful conception').

Claims by a child for damages from a medical practitioner for *'wrongful life' are very complex and raise significant ethical and legal issues.* Essentially the claim is based on the argument that, had the mother been properly advised about the option of terminating the pregnancy, the child would now not be alive and suffering. The issue to be determined by the court as stated by Kirby J in *Harriton v Stephens*[30] is:

> whether a child, born with profound disabilities, whose mother would have elected to terminate her pregnancy had she been aware that there was a real risk of the child being born with such disabilities, is entitled to damages where a medical practitioner negligently fails to warn the mother of the risk.

The appeal in the case of *Harriton* from the New South Wales Court of Appeal was heard by the High Court together with *Waller v James* and *Waller v Hoolahan*.[31] By a 6–1 majority the High Court dismissed each of the appeals making a determination that the alleged damage did not constitute a cognisable injury. Crennan J in the case of *Waller* (with whom Gleeson CJ, Gummow and Heydon JJ concurred), stated:

> The appellant's claimed damage in each of his appeals is his life with disabilities. This inevitably involves an assertion by the appellant that it would be preferable if he had not been born, irrespective of whether the conduct about which he complains occurred prior to, or during, his mother's pregnancy with him ... the appellant's life with disabilities is not legally cognisable damage in the sense required to found a duty of care towards him. This is so whether or not the proposed duty of care is formulated as a duty upon Dr James and the Sydney IVF to him as a 'prospective child' of the parents, or a 'potential child', or a 'potential person', or as a duty of care upon Dr Hoolahan to him as a foetus. For these reasons, and the reasons set out in *Harriton v Stephens*, the appellant's damage in each of the appeals is not actionable.

A claim for *'wrongful birth'* (as distinct from a claim for 'wrongful life') is initiated by the parent or parents of a child who has been born with a disability claiming in damages for the extra costs of raising their disabled child. The parents allege that had the medical practitioners diagnosed the abnormality or condition earlier, or at all, the mother would have had the opportunity to terminate the pregnancy.

In an action for '*wrongful conception*' the parents claim that the medical practitioner's negligence, in failing to properly perform a sterilisation or termination, or prescribing or supplying faulty contraception, led to the birth of a child they did not intend to have. In *Cattanach v Melchior*[32] the plaintiffs (the parents of the child) sued Dr Catternach, an obstetrician and gynaecologist who had performed a tubal ligation on Mrs Melchoir. Only one of Mrs Melchoir's fallopian tubes was clipped due to incorrect information given to Dr Cattanach by Mrs Melchoir and the inability of Dr Cattanach to have a clear view of the fallopian tubes during the procedure. Mrs Melchoir became pregnant and delivered a healthy baby some 5 years after the surgery. The High Court found Dr Cattanach negligent for accepting the information given by Mrs Melchoir without any further investigation. The majority held that, where a child was born as a result of a medical practitioner's negligence, the medical practitioner could be required to bear the cost of raising and maintaining a healthy child until they reached the age of 18 years. In Queensland, New South Wales and South Australia, legislation has been enacted to overcome the decision in *Cattanach v Melchoir*. As an example, ss 49A and 49B of the Civil Liability Act 2003 (Qld) state:

49A Failed sterilisation procedures

(1) This section applies if, following a procedure to effect the sterilisation of an individual, the individual gives birth to, or fathers, a child because of the breach of duty of a person in advising about, or performing, the procedure.

Examples of sterilisation procedures –

Tubal ligation and vasectomy

(2) A court cannot award damages for economic loss arising out of the costs ordinarily associated with rearing or maintaining a child.

49B Failed contraceptive procedure or contraceptive advice

(1) This section applies if, following a contraceptive procedure on an individual or the giving of contraceptive advice to an individual, the individual gives birth to, or fathers, a child because of the breach of duty of a person in advising about, or performing a procedure or giving the advice.

(2) A court cannot award damages for economic loss arising out of the costs ordinarily associated with rearing or maintaining a child.

Duty to rescue

The term 'good Samaritan' is often used to refer to a person who, in good faith and without the expectation of a fee, provides assistance or rescues another who has been injured, is at risk of being injured or requires emergency assistance. Though medical practitioners may feel ethically compelled to render aid in such circumstances, as a general proposition there is no common law obligation on any individual to render emergency aid, regardless of whether they are or are not a medical practitioner.[33] As stated by Windeyer J in *Hargrave v Goldman*:[34]

> The dictates of charity and of compassion do not constitute a duty of care. The law casts no duty upon a man to go to the aid of another who is in peril or distress, not caused by him. The call of common humanity may lead him to rescue. This the law recognises, for it gives the rescuer its protection when he answers the call. But it does not require that he do so. There is no general duty to help a neighbour whose house is on fire.

The decision in the New South Wales Court of Appeal case of *Lowns v Woods*[35] was a significant departure from the traditionally held assumption that in Australia there was, at common law, no duty to rescue or assist in an emergency. Further exceptions to the general principle that there is no duty to rescue would include those discussed below.

- **Where there is legislation specifically directed to the imposition of a legal duty to render assistance**

As an example, under s 155 of the Northern Territory Criminal Code:

> any person who, being able to provide rescue, resuscitation, medical treatment, first aid or succour of any kind to a person urgently in need of it and whose life may be endangered if it is not provided, callously fails to do so is guilty of a crime and is liable to imprisonment for 7 years.

Though the Northern Territory is the only Australian jurisdiction to impose such a general duty on 'any person', where the person is the 'driver' of a motor vehicle involved in an accident, the relevant legislation in each of the states or territories may impose an obligation to stop and provide reasonable assistance. Section 92(1) of the Transport Operations (Road Use Management) Act 1995 (Qld), for instance, requires that:

> [T]he driver of any vehicle … involved on any road, or of any motor vehicle involved elsewhere than on the road in a accident resulting in injury to or death of any person or

damage to property ... shall ... immediately stop the vehicle ... remain at or near the scene of the accident and immediately render such assistance as the driver can to the injured person ... (making) reasonable endeavours to obtain such medical and other aid as may reasonably be required for the injured person.

It is noteworthy that the legislative obligation imposes the duty to stop and render assistance only on the 'driver' of the vehicle involved in the accident and not on the drivers of other vehicles who come upon the accident. In addition, legislation may also impose an obligation on specific health professionals to provide assistance. The New South Wales Medical Practice Act 1992 imposed the obligation on medical practitioners to render assistance. Section 36(1) included, as the grounds for 'professional misconduct', that the medical practitioner has refused or failed:

... without reasonable cause, to attend (within a reasonable time after being requested to do so), on a person for the purpose of rendering professional services in the capacity of a registered medical practitioner in any case where the practitioner has reasonable cause to believe that the person is in need of urgent attention by a registered medical practitioner, unless the practitioner has taken all reasonable steps to ensure that another registered medical practitioner attends instead within a reasonable time.

• **Where the person has assumed responsibility for the supervision or care of another**.

In a healthcare context, this situation would most frequently arise in circumstances where a medical practitioner or nurse accompanies a patient away from the hospital or institutional environment.

• **Where the person requiring assistance is in an existing and special relationship with the rescuer**.

In circumstances, for example, where a parent is able to save their child's life, the law would anticipate that the parent would make all reasonable attempts to do so. In the case of *Horsley v McLaren (The Ogopogo)*,[36] Laskin J referred to the relationships of parent and child, employer and employee, doctor and patient, and passenger and carrier as giving rise to a duty to rescue.

• **Where the employer has, as part of the policy of the institution, a stated expectation that employees, in particular circumstances, will stop and render assistance**.

For example, it is not uncommon that the respective state and territory departments of health require employees who drive department vehicles to stop and provide assistance should they come upon an accident while on department business.

When a medical practitioner does stop at the scene of an accident for the purpose of rendering assistance, a duty of care arises. The standard of care, however, will be reflective of the circumstances in which the emergency care is provided. As an example, the standard of care would be that of 'any reasonable rescuer' in the environment in which the accident or injury has occurred. There is no expectation that the medical practitioner, at an accident site, could deliver the same standard of care that would be anticipated in the hospital setting. Where the rescuer is confronted with an unfamiliar emergency situation that requires life and death decisions to be made urgently, the courts have been reluctant to find the rescuer liable in negligence. In *Leishman v Thomas*,[37] it was held:

> ... a man is not to be charged with negligence if he, not being the creator of the crisis or emergency which has arisen, finds himself faced with a situation which requires immediate action of some sort and if, in the so called 'agony of the moment', he makes an error of judgment and takes a step which wiser counsels and more careful thought would have suggested was unwise.

Historically, the courts have taken a lenient attitude to rescuers, provided that they have acted in good faith and not in a manner that is reckless, negligent or demonstrates a lack of reasonable care and skill, thereby causing damage to the person being assisted. This seems to be the case even where the care has resulted in harm. The courts have held that the rescue itself is the 'natural and probable consequence of the original accident and therefore does not operate to break the chain of causation'.[38]

Both Queensland and New South Wales have legislation protecting specified health professionals from legal action in the rescuer role. In Queensland s 16 of the Law Reform Act 1995 protects medical practitioners, nurses or other people prescribed under a regulation who render medical care, aid or other assistance to an injured person in circumstances of a emergency and which is reasonable, given in good faith and without gross negligence or the expectation of a fee. In New South Wales the Health Services Act 1997 protects only members of staff of the New South Wales Ambulance Service and honorary ambulance officers.[39]

The following is an overview of the legislation and provisions relevant to potential claims against rescuers, good Samaritans and not-for-profit organisations.[40] Table 5.1 sets out the legislation addressing rescuers in each of the Australian jurisdictions.

Table 5.1 Legislation applicable to rescuers	
ACT	Civil Law (Wrongs) Act 2002 s 5
NSW	Civil Liability Act 2002 ss 56 and 57
NT	Personal Injuries (Liabilities and Damages) Act 2005 s 8
Qld	Law Reform Act 1995 s 16 and Civil Liability Act 2003 s 26
SA	Civil Liability Act 1936 s 74
Vic	Wrongs Act 1958 s 31B
WA	Civil Liability Act 2002 Part 1D

Good Samaritans

- In the **ACT** a good Samaritan or medical practitioner who acts honestly and without recklessness will be exempt from liability while rendering assistance or giving advice in an emergency. Similar protection is afforded volunteers in these circumstances, but the community organisations themselves may be held liable for the actions of their volunteers.[41]
- In **New South Wales** rescuers and good Samaritans will not incur personal civil liability in giving emergency aid except where their conduct evidences a degree of impairment or a failure to exercise reasonable care and skill. A person undertaking a rescue as a volunteer will similarly not be held personally liable where they act in good faith in carrying out community work or as an office-holder of a community organisation.[42]
- In the **Northern Territory** volunteers, good Samaritans and medically qualified people acting in good faith and without recklessness in an emergency situation are exempt from civil liability.[43]
- In **Queensland** the Civil Liability Act 2003 states there will be no personal liability for first aiders who are performing duties in an emergency acting in good faith and without reckless disregard for safety. In addition, a person providing first aid or other aid or assistance while performing duties to enhance public safety or for an entity prescribed under a regulation that prescribes services to enhance public safety will not be held liable for acts done or omitted to be done in the course of rendering that aid or assistance.[44]

- In **South Australia** the legislation refers to both the good Samaritan and the medically qualified person who, in assisting in an emergency, do so in good faith and without the expectation of being paid a fee.[45]

- In **Tasmania** there are no legislative provisions, which specifically address the legal obligations or protection offered to a rescuer in Tasmania. The law is therefore to be found in the case law which requires a standard that is generally consistent with that legislatively prescribed in the other states and territories.

- In **Victoria** a person acting as a good Samaritan is not personally liable in any civil proceedings where they have acted in good faith to provide assistance, advice or care in an emergency or accident where the recipient is actually or apparently at risk of death or injury.[46] A volunteer is also not personally liable where they are undertaking a service that has been organised by the community organisation or is part of the services provided by that organisation.[47]

- In **Western Australia** volunteers are exempt from liability in civil actions arising out of their service for community organisations. It is noteworthy that the Western Australian legislation imposes on the government the obligation of insuring essential not-for-profit organisations.[48]

There are no cases in Australia in which a medical practitioner has been held liable for the outcome of a voluntary rescue attempt.

Breach of the duty of care

Once it is established that a person (the defendant) owed a duty of care to another person (the plaintiff) it must then be proven, to the civil standard, that their action or omission amounted to a breach of a standard considered appropriate. The benchmark to determine a general breach of the duty of care, that is, whether the conduct fell below the requisite standard, is the 'reasonable man' test. As an example, the question is: 'What would the reasonable man or, as has been described, the "man on the Bondi bus" consider as reasonable in the circumstances?' This is an objective test. Provisions under the civil liability Acts[49] in a number of Australian jurisdictions have provided a legislative basis for the determination of the reasonable standard of care in personal injury claims. In the wider context, the legislation provides that a person will not be negligent where they fail to take precautions against a foreseeable risk; that is, unless the risk itself would be considered as 'not insignificant' and a reasonable person in the same position as the defendant would have taken the precautions. This notionally incorporates an assessment of the probability or likely seriousness of the harm, the burden of taking the precautions and the social utility of the activity associated with that risk. *The principle for breach of the general duty has been legislated in all jurisdictions other than the Northern Territory.* The Queensland Civil Liability Act 2003 provides at s 9:

(1) A person does not breach a duty to take precautions against a risk of harm unless –

    (a) the risk was foreseeable (that is, it is a risk of which the person knew or ought reasonably have known); and

    (b) the risk was not insignificant; and

    (c) in the circumstances, a person in the position of the person would have taken the precautions.

(2) In deciding whether a reasonable person would have taken precautions against a risk of harm, the court is to consider the following (among other relevant things) –

    (a) the probability the harm would occur if the care were not taken;

    (b) the likely seriousness of the harm;

    (c) the burden of taking precautions to avoid the risk of harm;

    (d) the social utility of the activity that creates the risk of harm.

When the issue involves the standard of care required of skilled professionals, and more particularly medical practitioners, the case law and civil liability legislation provide the benchmark against which the alleged conduct will be considered. Questions such as 'What is the standard?', 'Is the standard the same for all professions?', and 'Does it apply to all aspects of the medical practitioner's duty of care'? are fundamental and require further investigation. These questions are also integral to the decision-making practices of medical practitioners when they determine which diagnostic tests are appropriate, which procedures are to be undertaken, what treatment regimes should be ordered and carried out, and how much information is to be provided to a patient in relation to the risks inherent in medical treatment and care.

DETERMINATION OF A STANDARD OF CARE FOR PROFESSIONALS

Allegations made against medical practitioners involving a breach of the duty of care will most frequently arise in the context of technical practice issues (that is, about assessment, diagnosis or treatment decisions and/or action) or, in the context of providing, or failing to provide, information as to the risks associated with a particular procedure or treatment. The case law and the legislation distinguish between these two contexts (technical practice and failure to warn of risks) therefore each context will be considered separately.

Technical practice issues

The test to determine whether a medical practitioner has been negligent was advanced in the United Kingdom in the case of *Bolam v Friern Hospital Management Committee*,[50] McNair J stating:

> Where you get a situation which involves the use of some special skill or competence, then the test whether there has been negligence or not … is the standard of the ordinary skilled man exercising and professing to have that special skill … in the case of a medical man, negligence means failure in accordance with the standards of reasonable competent medical men at the time.[51]

And:

> A doctor is not in breach of his duty in the matter of diagnosis and treatment if he acts in accordance with a practice accepted at the time as proper by a reasonable body of medical opinion even though other doctors may adopt a different practice.[52]

The test identifies the standard for professionals, and was adopted by the High Court of Australia in the case of *Rogers v Whitaker*[53] which involved a claim made by a patient against her ophthalmologist. The test does not require that the medical practitioner 'possess the highest expert skill'.[54] The appropriate standard is determined by what a reasonable body of medical opinion accepts, at the time, as proper, reasonable, competent practice. The standard applies to the provision of all patient care and will, in each case, be determined by the level of expertise of the individual and the particular circumstances surrounding the alleged event. As an example, where a medical practitioner has worked in a particular clinical area for a prolonged period of time and undertaken specialist postgraduate qualifications, the standard will be commensurate with that level of skill and experience. In circumstances in which a medical practitioner has only recently graduated, the standards would be that of any other qualified medical practitioner. In the case of *Wilsher v Essex Area Health Authority*[55] a neonate sustained injuries resulting in almost total blindness from excessive amounts of oxygen administered while being treated in an intensive care unit. The premature neonate had, in addition to other illnesses, an oxygen deficiency. A junior doctor attempting to check the neonate's oxygen levels mistakenly inserted a catheter into the vein rather than the artery. The registrar who was asked to check not only failed to identify the error but also made the same mistake himself at a later time. One of the issues before the court was the standard of care owed to the child. On appeal to the House of Lords the standard of care accepted was that of the position or post occupied. That is, the standard of the ordinary person exercising or professing to have that special skill, in this case the skill of a medical practitioner. As stated by Lord Glidewell:

> The law requires the trainee or learner to be judged by the same standards as his experienced colleague. If it did not, inexperience would frequently be urged as a defence to an action in professional negligence.

In the case of a medical student it is imperative therefore that the student does not undertake any clinical activities for which they have not attained the requisite level of competency. The level of supervision for medical students must ensure that all tasks are carried out at an appropriate standard and a medical student must not undertake any task for which they are not clinically qualified without adequate and appropriate supervision.

Indicators as to the standard of care accepted at the time as proper, reasonable and competent may include relevant research data, affidavits and testimony of peers and experts in the particular clinical area, policy and procedure documents of the particular clinical unit and employing institution, policy documents of the respective departments of health and regulatory authorities in the particular state or territory, and standards set by specialist organisations and colleges. As an example, in the Queensland Court of Appeal case of *Langley v Glandore Pty Ltd (in liq)*,[56] two surgeons appealed against a jury decision finding them negligent in their failure to ensure the removal of a surgical swab from the abdomen of a patient undergoing a hysterectomy. The surgeons appealed on the grounds that, as the surgical swab was left in the wound, the swab count must have been incorrect. Therefore, the finding that there was no negligence on the part of the scrub nurse or the circulating nurse, and thereby the hospital, should be overturned. The surgeons argued that:[57]

> ... under the procedures in place and relied upon by all concerned in the operation, the primary duty that a correct count had been made of all instruments, sponges, packs and the like to establish that they had all been removed from the patient's body at the conclusion of the operation, lay with the nurses.

Macrossan CJ and Byrne J considered the conduct of the nurses against standards for swab and instrument counts established by the Australian Confederation of Operating Room Nurses. These standards, produced in evidence during the trial, had been accepted as benchmarking the required standard for the procedures. The court overturned the earlier decision and the nurses were found to be negligent:[58]

> [T]he nurses clearly, under the procedure described, had the primary duty for making an accurate count to ensure that all the sponges used had been recovered from the plaintiff's body.

Civil liability legislation in Australia now prescribes the standard of care for professionals. While the legislation adopts the general principle laid down in *Bolam's* case (above) it lacks uniformity between the jurisdictions and medical practitioners must familiarise themselves with the legislative provisions in the particular jurisdiction in which they conduct their practice. The following therefore sets out the relevant sections of the legislation in each of the jurisdictions (other than the Northern Territory where there are no specific legislative provisions for professionals):

Queensland

The Civil Liability Act 2003 states, in s 22:

22 Standard of care for professionals

(1) A professional does not breach a duty arising from the provision of a professional service if it is established that the professional acted in a way that (at the time the service was provided) was widely accepted by peer professional opinion by a significant number of respected practitioners in the field as competent professional practice.

(2) However, peer professional opinion can not be relied on for the purpose of this section if the court considers that the opinion is irrational or contrary to a written law.

(3) The fact that there are differing peer professional opinions widely accepted by a significant number of respected practitioners in the field concerning a matter does not prevent any one or more (or all) of the opinions being relied on for the purposes of this section.

(4) Peer professional opinion does not have to be universally accepted to be considered widely accepted.

(5) This section does not apply to liability arising in connection with the giving of (or the failure to give) a warning, advice or other information, in relation to the risk of harm to a person, that is associated with the provision by the professional of a professional service.

New South Wales

The Civil Liability Act 2002 s 5O states:

5O Standard of care for professionals

(1) A person practising a profession (a professional) does not incur a liability in negligence arising from the provision of a professional service if it is established that

the professional acted in a manner that (at the time the service was provided) was widely accepted in Australia by peer professional opinion as competent professional practice.

(2) However, peer professional opinion cannot be relied on for the purposes of this section if the court considers that the opinion is irrational.

(3) The fact that there are differing peer professional opinions widely accepted in Australia concerning a matter does not prevent any one or more (or all) of those opinions being relied on for the purposes of this section.

(4) Peer professional opinion does not have to be universally accepted to be considered widely accepted.

Australian Capital Territory

The Civil Law (Wrongs) Act 2002 s 42 does not limit the application of the provision to persons who hold themselves out as having special skills or practicing a professional. The section states:

42. For deciding whether a person (the defendant) was negligent, the standard of care required of the defendant is that of the reasonable person in the defendant's position who was in possession of all the information that the defendant either had, or ought reasonably to have had, at the time of the incident out of which the harm arose.

Victoria

The Wrongs Act 1958 ss 58 and 59 state:

58. Standard of care to be expected of persons holding out as possessing a particular skill

In a case involving an allegation of negligence against a person (the defendant) who holds himself or herself out a possessing a particular skill, the standard to be applied by a court in determining whether the defendant acted with due care is, subject to this Division, to be determined by reference to:

(a) what could reasonably be expected of a person possessing that skill; and

(b) the relevant circumstance as at the date of the alleged negligence and not a later date.

59. Standard of care for professionals

(1) A professional is not negligent in providing a professional service if it is established that the professional acted in a manner that (at the time the service was provided) was

widely accepted in Australia by a significant number of respected practitioners in the field (peer professional opinion) as competent professional practice in the circumstances.

(2) However, peer professional opinion cannot be relied on for the purposes of this section if the court determines that the opinion is unreasonable.

(3) The fact that there are differing professional opinions widely accepted in Australia by a significant number of respected practitioners in the field concerning a matter does not prevent any one or more (or all) of those opinions being relied on for the purposes of this section.

(4) Peer professional opinion does not have to be universally accepted to be widely accepted.

(5) If, under this section, a court determines peer professional opinion to be unreasonable, it must specify in writing the reason for the determination.

(6) Subsection (5) does not apply if a jury determines the matter.

Tasmania

The Civil Liability Act 2002 at s 22 states:

22. Standard of care for professionals

(1) A person practising a profession (a 'professional') does not breach a duty arising from the provision of a professional service if it is established that the professional acted in a manner that (at the time the service was provided) was widely accepted in Australia by peer professional opinion as competent professional practice.

(2) Peer professional opinion can not be relied on for the purpose of this section if the court considers that the opinion is irrational.

(3) The fact that there are differing professional opinions widely accepted in Australia concerning a matter does not prevent any one or more of those opinions being relied on for the purpose of subsection (1).

(4) Peer professional opinion does not have to be universally accepted to be considered widely accepted.

(5) This section does not apply to liability arising in connection with the giving of (or the failure to give) a warning, advice or other information in relation to the risk of harm associated with the provision by a professional of a professional service to a person.

Western Australia

The Civil Liability Act 2002 states at s 5PB:

5PB Standard of care for health professionals

(1) An act or omission of a health professional is not a negligent act or omission if it is in accordance with a practice that, at the time of the act or omission, is widely accepted by the health professional's peers as competent professional practice.

(2) Subsection (1) does not apply to an act or omission of a health professional in relation to informing a person of a risk of injury or death associated with –

(a) the treatment proposed for a patient or a foetus being carried by a pregnant patient; or

(b) a procedure proposed to be conducted for the purpose of diagnosing a condition of a patient or a foetus carried by a pregnant patient.

(3) Subsection (1) applies even if another practice that is widely accepted by the health professional's peers as competent professional practice differs from or conflicts with the practice in accordance with which the health professional acted or omitted to do something.

(4) Nothing in subsection (1) prevents a health professional from being liable for negligence if the practice in accordance with which the health professional acted or omitted to do something is, in the circumstances of the particular case, so unreasonable that no reasonable health professional in the health professional's position could have acted or omitted to so something in accordance with the practice.

(5) A practice does not have to be universally accepted as competent professional practice to be considered widely accepted as competent professional practice.

(6) In determining liability for damages for harm caused by the fault of a health professional, the plaintiff always bears the onus of proving, on the balance of probabilities, that the applicable standard of care (whether under this section or any other law) was breached by the defendant.

South Australia

The Civil Liability Act 1936 at s 41 states:

41 Standard of care for professionals

(1) A person who provides a professional service incurs no liability in negligence arising from the service if it

is established that the provider acted in a manner that (at the time of the service was provided) was widely accepted in Australia by members of the same profession as competent professional practice.

(2) However, professional opinion cannot be relied on for the purposes of this section if the courts consider that the opinion is irrational.

(3) The fact that there are differing professional opinions widely accepted in Australia by members of the same profession does not prevent any one or more (or all) of those opinions being relied on for the purposes of this section.

(4) Professional opinion does not have to be universally accepted to be considered widely accepted.

(5) This section does not apply to liability arising from connection with the giving of (or the failure to give a warning, advice or other information in respect of a risk of death of or injury associated with the provision of a healthcare service.

It is evident from the foregoing that, as a general principle, professionals will not be found liable in negligence if they practise in a manner that is widely accepted in Australia by peer professional opinion as competent professional practice. While the provisions apply to professionals across all disciplines, health-related or otherwise, the following is of note and should highlight the importance of identifying the provisions of the civil liability legislation in the particular state or territory in which a medical student is studying and intends to later practice in.

To whom does the section apply:

- **Western Australia** is the only state to refer specifically to the standard of 'a health professional'
- in **Queensland**, the section refers to a 'professional'
- and in **Tasmania** and **New South Wales** the legislation refers to the standard for a 'person practising a profession'
- the **South Australian** legislation applies to a person providing a 'professional service'
- and in **Victoria**, to 'persons holding out as possessing a particular skill'.

What amounts to a breach:

- in **Queensland** and **Tasmania** the legislation states that a professional will not be in 'breach of a/the duty arising from the provision of a professional service'

- in **New South Wales** and **South Australia** the respective sections state the professional 'does not incur liability'
- in **Victoria** and **Western Australia** the respective sections provide the professional is 'not negligent' or the conduct will not be 'a negligent act or omission'.

The New South Wales case of *Halverson & Ors v Dobler Halverson by his tutor v Dobler*[59] highlights the significance of different terminology when courts apply the test (of a professional's standard of care) as set out under the civil liability legislation in making a determination as to whether the medical practitioner breached their duty of care to the patient. In this case, Kurt Halverson (by his tutor) sued his general practitioner, Dr Dobler, in negligence for failing to exercise due care in his treatment of Kurt between 1995 and 10 February 2001. Halverson alleged that Dr Dobler should have identified his cardiac problems before he suffered a cardiac arrest on 11 February 2001 and, due to the resulting hypoxic brain damage, sustained catastrophic injuries. Halverson submitted that Dr Dobler breached his duty of care by failing to carry out an ECG or refer him to a cardiologist after Dr Dobler detected Kurt's heart murmur on 1 February 2001 and after Kurt suffered a period of loss of consciousness (a syncopal attack) on 4 February 2001. His Honour McClennan CJ considered the concurrent expert evidence of five general practitioners and then the concurrent evidence of five expert cardiologists. McClennan CJ preferred the evidence of the plaintiff's experts. In relation to the peer acceptance test under s 5O of the Civil Liability Act 2002 (NSW), his Honour found the test did not operate to replace the standard as accepted in the case of *Rogers v Whitaker.* In finding that s 5O of the New South Wales Civil Liability Act 2002 was a defence, McClennan CJ stated:

> Accordingly, the standard of care is still the standard that was endorsed in *Rogers v Whitaker*, but if a defendant is found to be negligent under this standard he or she can avoid liability if they can establish that they acted in a manner which was widely accepted in Australia as peer professional opinion as competent professional practice.[60]

And:

> In my view the section is intended to operate as a defence. The section is expressed so that 'a person practising a profession … *does not incur a liability in negligence*' if a certain state of affairs can be 'established'. The italicised word goes to the issue of liability, not to the issue of negligence.[61]

The wording of the New South Wales legislation is different from that of other jurisdictions such as Queensland in that it refers to incurring 'liability in negligence' rather than being in 'breach of the duty'. In addition, it is noted that in all jurisdictions other than Queensland ('widely accepted by peer professional opinion') and Western Australia ('in accordance with a practice ... widely accepted by the health professional's peers') the standard is determined by specific reference to that which is 'widely accepted in Australia'. This clearly influences the weight to be accorded to expert evidence from outside Australia. In all jurisdictions the civil liability legislation confirms that the court will not involve itself with the peer professional opinion unless it considers that opinion to be 'irrational', or in Western Australia and Victoria, to be 'unreasonable'.

'At the time'

The determination by the courts as to whether there has been a breach of the duty of care will require *consideration of the conduct in light of the standards of practice 'at the time' the incident occurred.*[62] The courts have been consistent in recognising that, with hindsight or the development of new technologies, conduct that is later found to be harmful may have been avoided. However, the courts will not hold a medical practitioner liable if at the time the event occurred it was not known that there was potential for damage or injury. The standard of care in negligence will be determined by the standards applicable when the conduct was alleged to have occurred, and not the standard at the time of the trial. The civil liability legislations in New South Wales, Queensland, South Australia, Tasmania, Victoria and Western Australia provide that the liability of a professional, in providing a professional service, will be determined by the peer professional opinion 'at the time' the service was provided or at the time the act or omission occurred.

It is therefore of the utmost importance that medical practitioners maintain their clinical competency and an up-to-date knowledge base in their particular area of clinical expertise. If, on the evidence, it would be reasonable to assume that the competent clinician at the time would have known of the potential for harm from a procedure or treatment, then ignorance as to that fact will not provide a defence.

Failure to disclose risk

In addition to the breach of the duty of care by a technical blunder (an error in relation to technical practice) there is also the possibility that the medical practitioner may breach the duty of care by failing to disclose to a patient, or warn a patient, of risks. A medical practitioner has a duty to provide the information that a patient would require to make an informed decision about whether or not to undergo a diagnostic test or procedure. A failure to provide such information may result in a successful claim in negligence for breach of the duty of care where the patient proves that they would not have undergone the test or procedure had they been given the information and, as a result, they have sustained an injury. In relation to this duty to warn patients of risks associated with treatments and procedures, there is a lack of uniformity across the Australian states and territories. In some jurisdictions the civil liability legislation prescribes the obligations of medical practitioners to provide information as part of the process of obtaining consent. In the remaining jurisdictions the case law applies. The following will therefore address both the legislative framework and the common law (cases) applicable to the practical issue of disclosure of risk in the provision of healthcare services. It is noteworthy that a number of legal commentators[63] have, on examination of the legislation, expressed the view that the changes introduced under the civil liability legislation might be little more than a restating of the common law and in 'failure to inform' cases the defendant medical practitioner may have lost the ability to have evidence of peers considered in the defence.[64] Section 22(5) of the Civil Liability Act 2003 (Qld), for example, expressly removes the protection of 'peer professional opinion ... in connection with the giving of or the failure to give a warning, advice or other information about a relevant risk of harm'.

Medical practitioners are subject to a prescribed duty to inform both proactively and reactively on the basis that they are to take reasonable care to provide information required to enable a patient to make a decision as to whether or not to undergo treatment. Section 21 of the Civil Liability Act 2003 (Qld), which is similar to the Tasmanian[65] provision, states:

21. Proactive and reactive duty of doctor to warn of risk

(1) A doctor does not breach a duty owed to a patient to warn of risk, before the patient undergoes any medical form of treatment (or at the time of being given medical advice) that will involve a risk of personal injury to the patient, unless the doctor at that time fails to give or arrange to be given to the patient the information about the risk –

(a) that a reasonable person in the patient's position would, in the circumstances, require to enable the person to make a reasonable decision about whether to undergo the treatment or follow the advice; and

(b) that the doctor knows or ought reasonably to know the patient wants to be given before making the decision about whether to undergo the treatment or follow the advice.

In New South Wales, Queensland, South Australia, Tasmania, Victoria and Western Australia there is no duty to warn another of an 'obvious risk'.[66] However, medical practitioners should be aware that in a number of jurisdictions legislative limits in relation to the disclosure of information have direct relevance to a healthcare context. As an example, the Civil Liability Act 2002 (NSW) s 5H provides:

5H No proactive duty to warn of obvious risk

(1) A person ('the defendant') does not owe a duty of care to another person ('the plaintiff') to warn of an obvious risk to the plaintiff.

(2) This section does not apply if:

(a) the plaintiff has requested advice or information about the risk from the defendant, or

(b) the defendant is required by a written law to warn the plaintiff of the risk, or

(c) the defendant is a professional and the risk is a risk of the death of or personal injury to the plaintiff from the provision of a professional service by the defendant.

(3) Subsection (2) does not give rise to a presumption of a duty to warn of a risk in the circumstances referred to in that subsection.

Allegations in negligence based on a 'failure to warn' are conducted in two stages. The first stage is to convince the court to the requisite standard that the relevant information was not communicated by the health professional to the patient. The second stage is to argue that had the information been given, the patient would not have consented to the treatment or procedure. In New South Wales, the plaintiff is precluded from leading this evidence under s 5D(3) of the Civil Liability Act 2002 which states:

(3) If it is relevant to the determination of factual causation to determine what the person who suffered harm would have done if the negligent person had not been negligent:

(a) the matter is to be determined subjectively in light of all relevant circumstances, subject to paragraph (b); and

(b) any statement made by the person after suffering the harm about what he or she would have done is inadmissible except to the extent (if any) that the statement is against his or her interest.

At common law, the determination of the duty to advise of risks of treatment within the Australian context was a gradual process that culminated in the High Court decisions in *Rogers v Whitaker*,[67]

Chappel v Hart[68] and *Rosenberg v Percival*.[69] An analysis of the cases preceding these judgments serves to illustrate why the Australian courts formulated and implemented the standard of care that requires the disclosure of 'material risk' and focuses on the rights of patients to self-determination and autonomy.

As described above, negligence cases involving medical practitioners are commonly associated with procedural and diagnostic errors known as technical blunders. However, in the case of *Chatterton v Gerson* the court concluded that there was a duty on the medical practitioner to 'explain what he intends to do, and its implications, in the way a careful and responsible doctor in similar circumstances would have done'.[70] The failure by the medical practitioner to provide such an explanation prior to a procedure or treatment would not constitute trespass[71] (refer to Chapter 6, Consent, for an explanation of the action trespass to the person (civil assault or battery)), but rather a breach of the duty of care amounting to negligence. The test in *Bolam's* case[72] was therefore extended from the traditional application in technical blunder cases to cases where failure to warn of the risk was alleged.[73]

In *Sidaway's* case,[74] the plaintiff came under the care of a neurosurgeon in seeking relief from chronic arm pain. After 14 years of treatment the doctor performed a laminectomy at the level of cervical 4 and 5 of the spinal column. Though the procedure was competently performed, the plaintiff became paraplegic. There was no evidence that the plaintiff had ever asked for information as to the risks associated with this procedure and by the time the case came to trial the neurosurgeon had died. The action in negligence was based on the alleged failure by the doctor to warn the plaintiff of the risks prior to obtaining her consent to perform the surgery. The majority judgment held that the test in *Bolam's* case applied to all aspects of a medical practitioner's duty of care whether this was a technical activity such as diagnosis and treatment or the duty to warn of risk.

The dissenting judgment of Lord Scarman in this case is credited with being the origin of the view that the *Bolam* test does not apply to cases where the alleged negligence is a failure to warn of the risks.[75] Lord Scarman acknowledged that the *Bolam* principle was applicable to diagnosis and treatment and in such cases 'the law imposes the duty of care but the standard of care is a matter of medical judgment'.[76] Lord Scarman concluded that in cases alleging negligence by the medical practitioner for failure to disclose risk:

> [t]he critical limitation is that the duty is confined to material risk. The test of materiality is whether in the circumstances of the particular case the court is satisfied that the reasonable

person in the patient's position would be likely to attach significance to the risk.[77]

This approach by Lord Scarman focused on the needs of a reasonable patient to have information, with a recognition that only the particular patient could fully appreciate their own particular needs and circumstances. It is noteworthy that the court imposed a duty to warn the patient of the material risks inherent in a procedure. *The risks were considered to be material if 'a reasonable person in the patient's position, if warned of the risk, would be likely to attach significance to it' or the medical practitioner ought to know that this patient would consider the information significant if told.*[78]

The meaning of the terms 'material risk', 'significant risk' and 'risks inherent in the proposed treatment' are significant to the practice of medical practitioners. They flag the existence of the duty to disclose relevant information to the particular patient or client. While a number of factors have been identified as indicative of a 'material risk' the courts have not concluded that one element is more significant than any other and, therefore, all factors would be considered.[79]

The issue of the *'likelihood of the occurrence of the risk'* has been raised as an indicator of the risk being 'material' and therefore necessary to disclose to the patient. Gaudron J, in *Rogers v Whitaker,*[80] stated that real and foreseeable risks must be disclosed; however, there was no obligation to disclose those which were 'far-fetched' and 'fanciful'. In *Causer v Stafford-Bell,*[81] the patient suffered from menstrual problems and was advised to undergo an abdominal hysterectomy. The risk to her of developing a vesico-vaginal fistula and urinary incontinence from the procedure was estimated as being between 1:1000 and 1:10 000. Post-operatively the patient indeed suffered the complications and initiated an action in negligence against the obstetrician and gynaecologist, alleging a failure to disclose the risk. The medical practitioner was held not to be in breach of the duty to warn, as the risk of developing a fistula was not significant or material so as to give rise to the duty. However, *the fact that the risk of an occurrence is low must not be taken as indicating that it was not significant and material.* In *Rogers v Whitaker,* where the plaintiff successfully sued the ophthalmic surgeon for failure to warn, the risk of suffering post-operative sympathetic ophthalmia was estimated as 1:14 000.[82]

The *gravity of the harm* to the patient will significantly influence the information to be disclosed prior to obtaining consent for the treatment or procedure. In *Rogers v Whitaker,*[83] the patient was rendered blind in her only sighted eye as a result of the post-operative complications that had not been disclosed pre-operatively. The case of *Uebel v Wechsler*[84] also involved an ophthalmic surgeon, sued by the patient for failure to warn of the risks associated with a corneal graft operation. The patient ultimately lost his eye and succeeded in his legal action on the grounds that the doctor was in breach of the duty of care in failing to disclose the risks that eventuated.

Other factors to be taken into account include the *need of the patient to have the treatment*,[85] *the prior experience of the health professional*,[86] the *attitude and temperament and health of the patient* (which includes their desire to have the information),[87] the *medical knowledge available*[88] in relation to the treatment or procedure and whether the client has had *access to other sources of information*.[89]

In the case of *Bustos v Hair Transplant Pty Ltd and Peter Wearne*[90] his Honour, Judge Cooper, applied *Rogers v Whitaker* and *Ellis v Wallsend District Hospital*.[91] The allegations of negligence involved the performance of a hair transplant operation and the failure of Dr Wearne to warn the plaintiff of the 'material risks'[92] associated with the treatment. A material risk in these circumstances was taken to include anything associated with the procedure. This was due to the fact that, first, the procedure was elective and, secondly, it was for the purpose of improving the plaintiff's physical appearance. The plaintiff, in the particular circumstances of the case, was unable to prove that if he had been informed of the risks he would not have undergone the procedure. Similarly, in *Rosenberg v Percival*,[93] the appellant was unable to persuade the High Court that, had she been advised of the material risks, she would not have undergone the surgery. In this case a nurse (the appellant), who consulted a maxillofacial surgeon (the respondent) complaining of increasing malocclusion, underwent a sagittal split osteotomy. Post-operatively she suffered chronic pain and sued the surgeon in negligence, alleging he had failed to advise her of the risk of temporomandibular joint problems prior to obtaining her consent. In reaching a decision, the High Court clarified the scope of the doctor's duty to warn, with Gleeson CJ reiterating that the High Court does not consider the term 'informed consent' suitable within the Australian context. On the issue of causation Gleeson CJ stated:

> Information about risk is being considered in the context of a communication between two people who have a common view that there is serious reason in favour of the contemplated surgery. The more remote a contingency which a doctor is required to bring to the notice of a patient, the more difficult it may be for the patient to convince the court that the existence of the contingency would have caused the patient to decide against the surgery.[94]

Gummow J observed that the risk must be precisely identified before it can be determined whether it was a 'material' risk. A material risk could be defined 'by reference to the circumstances in which the injury can occur, the likelihood of the injury occurring and the extent or severity of the potential injury if it does occur'.[95] Whether the failure to warn of a material risk caused the damage, Gummow J determined, was a two-stage process. In the first instance the risk must be related 'in a physical sense to the injury that was suffered' and, secondly, there must be a causative link between the failure to warn of the risk and the occurrence of the injury.

Of great practical assistance is the case of *Karpati v Spira*.[96] The decision in this case gives all health professionals, including medical practitioners, a clearer indication of what factors the court will consider in determining whether a breach of the duty of care has occurred.[97] Spender J considered that, in 'failure to warn' cases such as this one, even if the doctor or doctors had adequately warned the patient, this advice should be conveyed in percentage terms or within a band or range of figures. The use of subjective terms such as 'low', 'slight' or 'rare' do not 'adequately or relevantly convey the true nature of the risk'.[98] The taking and keeping of thorough and detailed medical records and notes, by implication, may assist the court in making a determination as to the reasonableness of the conduct of the health professional.

While the medical practitioner has the duty to provide the information necessary for the patient to make an informed decision it is for the court to determine what information a reasonable doctor would disclose in the particular case. The question for determination by the court is not whether the doctor's conduct accords with medical judgment and practice but whether it accords with a reasonable standard of care as determined by the courts. This is confirmed in the New South Wales Civil Liability Act NSW 2002 at s 5P which states:

> Both the courts and the legislature have been mindful of the effect that the occurrence of an injury may have on the plaintiff's perception of what they would have done had they been warned of the risk prior to consenting to the procedure or treatment.

In the case of *Hoyts v Burns*[99] a cinema patron claimed compensation for injuries she sustained when she fell, having failed to replace her seat which automatically lifted when she stood up. The woman claimed that, had the cinema provided a sign warning of the risk, she would not have sustained the injury. Justice Kirby stated:

> … trial counsel for the Appellant protested that the 'evidence' about what would have been done if a sign had been displayed

was a matter of 'speculation'. So indeed it was. Whether or not, strictly, such evidence is admissible, it is commonly received in Australian courts. Presumably, this practice emerged once it was established that the relevant test of causation applicable in Australia was a subjective one. Nevertheless, the evidence of what a Claimant would have done if a non-existent warning had been given by a hypothetical sign is so hypothetical, self-serving and speculative as to deserve little (if any) weight, at least in some circumstances.

The New South Wales Civil Liability Act 2002 s 5D (3) (b) provides:

(3) If it is relevant to the determination of factual causation to determine what the person who suffered harm would have done if the negligent person had not been negligent:

(a) the matter is to be determined subjectively in light of all relevant circumstance, subject to paragraph (b); and

(b) any statement made by the person after suffering the harm about what he or she would have done is inadmissible except to the extent (if any) that the statement is against his or her interest.

Damage

As discussed, *the damage is the 'gist' of an action in negligence*. No matter how reckless a medical practitioner may have been in the care of a patient, if the patient has not sustained any injury as a result of that conduct, there can be no claim for damages. For example, the medical practitioner may administer the incorrect dose of a drug. Such an act may amount to a breach of the standard of care; however, if the patient sustains no injury they cannot obtain compensation through a claim in negligence. The philosophy behind compensation is that it aims to place the plaintiff in the position they would have been in had the injury not been sustained, as far as money is able to do this. Legislative provisions enable the relatives and dependants of a person who has died due to the negligence of a health professional to initiate an action for damages: Compensation to Relatives Act 1897 (NSW); Wrongs Act 1958 (Vic); Wrongs and Other Acts (Law of Negligence) Act 2003 (Vic); Common Law Practices Act 1867 (Qld); Wrongs Act 1936 (SA); Fatal Accidents Act 1959 (WA); Fatal Accidents Act 1934 (Tas); Compensation (Fatal Injuries) Act 1968 (ACT); Compensation (Fatal Injuries) Act 1974 (NT). As an example, in the case of *Alexander v Heise*[100] (referred to in the section in this chapter under Reasonable foreseeability) the wife of the deceased claimed under the Compensation to Relatives Act 1897

(NSW) for the death of her husband due to a cerebral haemorrhage. The wife made an appointment for her husband for a medical check up with her GP, however he died of an aneurysm the day before the appointment. The wife claimed unsuccessfully that had her husband been seen by the GP sooner than the arranged appointment date he may not have died.

Following are the types (also referred to as 'heads') of damage recognised by the court:

1 *physical injury*: harm to the body, the assessment of which will depend on the particular circumstances of the case and the quantum awarded in previous cases

2 *pure economic loss*: a purely financial loss which a plaintiff suffers due to the negligence of another

3 *psychological and/or mental harm (nervous shock)*: this does not include grief but rather refers to a clinically demonstrable mental illness or disorder that renders the person unable to maintain their pre-event lifestyle.[101] In the cases of *Tame v New South Wales*[102] and *Annetts v Australian Stations Pty Ltd*,[103] the High Court held it is not a requirement of recovery in cases of pure psychiatric injury that there be a sudden 'shock'. It is not necessary that the plaintiff sustain a physical injury in conjunction with the psychological damage to have it compensated.[104]

A number of jurisdictions[105] have reinstated the '*normal fortitude*' rule in relation to psychological/mental harm. For example, s 32 of the Civil Liability Act 2002 (NSW) provides:

32 Mental harm-duty of care

(1) A person ('the defendant') does not owe a duty of care to another person ('the plaintiff') to take care not to cause the plaintiff mental harm unless the defendant ought to have foreseen that a person of normal fortitude might, in the circumstances of the case, suffer a recognised psychiatric illness if reasonable care were not taken.

(2) For the purposes of the application of this section in respect of pure mental harm, the circumstances of the case include the following:

(a) whether or not the mental harm was suffered as the result of a sudden shock,

(b) whether the plaintiff witnessed, at the scene, a person being killed, injured or put in peril,

(c) the nature of the relationship between the plaintiff and any person killed, injured or put in peril,

(d) whether or not there was a pre-existing relationship between the plaintiff and the defendant.

(3) For the purposes of the application of this section in respect of consequential mental harm, the circumstances of the case include the personal injury suffered by the plaintiff.

(4) This section does not require the court to disregard what the defendant knew or ought to have known about the fortitude of the plaintiff.

The assessment of damages is complicated and must be meticulously attended. This is because the system of compensation in Australia is in the form of a 'once and for all' lump sum payment. The plaintiff cannot come back to the court at a later time if the quantum of the damages was insufficient to meet the plaintiff's needs or if it has been invested or spent inappropriately.

Damages are divided into specific damages and general damages. *Specific damages* are the actual costs the plaintiff has incurred, such as expenditure or lost wages as a result of the damage, from the time of the injury and at the time of the trial. This portion of the damages is the amount of expenditure already incurred and can be specifically identified. *General damages* are estimates of expenditure in the future flowing from the injury. These will include loss of future earnings, pain and suffering, loss of enjoyment of life, loss of expectation of life, anticipated costs of medical, nursing, diagnostic services, pharmaceutical, physiotherapy and rehabilitation. Recent legislative changes have imposed 'thresholds' and 'caps' on the award of damages.

The defendant will be liable for that damage which could reasonably be foreseen as a real risk; that is, damage which is not considered as too remote. The test of reasonable foreseeability serves to limit the damages for which the defendant will be liable.[106] Where the plaintiff has a particular susceptibility to injury, the defendant will be held responsible for the full extent of the damage which occurs. This is referred to as the *egg shell skull* principle, the rule that the plaintiff takes the victim as they find them and will be liable for the injury regardless of the severity, provided the type of injury itself was reasonably foreseeable. In 2003, the High Court of Australia handed down its decision in the case of *Cattanach v Melchior* (refer to the section in this chapter under duty to the unborn).[107] This case, on appeal from the Queensland Court of Appeal, involved a claim by parents to recover the costs of raising and maintaining their child who was unintentionally conceived due to the negligence of their medical practitioner. Mrs Melchior, who informed her doctor that she had had her right fallopian tube removed, underwent a tubal ligation on her left fallopian tube only. In fact, her right tube had not been removed, she became pregnant and successfully sued her doctor in negligence. In addition to compensation awarded for pain and suffering, loss of amenities, economic loss and special damages, the Supreme Court of Queensland awarded the plaintiff $105 249.33 for the costs associated with the raising of the child. The doctor appealed unsuccessfully to the Queensland Court of Appeal and to the High Court on the question as to whether the damages for past and future costs of raising a child were reasonable. The High Court held that the costs of raising a healthy child, who was unwanted, were recoverable. As previously noted (refer to the section in this chapter under duty to the unborn) such a claim is now precluded under civil liability legislation in a number of jurisdictions.

Exemplary damages where described by the High Court in *Gray v Motor Accident Commission*[108] as 'intended to punish the defendant and presumably to serve one or more of the objects of punishment, namely moral retribution or deterrence'.[109] Punitive damages, though invariably sought in medical negligence actions, are rarely successful and were not awarded in Australia until the case of *Backwell v AAA (Backwell)*.[110] Punitive or exemplary damages are awarded to the plaintiff where the conduct of the defendant has been so excessively outrageous, gross or wanton as to warrant a penalty and warning from the court in the form of damages. Section 21 if the Civil Liability Act 2002 (NSW) preclude the award of exemplary or punitive damages, or damages in the nature of aggravated damages, in personal injury cases where the act or omission that caused the injury or death was negligence. In Queensland exemplary, punitive or aggravated damages cannot be awarded in personal injury damages unless the act causing the personal injury was an unlawful intentional act that intended to cause the injury sustained, or an unlawful sexual assault or other sexual misconduct.[111]

Causation

The plaintiff must establish a causal relationship between the negligent conduct of the medical practitioner and the damage sustained by the plaintiff. The breach of the duty of care must be causally linked to the injury or no compensation will be payable. Questions of causation are questions of fact. In a healthcare context, this is often the most difficult element for the plaintiff to prove. The plaintiff must be able to prove that, on the balance of probabilities, the damage now claimed has been caused by the defendant's conduct and is not in fact the natural progression of the underlying pathology, or the result of the plaintiff's illness, disease or disorder.

The decision in the case of *Barnett v Chelsea and Kensington Hospital*[112] established the 'but for' test as a means to determine if there was a causal relationship between the breach and the damage.

Could the plaintiff prove that 'but for' the defendant's negligence the plaintiff would not have suffered the injury? This test is now considered in combination with the 'common sense' approach[113] as a means to determine the liability of the defendant.

In the Queensland Court of Appeal case of *Green v Chenoweth*,[114] the plaintiff claimed damages against a surgeon for failure to warn of the post-operative risk of adhesions following a myomectomy. The trial judge at first instance found on the evidence that even if the plaintiff had known of the risk she would have undergone the procedure. The Court of Appeal held that even if the plaintiff had received a warning she would still have consented to the surgery, although there was a chance she may have refused. Further, the negligent failure to warn of material risks cannot, standing alone, give rise to a cause of action. It must be proven, on the balance of probabilities, to have caused in some form of action or inaction the damage claimed by the plaintiff. The plaintiff's appeal was dismissed.

In *Black v Lipovac*,[115] a fourteen-month-old child was prescribed aminophylline suppositories. After the administration of one of the suppositories the child suffered a fit and sustained significant neurological damage. The child by his 'next friend' (his parents) sued the general practitioner who had prescribed the aminophylline suppositories, the doctor who had administered an intramuscular injection of phenobarbitone soon after the fitting commenced, the ambulance officer who transported the child to the hospital and the manufacturer of the aminophylline. The action against the manufacturer alleged negligence in failing to provide adequate warning of the dangers of the drug on the packaging, and advise medical practitioners of the potential toxic side effects. The trial judge found on the evidence that only the child's general practitioner who had initially prescribed the aminophylline suppositories had been negligent. Though the evidence confirmed that the manufacturer had failed to provide a warning as to the weight-related dependency of the dosage, and had failed to provide adequate written warnings on the packaging of the drug, they were not found to be liable for the child's damage. The Court of Appeal upheld the initial decision as it could not be established that the lack of warning to either the doctor or the parents was causally linked to the damage that followed from the prescription for and administration of the drug.

As previously noted, the issue of causation has been specifically addressed by legislation in a number of jurisdictions. The panel reviewing the law of negligence in Australia in the late 1990s and early 2000 proposed the following recommendations:

- the plaintiff always bears the onus of proving, to the requisite civil standard, any fact relevant to causation

- there are two elements that need to be established regarding
a causal link between the alleged conduct and the damage:

1 factual causation: factually whether the negligent conduct
played a part in bringing about the harm. The 'but for
test' is not to be considered in isolation

2 scope of the liability: once it is established that negligence is
the factual cause of the damage, the question is: what is the
scope of the negligent person's liability for that damage?

These recommendations have been adopted into legislation in
Queensland,[116] Western Australia,[117] Tasmania,[118] the Australian Capital
Territory,[119] South Australia[120] and New South Wales.[121] In Victoria,[122]
the plaintiff bears the burden of proving, on the civil standard of the
balance of probabilities, any facts relevant to the issue of causation. As an
example, s 13 of the Tasmanian Civil Liability Act 2002 states:

Division 3 — Causation 13. General principles

(1) Prerequisites for a decision that a breach of duty caused
particular harm are as follows:

(a) the breach of duty was a necessary element of the
occurrence of the harm ('factual causation');

(b) it is appropriate for the scope of the liability of the
person in breach to extend to the harm so caused
('scope of liability').

(2) In deciding in an exceptional case, in accordance with
established principles, whether a breach of duty, being
a breach of duty that is established but which cannot be
established as satisfying subsection (1)(a), should be taken as
satisfying subsection (1)(a), the court is to consider (among
other relevant things) whether or not and why responsibility
for the harm should be imposed on the party in breach.

In application therefore, factual causation is determined by whether
'the breach of the duty was a "necessary condition" of the occurrence
of the harm'.[123] In the case of *Finch v Rogers*[124] the question before
the New South Wales Supreme Court was precisely that, whether, as a
matter of scientific fact, the breach of duty by the medical practitioner
was a 'necessary condition' of the harm suffered by the patient. In
this case the plaintiff was a patient who had undergone surgery for
the removal of a testicle following a diagnosis of testicular cancer. The
allegations of negligence were based on the failure of the medical
practitioner to properly follow up and investigate the possibly that the
tumour had metastasised. The plaintiff alleged that as a result of the
delay by the medical practitioner he had been required to undergo an
extra cycle of chemotherapy, which was accompanied by permanent

tinnitus and peripheral neuropathy. The court held in relation to s 5D Civil Liability Act 2002 (NSW) at 147–8:

> Addressing the issue of factual causation, but for the breach, and the delay which was the consequence of the breach, the following can be said. First, that Mr Finch would probably have been given Indiana BEP chemotherapy on Monday, 30 December 1996 or at the latest, Monday 6 January 1997. Second, that on either day, he would have been regarded as a good prognosis patient. Third, that given his response to chemotherapy (which was good) he would have needed only three cycles, not four; fourth, that he would not have suffered the disabling consequences of ototoxicity and neurotoxicity which were evident after the fourth cycle ... I consider, that the Defendant's negligence was a necessary condition of the harm that ensued ... that it is appropriate that the scope of the defendant's liability extend to the harm so caused ... The consequences were in each case a foreseeable risk of the breach.

APOLOGIES

Following an adverse event it had been the practice of many disciplines of health professionals to deny any knowledge of (or involvement in) the adverse event or refuse to admit that an adverse event had occurred. This was usually due to the perception that to recognise the adverse event or involvement in an adverse outcome is an admission of liability and may be used in future legal actions. All Australian states and territories have introduced statutory reform giving recognition to an *expression of regret* or *apology*. It is important that medical practitioners are familiar with the legislative provisions in the states or territories in which they practice. As can be seen by the following, the use of particular language is very significant in ensuring that the apology or expression of regret is not an admission of liability. All health professionals, including medical practitioners, must familiarise themselves and understand the inter-relationship between the expression of regret or apology and the National Disclosure Policy (refer to Chapter 2, Safety and quality in health). The following provides an overview of the legislation pertaining to expressions of regret and apologies. Section 75 of the Civil Liability Act 1936 (SA) states:

75 Expression of regret

> In proceedings in which damages are claimed for a tort, no admission of liability or fault is to be inferred from the fact that the defendant or a person for whose tort the defendant is

liable expressed regret for the incident out of which the cause of action arose.

Under s 7 of the Tasmanian Civil Liability Act 2002:

(1) An apology made by or on behalf of a person in connection with any matter alleged to have been caused by the fault of the person –

  (a) does not constitute an express or implied admission of fault or liability be the person in connection with that matter; and

  (b) is not relevant to the determination of fault or liability in connection with the matter.

(2) Evidence of an apology made by or on behalf of a person in connection with any matter alleged to have been caused by the fault of the person is not admissible in any civil proceedings as evidence of the fault or liability of the person in connection with that matter.

(3) In this section,

'apology' means an expression of sympathy or regret, or of a general sense of benevolence or compassion, in connection with any matter, which does not contain an admission of fault in connection with the matter.

While the civil liability legislation in New South Wales and the Australian Capital Territory define an apology in a way that includes an admission of fault, in Queensland, Tasmania, Victoria, Western Australia and the Northern Territory an admission of fault is expressly excluded. The consequences of an apology or expression of regret are listed in Table 5.2.

DEFENCES TO AN ACTION IN NEGLIGENCE

There are five commonly raised strategies in defending an action in negligence. The first is to deny or rebut at least one of the elements of the action. That is, the medical practitioner:

1 denies that a duty of care existed; or
2 establishes that the conduct and behaviour at the time of the incident was of a reasonable standard for a skilled professional; or
3 establishes that there was no damage suffered by the plaintiff; or
4 denies that there was a causal link between the conduct and the damage; or
5 establishes that the damage was not reasonably foreseeable.

The second defence lies in attempting to establish contributory negligence on the part of the plaintiff. Historically, contributory negligence amounted to a total defence. However, the defence is

Table 5.2 Consequences of an apology or expression of regret

Legislation	Consequence	Admissibility in proceedings
Queensland Civil Liability Act 2003 s 72	Allows an individual to express regret without concern that the expression of regret will be construed or used as an admission of liability.	Expression of regret is not admissible in proceedings.
New South Wales Civil Liability Act 2002 s 69	Does not constitute express or implied admission of fault or liability. Is not relevant to the determination of fault or liability.	Not admissible in any civil proceedings as evidence of fault or liability.
Tasmania Civil Liability Act 2002 s 7(1)	Does not constitute express or implied admission of fault or liability. Is not relevant to the determination of fault or liability.	Not admissible in any civil proceedings as evidence of fault or liability.
Western Australian Civil Liability Act 2002 s 5AH	Does not constitute express or implied admission of fault or liability. Is not relevant to the determination of fault or liability.	Not admissible in any civil proceedings as evidence of fault or liability.
Victorian Wrongs Act 1958 s 14J (1)	In civil proceedings where death or injury is in issue or is relevant to an issue in fact or law the apology does not constitute liability for death or injury or admission of unprofessional conduct, carelessness, incompetence, or unsatisfactory professional performance.	Nothing in the section affects the admissibility of a statement with respect to a fact in issue or tending to establish a fact in issue.
Northern Territory Personal Injuries (Liability and Damages) Act 2003 s 13	Section silent on consequence.	Not admissible as evidence.
South Australian Civil Liability Act 1936 s 75	No admission of liability or fault to be inferred.	Section silent on admissibility.
Australian Capital Territory Civil Law (Wrongs) Act 2002	Is not (and must not be taken as) an express or implied admission of fault or liability. Not relevant to deciding fault or liability.	Not admissible in any civil proceedings as evidence of fault or liability.

now referred to as a 'partial defence' which, if successful, results in the damages being divided amongst the number of persons held liable for the damage. This may include the plaintiff where their own conduct has in some way caused or contributed to the damage they are now claiming. The plaintiff effectively is under a duty of care to avoid being injured. The defendant seeking contribution from the plaintiff must establish, on the balance of probabilities, that the plaintiff contributed to their own injuries. As stated by Denning J in *Froom v Butcher:*[125]

Negligence depends on a breach of duty, whereas contributory negligence does not. Negligence is a man's carelessness in breach of duty to others. Contributory negligence is a man's carelessness in looking after his own safety. He is guilty of contributory negligence if he ought reasonably to have foreseen that, if he did not act as a reasonable prudent man, he might be hurt himself ...

It is for the judge to determine the percentage of the blame to be allocated to the plaintiff and the amount to be deducted from the damages. While contributory negligence is frequently raised in personal injury claims where seatbelts or motorbike helmets have not been worn at the time of the injury, it is most uncommon in a healthcare context. The defendant would be required to show that the patient conducted themselves in a negligent manner and thereby contributed to their own injuries. As an example, in the American case of *Brockman v Harpole*,[126] the Oregon Supreme Court held that a patient who had badgered the registered nurse about not wanting to wait while she was attempting to syringe his ear had contributed to the damage that occurred when his eardrum was punctured.

The third defence is known as *volenti non fit injuria* or voluntary assumption of risk. The defence requires that the plaintiff voluntarily assumed the risk of being injured by participating in the activity and therefore their injuries cannot found an action in negligence. This defence has its origins in employment law and has now been confined effectively to sporting activities. The defence is raised where a player is injured during a game or activity and all players are playing at the time by the rules. The defence is that the injured player voluntarily assumed the risk of injury in playing the game. Obviously patients and clients do not enter a hospital or health facility voluntarily assuming the risk of being injured. Therefore, the defence has no application in a healthcare context.

The fourth strategy is to claim that the action is out of time or statute barred. All jurisdictions have limitation periods after which, no matter how significant and severe the injury, an action cannot be initiated. As a general principle the time starts to run from when the plaintiff sustains the damage. However, the court has the discretion to extend the time in particular circumstances.[127] It has been recommended that the limitation period be calculated by what was referred to as the 'date of discoverability', which identifies the starting time as that date on which the plaintiff knew, or ought to have known, that the injury had occurred. Historically, the limitation period for minors did not start to run until the age of majority, which in all jurisdictions is 18 years. Therefore, in those states and territories with a 3-year limitation period, the person would have until they were twenty-one to commence an action in negligence and, in the other jurisdictions, until they were 24 years of age. The special rules that now apply to children and those with a disability are specific to each jurisdiction and all medical practitioners should consult the legislation in their particular jurisdiction.[128] The limitation period for personal injuries in all Australian jurisdictions is 3 years from the date on which the cause of action accrued or the date of discovery. As there are differences between the individual jurisdictions health professionals are advised to familiarise themselves with the provisions relevant to the state or territory in which they conduct their practice.

Finally, the defendant may join another defendant and show that, through that person or institution's negligence, they are jointly liable for the damage. In the case of *Jones v Manchester Corporation*,[129] both the resident medical officer and the hospital board were held jointly liable for the negligence that resulted in the death of the patient. The medical officer had graduated from university some 6 months prior to her overdosing a patient with an intravenous anaesthetic. The hospital board, aware of her lack of experience, nevertheless rostered her to work alone in the Emergency Department overnight.

VICARIOUS LIABILITY

The doctrine of vicarious liability is a common law concept and serves to shift the financial responsibility from the individual who has been found liable for the damage to another individual or entity that has a greater financial capacity to bear the loss. The policy consideration underpinning the doctrine is the recognition that an employer will be financially more capable than an employee of meeting the cost of compensating the plaintiff. Thus, within the healthcare system, *the doctrine of vicarious liability transfers the responsibility for compensating the patient's damages from the medical practitioner to the employer*, who will be a hospital, healthcare facility, government agency or owner of a private healthcare provider.

The doctrine applies when an employee, in the course or scope of their employment, negligently injures a patient. An employer is vicariously liable for the torts of the employees but assumes no liability for independent contractors. The two tests therefore are:

1   Is the negligent individual an employee?
2   Did the negligent conduct occur within the course and scope of the employment?

Whether an individual is an employee will be determined through an examination of the relationship with the employer. Three tests are applied: the control test, the part and parcel of the organisation test and the multiple test. Historically, the control test determined the issue. However, the court now examines wider *indicia* to establish whether or not the person is an employee or an independent contractor.

The control test

The court looks to whether the employer has the legal authority to control the person, regardless of whether or not there is any attempt to exercise that control. In the case of *Zuijs v Wirth Bros*,[130] the High Court held that a trapeze artist was an employee for the purpose of workers' compensation. The employer had attempted to escape liability by arguing that the work performed by the artist was beyond their control. The court stated:

> The duties to perform may depend so much on professional skill or knowledge ... or the necessity of the employee acting on his own responsibility may be evident, that little room for direction or command in detail may exist. But this is not the point. What matters is the lawful authority to command so far as there is scope for it.

From the perspective of a highly skilled medical practitioner, this decision is of great significance. The judgment clearly indicates that the employer will not be able to escape liability by arguing that the work is so complicated, specialised and technical that they did not have control and therefore are not in an employer–employee relationship. Provided the employer has the legal right to tell the individual where, when and how the work is to be done, the control test will be satisfied.

Part and parcel of the organisation test

This may be referred to as the 'integration test' or the 'organisation test' and alone will not determine the existence of an employer–employee relationship if the control test indicates an independent contractor rather than an employee. The test is applied in combination with other *indicia* of employment.[131] Effectively the court examines whether the person is part of the employer's organisation.

In the case of *Albrighton v Royal Prince Alfred Hospital*,[132] a 15-year-old girl was admitted to the Royal Prince Alfred Hospital for corrective surgery to her spine. The procedure involved the application of a halopelvic traction. On her lower back she had a large hairy naevus over her spine which, it was suggested, indicated tethering to the spinal cord and adjacent structures with the risk of rupture and possible paraplegia if traction were applied. During the admission, she was seen by a neurosurgeon, who requested a second opinion. The traction was fitted prior to the examination by the consultant neurosurgeon and after five days the spinal cord was severed and the girl became a paraplegic. The girl sued the two doctors and the hospital as being vicariously liable for its employees. The hospital attempted to escape liability by claiming that the consultant neurosurgeon was not an employee but rather an independent contractor, a private practitioner beyond its control. On appeal, the Court of Appeal of the Supreme Court of New South Wales held that the hospital was vicariously liable for the doctor, stating as follows:[133]

> The control test is not now acceptable in its full vigour. Today, the uncontrollability of a person forming part of an organisation, as to the manner in which he performs his task, does not preclude recovery from the organisation, and does not preclude the finding of a relationship of master and servant, such as to make the former vicariously liable for the negligence of the latter.

The issue was also raised in *Ellis v Wallsend Hospital*.[134] In this case, the plaintiff successfully sued the surgeon for failing to warn her of possible paralysis pre-operatively.

Unfortunately, the doctor died, and his estate and insurance cover were not adequate to meet the claim. Mrs Ellis therefore sought to be compensated, under the doctrine of vicarious liability, by the hospital where the doctor had admitted her as a patient. In holding that the doctor was an independent contractor, the court considered the totality of the relationship between the doctor and the hospital. The court heard evidence that the doctor at all times carried on his own business, received no remuneration from the hospital, was paid directly by his patients and exchanged his medical services for the use of the hospital beds. Samuels JA stated:[135]

> I conclude that it [the totality of the relationship between the parties] points convincingly to the conclusion that in treating the appellant Dr Chambers was engaged in his own business

and not the hospital's. He was conducting his independent practice as a neurosurgeon and his relationship with the hospital was not one of employer and employee.

The multiple test

This is not a test as such but rather a collection of *indicia* that are consistent with the employer–employee relationship. The five elements considered by the court are as follows.

1 Is tax taken from the pay prior to receipt by the person?
2 Does the person receive sick leave?
3 Is there a superannuation contribution by the employer?
4 Does the employer provide the plant and equipment?
5 Is there an expectation of personal service?

The liability of the employer under the doctrine of vicarious liability is confined to the negligence of an employee in the 'course and scope of their employment'. The term 'course and scope of the employment' is given a very broad application by the courts and includes all activities that the employee is authorised to do, even if carried out in an unauthorised manner. It is important, therefore, for medical practitioners to be clear about the activities they are and are not authorised to undertake. This will vary not only from institution to institution but also between different clinical units within the same institution. Hospital protocols and policies and guidelines are invaluable documents in relation to this element.

To be outside the course and scope of the employment, the health professional must be undertaking some activity that is so totally unrelated to the employment that they are a 'stranger vis-a-vis the employer'.[136]

NON-DELEGABLE DUTY OF CARE

Hospitals and healthcare facilities hold themselves out as providing a service to the consumers of healthcare. As such, hospitals owe a non-delegable duty of care to patients and clients. This duty is based on the relationship between the institution and the patient and therefore cannot be delegated to others.

In *Kondis v State Transport Authority*,[137] it was held that the employer owed a non-delegable duty of care to employees to maintain a safe system of work. In this case, an independent contractor injured an employee while operating a crane and the employer was held to be liable for the damage. The non-delegable duty is also owed to patients and cannot be devolved to employees. It is therefore separate and distinct from vicarious liability. As stated by Mason J in *Kondis's* case[138] the non-delegable duty arises:

> because the person on whom it is imposed has undertaken the care, supervision or control of the person or property of another or is so placed in relation to that person or his property as to assume a particular responsibility for his or its safety, in circumstances where the person affected might reasonably expect that due care will be exercised.

A 'special relationship' giving rise to the existence of a non-delegable duty of care is said to exist between the hospital and the patient. This 'special relationship' exists because the hospital assumes the responsibility for the control, care and supervision of a patient or is so placed, in relation to a particular patient, as to assume a particular responsibility. The vulnerability and dependence of the patient on the hospital is fundamental to the 'special relationship' that goes to the existence of the non-delegable duty of care.[139] In *Elliott v Bickerstaff*,[140] it was held that this latter element was satisfied in the hospital–patient relationship as:

> the patient is usually specially dependent or vulnerable in that ... [they have] no relevant expertise and, rather like an employee, must put up with whatever the hospital subjects him to in fulfilling its undertaking, and perhaps it is thought that, by its arrangements, the hospital has ultimate control over what the patient is subjected to even though it does not control how the medical officers do their work.

In the healthcare context, this non-delegable duty imposes on the hospital or healthcare facility the obligation to employ adequate numbers of appropriately trained and skilled staff, ensuring that the plant and equipment is operational and safe, and that the patients are not exposed to any undue risk. However, statutory defences in most jurisdictions give public authorities a measure of protection from liability from harm that is the outcome of decisions about the allocation of scarce resources.[141]

ALTERNATIVE ACTIONS

A patient or client may wish to pursue a claim for compensation through initiating an action under the Trade Practices Act 1974 (Cth). This use of consumer law, in a healthcare context, relieves the patient of the burden of having to prove that the medical practitioner behaved in a manner that was in breach of the standard of care. Section 52 of the Trade Practices Act 1974 (Cth) states: 'a corporation shall not in trade or commerce engage in conduct that is misleading or deceptive or is likely to mislead or deceive'.

The patient must bring the action within 3 years of acting upon the representation of the corporation. The plaintiff would argue that the corporation (the hospital) made a representation, for example, that the blood and blood products were not contaminated. The plaintiff then would have relied on the representation that was false and misleading and, as a result, sustained an injury.

The issue has been raised and resolved as to whether hospitals and other providers of healthcare services are corporations for the purpose of the legislation.[142] It has been held that, as hospitals trade in goods and services, they are corporations. This interpretation has been extended to individual health professionals across a number of disciplines including medicine. It appears that, if the services are exchanged for monetary reward, the professional will fall within the definition of 'trade and commerce' and become liable for action under the Act.[143]

SCENARIO AND ACTIVITIES

Mr Butter is admitted to Shine Hospital for the removal of his diseased kidney. On the morning of Mr Butter's surgery there has been a multi-vehicle accident. The operating theatre nurses and doctors have been working continually from 3 a.m. carrying out surgery on those injured in the accident. Two of the patients had sustained such significant injuries they had not survived their surgery. The operating theatres are still very busy as Mr Butter is checked in for his surgery. The nurse checked Mr Butter's identification and consent. The nurse does not notice, until Mr Butter is anaesthetised, that his medical records do not contain the required pre-operative physical assessment form. The surgeon, who has been working since 4 a.m., was also the doctor who assessed Mr Butter the preceding night. He decides that he will proceed without the assessment form as he thinks that he has a clear memory of the examination he carried out on Mr Butter. The surgeon considers that the time required to retrieve the missing assessment form will only cause further delay in the operating schedule. The doctor mistakenly removes the wrong kidney. Almost simultaneously Mr Butter has a respiratory arrest and though he can be resuscitated he now only has one diseased kidney which will require almost immediate removal.

- What is the legal action Mr Butter is most likely to pursue?
- Who are the individuals and/or organisation he is most likely to sue?

- Identify all the elements necessary to win in the legal action you think Mr Butter will take. Include for each element the legal principles (from the case law) and legislative requirements (from the Acts of Parliament) that apply for Mr Butter to succeed in his case.
- Identify the possible arguments that you, as the nurse, doctor or hospital may use to defend yourself if you were a defendant in this action.

REVIEW QUESTIONS

To ensure that you have identified and understood the key points of this chapter please answer the following questions.

1 What is the standard of proof in a civil action in negligence?

2 Identify the names of the parties in an action in negligence. For example, in most cases the patient will initiate the action and will be called the ..., and the medical practitioner who was responsible for the care of the patient when the injury occurred will be called the ... .

3 What are the elements necessary to succeed in an action in negligence?

4 What criteria must be satisfied to establish a duty of care between the patient and the medical practitioner?

5 In what circumstances may a medical practitioner owe a duty of care to an unborn infant?

6 Can you locate and identify the legislation in your particular jurisdiction which establishes the standard of care for professionals (www.austli.edu.au). Having done that, describe the standard of care required of a medical practitioner under that Act.

7 What sources of information would you access to identify the standard of care in a particular clinical area or in relation to a particular medical intervention?

8 In relation to the disclosure of risk, what information must be disclosed to a patient?

9 What types of damage does the court recognise for the purpose of assessing compensation in a negligence action?

> **10** What is the legislative definition of causation in your jurisdiction?
> **11** Describe the concept of a non-delegable duty of care.
> **12** Discuss the elements necessary to establish that an employing healthcare facility is vicariously liable for an intern (employee).
> **13** What are the provisions for giving an 'apology' or 'expression of regret' in relation to an incident from which a cause of action in negligence may arise in your state or territory.

Further reading

Australian Health and Medical Law Reporter, CCH Sydney.

Boston, T, 'A hospital's non-delegable duty of care' (2003) 10 *Journal of Law and Medicine* 364.

Brophy, E, 'Does a Doctor have a duty to provide information and advice about complementary and alternative medicine?' (2003) 10 *Journal of Law and Medicine* 271.

Butler, D, 'Once more into mire, dear friends: Determining the existence of a duty of care negligence' (2000) *National Law Review* 3. Online. Available: http://web.nlr.com.au.

Chambers, K, Krikorian, R, 'Review of the final Ipp Report and its impact on health claims' (2003) 11(4) *Australian Health Law Bulletin* 37.

Cockburn, T, Madden, B, 'Intentional torts claims in medical cases' (2006) 13 *Journal of Law and Medicine* 311.

Devereux, J, 'Medical law report' (1999) 6 *Journal of Law and Medicine* 331.

Devereux, J, *Australian Medical Law*, 3rd edn, Routledge-Cavendish, AbingdonOxon, 2007.

Hirsch, D, '*PD v Harvey*: Revisiting a doctor's duty of care to sexual partners' (2003) 11(10) *Australian Health Law Bulletin* 109.

Ipp J et al, *Review of the Law of Negligence,* Australian Government, Department of Treasury, 2002. Online. Available: http://revofn eg.treasury.gov.au/content/reports.asp.

Kennedy, E, 'Punitive damages for medical negligence' (1999) 8(3) *Australian Health Law Bulletin* 27.

Madden, B, 'Changes to the definition of negligence' (2003) 12 (1) *Australian Health Law Bulletin* 6.

Madden, B, Cockburn, T, 'Duty to disclose medical error in Australia' (2005) 15 *Health Law Bulletin* 19.

Magnussan, RS, 'Legal issues in teamwork: liability within medical teams and hierarchies in NSW' (2007) *Precedent* (79) 10–17.

McDonald, B, 'The common law of negligence' (2003) *Commercial Law Quarterly* 12.

McIlwraith, J, Madden, B, *Healthcare and the Law*, 4th edn, Lawbook Co, Sydney, 2006.

Mendelson, D, *A New Law of Torts*, Oxford University Press, Melbourne, 2007.

Parker, M, 'Reforming the law of medical negligence: solutions in search of a problem' (2003) *Torts Law Journal* 136–64.

Skene, L, *Law and Medical Practice*, 2nd edn, LexisNexis, Sydney, 2004.

Endnotes

1 Review of Professional Indemnity Arrangements for Healthcare Professionals. Compensation and Professional Indemnity in Healthcare Final Report, Australian Government Printing Service, Canberra, 1995 at 127.

2 Mann, A. 'Medical negligence litigation' (1989) 21(4) *Australian Journal of Forensic Sciences* 124.

3 Trebilcock, MJ, Dewees, DN, Duff, DG, 'The medical malpractice explosion: an empirical assessment of trends, determinants and impacts' (1990) 17 *Melbourne University Law Review* 539; Imershein, AW, Brents, AH, 'The impact of large medical malpractice awards on malpractice awardees' (1992) 13 *The Journal of Legal Medicine* 33; Hall, MA, 'The defensive effect of medical practice policies in malpractice litigation' (1991) 51(2) *Law and Contemporary Problems* 119.

4 Civil Law (Wrongs) Act 2002 (ACT); Civil Liability Act 2002 NSW; Civil Liability Act 2003 (Qld); Personal Injuries (Liabilities and Damages) Act 2003 (NT); Civil Liability Act 1936 (SA); Wrongs Act 1958 (Vic), Civil Liability Act 2002 (WA); Civil Liability Act 2002 (Tas).

5 Civil Liability Act 2002 (NSW), s 5; Civil Liability Act 2002 (ACT), s 32; Civil Liability Act 1936 (SA), s 3; Wrongs Act 1958 (Vic), s 43.

6 Civil Liability Act 1936 (SA).

7 Kennedy, I, Grubb, A, *Medical Law: Text with Materials*, Butterworths, London, 1994 at 465.

8 [1951] 1 All ER 574.

9 Above, n 7 at 467.

10 *Blyth v Birmingham Water Works Co* (1856) 11 Exch 781 at 784.

11 *Whitehouse v Jordon* [1981] 1 All ER 650 at 658 per Lord Denning MR; affirmed [1981] 1 All ER 267 (HL). However, it is noteworthy that the 'mere' error in clinical judgment will not alone succeed as a defence. As stated by Lord Frazer at 281: '[m]erely to describe something as an error of judgment tells us nothing about whether it is negligent or not ... If the [error] is one which would not have been made by a reasonably competent man professing to have the standard and type of skill the defendant held himself out as having, and acting with ordinary care, then it is negligent. If on the other hand it is an error that a man, acting with ordinary care, might have made, then it is not negligence'.

12 *Whitehouse v Jordan*; *Roe v Minister of Health* [1954] 2 QB 66; K Oliphant, 'Defining medical misadventure: lessons from New Zealand' (1996) *Medical Law Review* 1–31.

13 MacFarlane, P, *Health Law: Commentary and Materials*, The Federation Press, Sydney, 1995 at 99.

14 Above, n 7 at 400.

15 [1932] AC 562.

16 Ibid at 580.

17 *Sidaway v Board of Governors of the Bethlem Royal Hospital* [1985] AC 871 at 893; *Gover v South Australia and Perriam* (1985) 39 SASR 543 per Cox J, adopted per Mason CJ, Brennan, Dawson, Toohey and McHugh JJ in *Rogers v Whitaker* (1992) 109 ALR 625 at 628.

18 *Swain v Waverley Municipal Council* [2005] HCA 4 at [5].

19 *Chapman v Hearse* (1961) 106 CLR 112; *Bale v Seltsam Pty Ltd* [19996] QCA 288.

20 *X and Y (By her Tutor X) v Pal* (1991) 23 NSWLR 26 at 38–42 per Clarke JA (CA).

21 [2001] NSWCA 422 (27 November 2001).

22 *Holgate v Lancashire Mental Hospital Board* [1937] 4 All ER 19; *Dorset Yacht Co v Home Office* [1970] AC 1004; *Pallister v Waikato Hospital Board* [1975] 2 NZLR 725.

23 [1999] NSWSC 1082.

24 [2005] NSWSC 924.

25 [2003] NSWSC 487 (10 June 2003) BC200303031.

26 Ibid at para [82].

27 [1972] VR 353.
28 *Attorney-General for the State of Queensland (ex Rel Kerr) v T* (1983) 46 ALR 275 at 279.
29 [1982] VR 961.
30 (2006) 226 ALR 457.
31 (2006) 226 ALR 457.
32 (2003) 215 CLR 1.
33 Refer generally to Eburn, M, *Emergency Law*, Federation Press, Melbourne, 1999; Mendelson, D, 'Quo lure? Defendants' liability to rescuers in the tort of negligence' (2001) 9 *Torts Law Review* 130.
34 (1963) 110 CLR 40.
35 (1996) Aust Torts Reports 81–312.
36 [1971] 2 Lloyd's Rep 410.
37 (1985) 75 WN (NSW) 173 at 175.
38 *Haynes v Harwood* [1935] 1 KB 147; *Ward v TE Hopkins & Son Ltd* [1995] 3 All ER 225; K Tronc, 'A plaintiff lawyers guide to the liability of emergency services personnel and rescuers', Australian Plaintiff Lawyers Association conference, Surfers Paradise, 27 October 2000.
39 Section 67l.
40 Doepel, M, 'Tort reform throughout Australia: A brief review of recent amendments', paper given at the Medical Indemnity Forum, Sydney, October 2003.
41 Civil Law (Wrongs) Act 2003 (ACT); Civil Law (Wrongs) Amendment Act 2003 (ACT).
42 Civil Liability Act 2002 (NSW); Civil Liability Amendment (Personal Responsibility) Act 2002 (NSW).
43 Personal Injuries (Liabilities and Damages) Act 2003 (NT); Personal Injuries (Civil Claims) Act 2003 (NT).
44 Section 26 Civil Liability Act 2002.
45 Volunteers Protection Act 2001 (SA); Recreational Services (Limitation of Liability) Act 2002 (SA); Wrongs (Liability and Damages for Personal Injury) Amendment Act 2002 (SA).
46 Wrongs Act 1958 (Vic), s 31B.
47 Wrongs Act 1958 (Vic), s 37.
48 Civil Liability Act 2002 (WA); Volunteers (Protection from Liability) Act 2002 (WA); Insurance Commission of WA Amendment Act 2002 (WA).

49 Civil Law (Wrongs) Act 2002 (ACT), s 43; Civil Liability Act 2002 (NSW), s 5B; Civil Liability Act 2003 (Qld), s 11; Civil Liability Act 1936 (SA), s 32; Civil Liability Act 2002 (Tas), s 11; Wrongs Act 1958 (Vic), s 48; Civil Liability Act 2002 (WA), s 5B.

50 [1957] 1 WLR 582.

51 Ibid at 586.

52 Ibid at 587.

53 (1992) 175 CLR 479.

54 Ibid at 586.

55 [1988] 1 All ER 871.

56 (1997) Aust Tort Reports 81-448 at 64,560.

57 Ibid at 64,564.

58 Ibid at 64,566.

59 [2006] NSWSC 1307.

60 Ibid at [180].

61 Ibid at [182].

62 *Roe v Minister of Health* [1954] 2 QB 66; *Anna Koziol v Louise Anasson* [1997] 803 FCA; *H v Royal Alexandra Hospital for Children* (1990) Aust Torts Reports 81–000; *Black v Lipovac*, unreported, 4 June 1998, FCA.

63 Crofts, P, 'The more things change, the more they stay the same; the Civil Liability Act 2003 (Qld) — opportunity lost' (2003) 11(10) *Australian Health Law Bulletin* 113; Madden, B, 'Quiet changes in professional negligence' (2003) *September Law Society Journal* 72.

64 Crofts, P, 'The more things change, the more they stay the same; the Civil Liability Act 2003 (Qld) — opportunity lost' (2003) 11(10) *Australian Health Law Bulletin* 113.

65 Civil Liability Act 2002 (Tas).

66 Civil Liability Act 2002 (NSW), s 5H; Civil Liability Act 2002 (Qld), s 15; Civil Liability Act 1936 (SA), s 38; Civil Liability Act 2002 (Tas), s 17; Wrongs Act 1958 (Vic), s 53; Civil Liability Act 2002 (WA), s 5O.

67 (1992) 175 CLR 479.

68 [1998] HCA 55 unreported, High Court of Australia, 2 September 1998, Gaudron, McHugh, Gummow, Kirby and Hayne JJ, case number S88/1997.

69 (2001) 205 CLR 434.

70 [1981] 1 QB 432.

71 Ibid per Bristow J in referring to the Canadian decision of *Reibl v Hughes* (1978) 21 OR (2d) 14.

72 That the medical practitioner would not be found negligent if he or she had acted in accordance with proper practice by a responsible body of medical men skilled in the particular art.

73 Adopted in *Freeman v Home Office* [1983] 3 All ER 589 per McCowan J and *Hills v Potter* [1983] All ER 716 per Hirst J.

74 *Sidaway v The Board of Governors of the Bethlem Royal Hospital and Maudsley Hospital* [1985] 1 AC 871.

75 Cassidy, above, n 8 at 75.

76 Above, n 74 at 893.

77 Ibid at 889–90; *Rogers v Whitaker* (1992) 175 CLR 479 per Mason CJ, Brennan, Dawson, Toohey and McHugh JJ at 488: 'a risk is material if, in the circumstances of the particular case, a reasonable person in the patient's position, if warned of the risk, would be likely to attach significance to it …'.

78 Ibid at 488.

79 *Causer v Stafford-Bell* (unreported), Supreme Court of the Australian Capital Territory, Gallop J, BC 9706029, 14 November 1997.

80 (1992) 175 CLR 479 at 494.

81 Above, n 79.

82 Above, n 80.

83 (1992) 175 CLR 474 at 494.

84 Unreported, Supreme Court of New South Wales, Hulme J, BC 9803398, 2 July 1989.

85 *F v R* (1993) 33 SASR 189 at 192–3 per King CJ; *Tai v Saxon* (unreported), Supreme Court of Western Australia, Pidgeon, Franklyn, Ipp JJ, BC 9600521, 8 February 1996; *Anderson v Bowden* (unreported), Full Court of the Supreme Court of Western Australia, Malcolm CJ, Kennedy and Ipp JJ, BC 9707211, 4 December 1997; *Causer v Stafford-Bell* (unreported), Supreme Court of the Australian Capital Territory, Gallop J, BC 9706029, 14 November 1997.

86 *Tai v Saxon* (unreported), Supreme Court of Western Australia, Pidgeon, Franklyn, Ipp JJ, BC 9600521, 8 February 1996; *Anderson v Bowden* (unreported), Full Court of the Supreme Court of Western Australia, Malcolm CJ, Kennedy and Ipp JJ, BC 9707211, 4 December 1997; *Causer v Stafford-Bell* (unreported), Supreme Court of the Australian Capital Territory, Gallop J, BC 9706029, 14 November 1997.

87 *Rogers v Whitaker* (1992) 175 CLR 479 at 490 per Mason CJ, Brennan, Dawson, Toohey and McHugh JJ.

88 *Rogers v Whitaker* (1992) 175 CLR 479; *Perrin v Bleasel* (unreported), Supreme Court of New South Wales, McInerney J, BC 9804689, 15 July 1998.

89 *Percival v Rosenberg* (unreported), Full Court of the Supreme Court of Western Australia, Kennedy, Wallwork and Owen JJ, BC 9902820, 25 May 1999.

90 Unreported, District Court of NSW, 20 December 1994.

91 (1989) 17 NSWLR 553.

92 *Rogers v Whitaker* (1992) 175 CLR 479 at 487: 'The law should recognise that the doctor has a duty to warn a patient of a material risk inherent in the proposed treatment'.

93 (2001) 75 ALJR 734.

94 Ibid at 737.

95 Ibid at 746.

96 Unreported, Supreme Court of NSW, Spender AJ, 6 June 1995.

97 Robinson, WA, Yeldham, BA, 'The application of *Rogers v Whitaker* in the courts' (1996) 3 *Journal of Law and Medicine* 222.

98 Ibid.

99 (2003) 201 ALR 470.

100 [2001] NSWCA 422.

101 *Mount Isa Mines v Pusey* (1970) 125 CLR 383.

102 [2002] 211 CLR 317.

103 Ibid.

104 *Tame v New South Wales* and *Annetts v Australian Stations Pty Ltd* [2002] HCA 35.

105 Civil Law (Wrongs) Act 2002 (ACT), s 34; Civil Liability Act 2002 (NSW), s 32; Civil Liability Act 1936 (SA), s 33; Civil Liability Act 2002 (Tas), s 34; Wrongs Act 1958 (Vic), s 72; Civil Liability Act 2002 (WA), s 5S.

106 *Overseas Tankship (UK) Ltd v Morts Dock and Engineering Co Ltd (The Wagon Mound (No 1))* [1961] AC 388.

107 [2003] HCA 38 (16 July 2003).

108 (1998) 196 CLR 1.

109 Ibid at 4.

110 (1996) Aust Torts Reports 81–387. In the case of *Benkovic v Tan (Benkovic)* (unreported), District Court of NSW, No. 2644 of 1997, discussed in Kennedy, E, 'Punitive damages for medical negligence' (1999) 8(3) HLB 25.

111 Civil Liability Act 2003 (Qld), s 52.

112 [1969] 1 QB 428.

113 *March v E & M H Stramare Pty Ltd* (1991) 171 CLR 506; Aust Torts Reports 81–095.

114 [1998] 2 Qd R 572.

115 Federal Court of Australia, Miles, Heerey and Madgewick JJ, unreported, 4 June 1998.

116 Civil Liability Act 2003 (Qld); Personal Injuries Proceedings Act 2002 (Qld).

117 Civil Liability Act 2002 (WA).

118 Civil Liability Act 2002 (Tas); Civil Liability Amendment Act 2003 (Tas).

119 Civil Law (Wrongs) Act 2003 (ACT); Civil Law (Wrongs) Amendment Act 2003 (ACT).

120 Civil Liability Act 1936 (SA), s 34(1).

121 Civil Liability Act 2002 (NSW).

122 Wrongs and Other Acts (Law of Negligence) Act 2003 (Vic).

123 Civil Law (Wrongs) Act 2002 (ACT), s 45; Civil Liability Act 2002 (NSW), s 5D; Civil Liability Act 1936 (SA), s 34; Civil Liability Act 2002 (Tas), s 13; Wrongs Act 1958 (Vic), s 51; Civil Liability Act 2002 (WA), s 5C.

124 [2004] NSWSC 39.

125 [1976] QB 286 at 291.

126 444 P 2d (1968).

127 *Morton v Jools* (1991) Aust Torts Reports 81–123; Limitation Act 1969 (NSW).

128 Limitation Act 1985 (ACT); Limitation Act 1969 (NSW); Limitation Act 1981 (NT); Limitation of Actions Act 1974 (Qld); Limitation of Actions Act 1936 (SA); Limitation Act 1974 (Tas); Limitation of Actions Act 1958 (Vic); Limitation Act 2005 (WA).

129 [1952] 2 QB 852.

130 (1955) 93 CLR 561.

131 *Stevens v Brodribb Sawmilling Co Pty Ltd* (1986) 160 CLR 16.

132 [1980] 2 NSWLR 542.

133 Ibid at 543.

134 (1989) 17 NSWLR 553.

135 Ibid at 598–99.

136 Fleming, JG, *The Law of Torts*, 9th edn, Law Book Co, Sydney, 1998 at 345; Staunton, P, Whyburn, B, *Nursing and the Law*, 4th edn, Harcourt Brace Company, Sydney, 1997 at 82.

137 *Kondis v State Transport Authority* (1984) 154 CLR 672.
138 Ibid at 687 per Mason J.
139 Boston, T, 'A hospital's non-delegable duty of care' (2003) 10 *Journal of Law and Medicine* 364.
140 (1999) 48 NSWLR 214 per Giles J at 240–41.
141 Civil Liability Act 2002 (NSW), s 42; Civil Liability Act 2002 (Qld), s 35; Civil Liability Act 2002 (Tas), s 38; Wrongs Act 1958 (Vic), s 83; Civil Liability Act 2002 (WA), s 5W; Civil Law (Wrongs) Act 2002 (ACT), s 110.
142 *E v Australian Red Cross Society* (1991) ATPR 41-085.
143 *Bond Corporation Pty Ltd v Thiess Contractors Pty Ltd* (1987) ASC 55-557.

6

Consent

LEARNING OBJECTIVES

This chapter aims to introduce you to the potential legal consequences in circumstances in which a medical practitioner or medical student undertakes a procedure, treatment or surgical intervention without obtaining a legally valid consent. While reading this chapter you should focus on:

- identifying the types of consent applicable in a healthcare context
- identifying and understanding the elements that must be addressed in obtaining a valid consent; that is:
  - the voluntariness of the consent
  - the capacity of the patient or client to give a consent
  - the amount of information you are required to give a patient or client
  - the requirement that the consent obtained covers the specific procedure
- identifying the issues particularly relevant to obtaining a consent from a child/minor or a person with an intellectual disability
- understanding the issues raised when an adult of sound mind refuses treatment
- identifying the elements of false imprisonment and the criteria relevant to a decision by a medical practitioner to physically or chemically restrain a patient.

TRESPASS TO THE PERSON

It is a cultural expectation and social norm that a person is not touched without indicating either verbally or non-verbally that they consent to or invite such touching. It would therefore be considered, as a general principle, that obtaining the consent of a patient prior to commencing a procedure or treatment is respectful and should be undertaken as a matter of course by all health professionals. In addition, it is also a legal requirement that all health professionals obtain a legally valid consent from patients prior to any form of physical contact or medical intervention. Obtaining a patient's consent before touching them converts what would otherwise amount to an assault or battery into lawful touching. The law in this area is constantly becoming more complex in response to the changing attitudes of society towards the provision of healthcare services, the responsibility of health professionals in the provision of those services and the rapid increase in the scope of medical technology to offer new forms of treatment.

Medical practitioners are required, as part of their role in the provision of care and treatment, to come into physical contact with their patients and clients. The character of the physical contact will vary depending on the patient, the severity and presentation of the illness or injury and the specific work to be carried out by a medical practitioner. In all circumstances (other than those covered by the exceptions such as emergency treatment), *the expectation is that a legally valid consent will be obtained from the patient prior to any medical intervention or touching being initiated.*

It is obvious, therefore, that the law in relation to obtaining a valid consent is relevant to the practice of medical practitioners and part of the legal obligation requires that the medical practitioner *respects the autonomous wishes of their patients.* The law thereby seeks to protect the right of patients and clients to choose what is done to their body, through specific legislation in each jurisdiction, and actions such as negligence and trespass to the person (which includes assault, battery and false imprisonment).[1] Civil actions in assault and battery, though rare, may potentially be brought against a medical practitioner who fails to obtain a valid consent before touching their patients or clients. The legal requirement for a valid consent by the patient prior to any interference applies regardless of whether or not the patient would benefit from the treatment or be harmed by refusing the procedure.[2] All medical practitioners should therefore be mindful that they are legally prohibited, unless there is a lawful excuse, from doing anything to a patient without the patient's consent, or continuing with treatment after the consent has been revoked.[3]

The general principle

It is a basic legal principle that *all people have a legal right to determine what is done to their person.* As stated by Justice Cardozo in *Schloendorff v Society of New York Hospitals:*[4]

> Every human being of adult years and sound mind has a right to determine what will be done with his own body; and a

surgeon who performs an operation without his patient's consent commits an assault, for which he is liable in damages.

This legal principle is reinforced through the various Codes of Ethics and Codes of Conduct that have been adopted nationally by medical regulatory authorities. The *Good Medical Practice: A Code of Conduct for Doctors in Australia*, developed by a working party of the Australian Medical Council on behalf of the Medical Boards of the Australian states and territories in 2009, identifies the professional obligation on medical practitioners in '[e]ncouraging and supporting patients to be well informed about their health and to use this information wisely when they are making decisions'.[5] At s 3.3 of this national Code of Conduct for Doctors the effectiveness of communication between a medical practitioner and their patient includes a requirement that the medical practitioner inform 'patients of the nature of, and need for, all aspects of their clinical management, including examination and investigation, and giving them adequate opportunity to question or refuse intervention and treatment'. The provisions expressly recognise the significance to a patient of being provided with all the information pertinent to their particular condition, disease or injury as the basis upon which to exercise their right to be an autonomous decision-maker in relation to their medical care and treatment.

Assault

The *intentional tort of assault involves the creation in the mind of another the fear of imminent, unwanted physical contact.* The threat does not need to involve any actual touching, nor does it need to be explicitly communicated. It is sufficient if the patient believes, from the behaviour or conduct of the medical practitioner, that they will be touched against their wishes, or be subjected to some form of treatment or conduct to which they have not consented. That is, in facilities where the patients and clients are elderly or difficult to manage, it is an assault to threaten to medicate a patient if he or she does not comply with the medical practitioner's request. For example, where the medical practitioner raises their voice and shouts at the patient that if the patient does not stop wandering about in the garden they will prescribe high doses of a tranquilliser that will ensure the patient remains in their bed.

The allegation of assault is made out when the plaintiff proves that he or she had a reasonable belief that the defendant intended to carry out the threat and had the means to do so. As noted by Wallace, even though the action in civil assault involves 'subjective interpretation of conduct or behaviour', the test is based on what a reasonable person with the characteristics of the patient would believe.[6] As stated by Bray CJ in *Macpherson v Beathwould*:[7]

> The reasonableness of the apprehension [of immediate and unlawful physical contact] may or may not be necessary … [I]f the defendant intentionally puts in fear of immediate violence an exceptionally timid person known to him to be so then the unreasonableness of the fear may not be necessary.

Battery

Battery, the actual physical contact with the person of another, does not require that the plaintiff prove that such contact was harmful or offensive.[8] As in the example given above, if the medical practitioner then prescribed and administered the tranquillisers to the aged care patient without the patient's consent that constitutes the battery. Unlike negligence, where the damage is the 'gist' of, or fundamental to, the action, there is no requirement that the plaintiff sustain any injury as a result of the unlawful touching. It is the actual touching of the person without his or her consent which is unlawful and forms the basis of the action. It is unlikely, however, that the plaintiff would receive anything more than nominal damages where no injury has been sustained.

Intention required

The touching of the patient must be intentional. The requirement of intention serves to distinguish the deliberate action from the accidental physical contact that occurs as a part of everyday life and which would not constitute an action in battery. It is not, however, a defence for the medical practitioner to claim that he or she touched the patient for the purpose of bestowing some benefit. That the intentions of the medical practitioner are in the patient's best interest does not operate as a defence to the claim by the patient that he or she did not consent to the unlawful touching. This situation is most likely to occur where a medical practitioner forms the opinion that he or she knows what is in the best interests of the patient and proceeds to undertake treatments or procedures without obtaining prior consent.[9]

The patient does not need to be aware

While the touching must be intentional, *the patient does not need to be aware at the time that they were touched*. The patient may be asleep, comatose or anaesthetised when the unlawful touching occurs. There are common law and legislative provisions which deem consent in cases where the patient is unconscious or requires treatment as an emergency measure. All healthcare workers involved in implementing the therapeutic intervention without consent are equally liable. Thus, the medical practitioner who extends an operative procedure beyond that consented to by the patient and the nurse who participates in the extended operative procedure, knowing the patient has not given consent, may be equally liable.

TYPES OF CONSENT

Consent to medical treatment or intervention may be given in one of the following forms:

- implied consent
- verbal consent, and/or
- written consent.

Implied consent

In the normal daily activities of medical practitioners, consent by patients is most often implied rather than explicit. Consent to treatment is implied through the actions and postures of patients where, for example, they roll up their sleeve for an injection or turn to a position suitable for an examination. Consent by the patient to routine care interventions such as regular physical examination and the administration of medications is often implied to the medical practitioner through the patient's behaviour.[10]

However, there are obvious difficulties in relying on non-verbal communication as a method of obtaining consent where there is a possibility for confusion. Situations where it would be unwise for a medical practitioner to rely solely on the behaviour of the patient as indicative of consent include:

- at the initial presentation in an emergency department
- when the patient is a new admission to the clinical unit
- when the patient is anxious, in pain or distressed
- when the patient is from a different cultural or ethnic background from the medical practitioner.

In circumstances where the patient has not undergone a procedure or treatment previously, it is good practice to seek a very clear direction from the patient that they are indeed communicating their consent. Medical practitioners in clinical practice must ensure that their understanding of what the patient has consented to is consistent with the understanding of the patient.

The mere fact that the patient presents to a hospital or healthcare facility does not in itself provide a valid consent for medical practitioners to initiate diagnostic procedures or treatments. The attendance of the patient will not amount to an implied consent for medical intervention. In the case of *Hart v Herron*,[11] the plaintiff attended the admission unit of a psychiatric hospital in an agitated state. He was seeking information from his medical practitioner as to a procedure he was to undergo. The plaintiff alleged he had been offered a medication to 'calm him down' and later had undergone narcosis (deep sleep) treatment and electroconvulsive therapy without his consent. He sued both the hospital and the psychiatrist in negligence, assault, battery and false imprisonment. The hospital argued that the plaintiff, through his presentation to the admission unit, had consented to the treatment. Fisher J rejected the argument that attendance at the hospital constituted consent to the treatment.

Verbal (oral) consent

A more frequent and meaningful form of consent occurs when agreement to treatment is orally stated by the patient. In the clinical situation, medical practitioners obtain the consent by explaining to the patient what is about to occur and allowing the patient to consider the information before orally (verbally) agreeing or refusing. Ideally, this should occur in most communications between a medical practitioner and their patient. In relation to more invasive procedures, verbal consent generally takes place in the physician's or surgeon's rooms or outpatients' department prior to admission. The medical practitioner will discuss the procedure and the patient has the option to refuse or to agree to undergo the specified form of treatment. Where the procedure is invasive, this type of exchange is commonly followed by the completion of a written consent form.

Written consent

As part of a health department or hospital policy, a consent to invasive procedures may be required to be obtained in writing and witnessed. Where this is the case, it is the responsibility of the medical practitioner carrying out the procedure to ensure that a valid consent is obtained. That is, the medical practitioner may obtain the consent himself or herself, or may delegate the activity to another medical practitioner (the registrar or intern) or a registered nurse. The written consent form that has been signed by the patient and witnessed is a significant piece of evidence. The written consent is most important when non-routine treatments or procedures that have risks and complications attached to them are to be carried out. The benefit of having the consent in writing lies in the fact that it provides documentary evidence of the consent. Thus, a written consent makes proof of consent easier to establish. However, the existence of a written consent is not to be equated with a process of obtaining consent. If the process is defective, the consent will be held to be invalid or non-existent. Therefore, even when patients have signed the consent form, they are not precluded from initiating an action in assault, battery or negligence if they were insufficiently informed, did not understand the content or did not have the risks explained. The need for a written consent and its superiority over implied or oral (verbal) consent is questionable.

CONSENT FORMS

The most important function of a consent form is that it provides documentary evidence that consent has been given for a treatment to proceed. Generally speaking, the more extensive, invasive, specific and risky a procedure is, the more important it is to be able to establish that consent has been obtained. However, the documentation of consent does not necessarily establish that the consent given is legally valid and the consent can be withdrawn at any time, verbally or in writing. Consent forms also do not usually indicate the process by which the patient has been sufficiently informed. Evidence of this should be available from some other source; for example, in the progress notes of the patient's medical or nursing history. Blanket consents and 'catch all' clauses[12] within consent forms are of limited legal value and their use should be avoided.[13]

It is important to recognise that it is legally dubious and unsafe to assume that signing a consent form establishes that a valid consent has been obtained. It is also legally unsafe to assume that consent for one person to perform a procedure automatically permits another person to carry out the procedure (for example, permission for a consultant physician or surgeon to perform a procedure does not necessarily allow his or her registrar or resident medical officer to carry out the procedure).[14]

ELEMENTS OF A VALID CONSENT

Obtaining *a legally valid consent* from a patient prior to undertaking a medical treatment or intervention *is a defence to an action in trespass to the person* (civil assault/battery). The elements of a legally valid consent are:

- it is voluntarily given
- it covers the specific procedure
- it is based on the requisite amount of information
- the person consenting has the legal capacity to do so.

Voluntarily given

First, the consent must be *freely and voluntarily given*. All medical practitioners are obliged to ensure that the patient's consent is not obtained through coercion, duress, misrepresentation or fraud. The voluntariness of a consent may be challenged on the basis either that the patient felt there would be unpleasant consequences following on from a refusal or where the consent was obtained because of the patient's level of fatigue or stress. In the *Beausoleil* case,[15] the patient had specifically refused a spinal anaesthetic prior to receiving her premedication. Her consent was obtained after the premedication was administered and in response to pressure from the anaesthetists. The court held that the consent was not voluntary and was therefore invalid in the circumstances. Medical practitioners must be mindful not to give patients the impression that if they do not consent to a particular treatment or procedure their care will alter. That is, it would be inadvisable to suggest to patients that if they do not consent to the operation they will be discharged. Though this may be the clinical reality, particularly with the high demand for beds, it may be interpreted by the patient as a threat. The medical practitioner must not 'promise' an outcome from a procedure or treatment; for example, that the patient will be 'pain free' after the surgery. The patient who is not 'pain free' after the procedure may well allege that his or her consent was obtained through a misrepresentation.

Covers the procedure

The consent for one procedure *does not* extend to the carrying out of a different procedure. Where a medical practitioner is obtaining a consent from a patient, the specifics of the treatment or procedure must be discussed. Should the medical practitioner consider that it is necessary to undertake a different procedure, the consent requirement will only be waived where the circumstances indicate that the action was necessary to save the patient's life. That it was convenient to carry out the procedure at the time will not suffice: *Candutti v ACT Health an Community Care* and *Murray v McMurchy*.[16] In Candutti's case, the plaintiff was admitted to the hospital for a laparoscopic tubal ligation. She had consented to a laparotomy only if an emergency arose during her surgery. Due to some difficulty inflating the plaintiff's abdomen the surgeon proceeded to undertake the tubal ligation by way of a laparotomy. The plaintiff sued the medical practitioner in trespass to the person on the grounds that she had not consented to this more invasive procedure. The court, in upholding the plaintiff's claim, determined that the particular circumstances did not amount to an emergency and therefore the procedure was performed without the patient's consent. In *Murray v McMurchy*, the plaintiff consented to a caesarean section. During the procedure, the surgeon noted that the plaintiff had uterine fibroids which he considered could, at a later time, cause difficulties with future pregnancies. On this basis, the surgeon performed a tubal ligation without the consent of the plaintiff. The plaintiff successfully sued in assault and battery. The court was clear in indicating that the fact that it was convenient to undertake the surgery at the time was not enough to defend the action.

The issue of medical practitioners exceeding the scope of the consent was considered in *Walker v Bradley*.[17] In this case, the plaintiff underwent a laparotomy for the removal of an ovarian cyst. Though initially diagnosed as having uterine fibroids, an ultrasound confirmed the presence of an ovarian cyst and the plaintiff consented to having it removed. Prior to the surgery the gynaecologist recommended a hysterectomy. However, the plaintiff refused to consent to the removal of her uterus unless there was evidence of cancer. The plaintiff signed the consent form which read 'laparotomy, left ovarian cystectomy and ? hysterectomy'. During the operation, the uterus was found to be enlarged but symmetrical, with a cyst on the left ovary approximately five centimetres in diameter. The gynaecologist removed both the cyst from the ovary and the uterus. The court held that the doctor had exceeded the scope of the consent in performing a procedure for which the plaintiff had not given her consent. Based on the evidence, it was found that the question mark on the consent form was 'window dressing' and that the gynaecologist had determined to proceed with the surgery based on his initial diagnosis. He had done this, it was found, regardless of the fact that the plaintiff had expressly refused.

Requisite amount of information

Generally, the medical practitioner will be in breach of the duty of care if he or she fails to warn the patient of the 'material and significant' risks associated with treatments and procedures or fails to comply with the legislative provisions addressing the failure of the medical practitioner to warn (refer to Chapter 5, Negligence). There is a distinction between a lack of consent prior to performing a procedure, which may open the way for an action based on assault or battery to the person, and obtaining a consent which is not adequately informed in relation to material risks which could give rise to a negligence action.[18]

Historically, the legal position in relation to 'how much' information was required was unclear. The majority judgment of the Full Court of the High Court of Australia in *Rogers v Whitaker* has, to a large extent, clarified this situation.[19] In this case, a woman underwent surgery to improve the appearance, and possibly the sight, of her eye in which she had been almost totally blind since the age of 9 years. The evidence indicated that she had 'incessantly' questioned the surgeon as to adverse consequences associated with the surgery. The surgeon did not warn her of the risk of developing sympathetic ophthalmia.

The occurrence rate of this condition following eye surgery was assessed at 1:14 000. The surgery was performed without negligence.

However, the sight was not restored to the injured eye and the condition of sympathetic ophthalmia developed in the sighted eye, leading to blindness in that eye (refer discussion in Chapter 5, Negligence). The court held:[20]

> The law should recognise that a doctor has a duty, subject to therapeutic privilege, to warn a patient of a material risk inherent in the proposed treatment; a risk is material if, in the circumstances of the particular case, a reasonable person if warned of the risks, would be likely to attach significance to it or if the medical practitioner is or should reasonably be aware that the particular patient, if warned of the risk, would be likely to attach significance to it.

For the purpose of a defence to an action in assault and battery (not an action in negligence), that the medical practitioner has informed the patient in 'broad terms' of the nature of the procedure would appear to suffice for a valid consent. In the case of *Chatterton v Gerson*, Bristow J stated:[21]

> In my judgment once the patient is informed in broad terms of the nature of the procedure which is intended, and gives her consent, that consent is real and the cause of action on which to base a claim for failure to go into risks and implications is negligence, not trespass. In this case … she is under no illusion as to the general nature of what an intrathecal injection of phenol solution nerve block would be and in the case of each injection her consent was not unreal.

When making decisions about how much information to give the patient it is incumbent on the medical practitioner to ensure that, prior to obtaining consent, the patient understands the nature and effect of the information that has been given. In circumstances in which the patient does not have fluency in the English language, where there are particular communication needs, or an explanation of the medical procedure that involves the use of highly technical language, the medical practitioner must ensure the information that is given is understood. This may be achieved by engaging the services of a government-approved interpreter, providing more information or giving the patient a longer period of time to make a decision. In addition to, or in combination with, the foregoing there is also the possibility that a patient or client may not understand because they lack the capacity to do so.

Legal capacity

An adult of sound mind is said to have 'capacity' or to be legally 'competent' to provide a valid consent or to refuse to consent to treatment. As discussed, *once a patient with legal capacity makes a decision as to his or her treatment, it is an assault for the medical practitioner to do other than that for which the consent has been given.* However, when a patient is not capable of giving a valid consent, this does not automatically mean that the medical practitioner may initiate treatment regardless. It will not be a defence to an action in assault that the patient was incompetent. The legal capacity to consent is defined in various ways by statutes which have been codified to cover specific situations (for example, Mental Health Acts, various Guardianship and Administration Acts protecting the rights of intellectually disabled citizens, blood alcohol legislation and statutory protection for children at risk where the state may act on their behalf) and common law decisions. The law makes provision for substitute decision-makers where the patient by reason of age, mental or intellectual incapacity may not be considered competent to provide a valid consent.

The following discussion addresses the specific exceptions to the general rules that apply to obtaining a consent from an adult of sound mind.

Impaired intellectual decision-making capacity

Patients with an intellectual impairment (including an intellectual disability, dementia, acquired brain injury) have varying abilities to comprehend information and make decisions as to what is in their best interests. There is legislation in all Australian jurisdictions which addresses the issue of consent to medical and dental treatment, or health and lifestyle decisions, for persons with an intellectual disability. However, this legislation only applies when the person is not capable of understanding what it is that they are being asked to consider in terms of treatment or care. It may well be that in relation to some decisions, for example taking an X-ray or applying a plaster cast, the person with the intellectual disability or reduced intellectual capacity will be able to give a valid consent. However, in relation to more medically technical and complicated procedures, a substitute decision-maker may be required. *A patient's competence, or capacity, to make a legally valid decision about their healthcare may not be constant. The question is whether this particular patient has capacity to make this particular decision at this particular time.*

The threshold test of capacity, which is the determinative factor as to whether a substitute decision-maker is required, is whether the adult is able to understand the nature and effect of their decision, make that decision voluntarily and of their own free will, and communicate the decision to others.[22] This section will provide an overview of the relevant legislation in each of the jurisdictions.

Australian Capital Territory

Where a person has an impaired decision-making capacity, a health attorney or guardian will be the person from whom the medical practitioner obtains consent prior to treating the 'protected person'. In circumstances in which a health attorney refuses to consent, the decision must be referred to the Public Advocate. The health attorney for a 'protected person' may be their domestic partner, a carer, or a close friend or relative who does not receive remuneration or payment: s 32D. The guardian appointed by the ACT Civil and Administrative Tribunal (ACAT) under the Guardianship and Management of Property Act 1991 may also give consent to medical procedures and other treatments. 'Prescribed medical procedures' require the consent of the ACAT: s 70, and are defined under s 69 to mean:

- abortion
- reproductive sterilisation, hysterectomy
- a medical procedure concerned with contraception
- removal of non-regenerative tissue for transplantation to a living person
- treatment for mental illness, electroconvulsive therapy or psychiatric surgery (which a covered under the Mental Health (Treatment and Care) Act 1994 (ACT)
- any other medical or surgical procedure prescribed for this definition.

The ACAT may consent if it is satisfied the procedure is lawful, the person is not competent to give consent, the procedure will be in the 'protected person's' best interest and notice of the procedure has been given to the person, their guardian and any other person the ACAT considers should be notified: s 70. Where a medical practitioner treats a person with impaired decision-making capacity without knowledge that they are subject to an order, and has acted in good faith in the belief that the person was capable of giving a valid consent, there can be no action.

New South Wales

Under the Guardianship Act 1987 a Guardian may be appointed for a person who, 'because of a disability, is totally or partially incapable of managing his or her person'. The appointment takes effect at the time identified by the adult person making the appointment or at the time the adult person is 'in need' of the Guardian. The functions of an Enduring Guardian include making decisions about where the person is to live and the healthcare and personal services the person is to receive. The Enduring Guardian is also able to give consent under Part 5 of the Act which deals with medical and dental treatment.

Section 33A (under Part 5 of the Act) identifies the hierarchy of 'person responsible' for an adult, who is not under the care of the Director-General: the person's guardian, their spouse with whom they have a close and continuing relationship, a person who has care of the adult person, or a close friend or relative. The 'responsible person' thereby has the legal authority to consent to major and minor medical and dental treatment of the person who has lost their capacity to consent on their own behalf. The medical practitioner or dentist may carry out treatment if they consider the medical or dental treatment necessary as a matter of urgency, to save the patient's life, to prevent serious damage to the person's health and, except in cases of special treatment,[23] to prevent the person from suffering or continuing to suffer significant pain or distress. Minor treatment[24] may also be carried out if there is no 'responsible person', the 'responsible person cannot be contacted or they are unwilling or unable to make a choice'. The tribunal may also give consent to the medical and dental treatment of a person who has lost their capacity.

Northern Territory
Healthcare that is in the best interests of the person who is under a full or conditional guardianship order is consented to by a guardian appointed under the Adult Guardianship Act 1988. Under s 21 of the Adult Guardianship Act 1988 a medical practitioner or person with the right to practice under the Health Practitioners Act (NT) must not carry out any 'major' medical procedure on a represented person without the consent of the court. A major medical procedure is defined by the legislation as:

- a procedure which does not remove an immediate threat to the person's health and is generally accepted by medical and dental professions as a major procedure
- medical procedures relating to contraception and termination of a pregnancy.

Prior to consenting on behalf of the represented person, (if the court considers they are capable of giving or refusing to consent) the court will seek direction from the individual as to whether he or she wishes to undergo the major medical procedure.

Queensland
In Queensland, the Powers of Attorney Act 1998 provides for the appointment of an Enduring Power of Attorney for 'personal decisions' and for 'financial decisions': s 32. The legislation also creates a Statutory Health Attorney who assumes the decision-making power for a person (referred to as the principal) who has not created an Enduring Power of Attorney or who is legally incapable of

giving a valid consent in their own right or nominating an Enduring Power of Attorney. The person, therefore, who has an intellectual impairment significant enough to render them incapable of making health decisions, will have a suitable person nominated under the legislation to take responsibility for their decisions. This person is referred to as the 'substitute decision-maker'. This role will be assumed by a person who is over the age of 18 years and of sound mind and will usually be his or her spouse or next-of-kin, the person who has the voluntary (unpaid) role of primary carer or a close friend. For the medical practitioner this is the person from whom consent is obtained prior to initiating treatments or undertaking procedures on the intellectually impaired person. While the Statutory Health Attorney has power to make decisions about most matters that impact on the physical and mental condition of the person, they have no authority to make decisions on purely lifestyle matters or 'special health matters' such as (Sch 2):

- tissue donation
- sterilisation
- pregnancy termination
- participation in special medical research or experimental healthcare, or
- electroconvulsive therapy or psychosurgery.

In a situation where there is a dispute between those who are equally entitled to make decisions as the Statutory Health Attorneys of a person, the 'Adult Guardian' has the power to intervene. Where a person may not have anyone who could act as their Statutory Health Attorney, the legislation provides for an Adult Guardian who is an independent officer appointed by the government 'to protect the interests of people with decision-making disabilities'.[25]

The Guardianship and Administration Act 2000 (Qld) allows for the appointment of a Guardian for personal matters (of which health is a sub-set) and an Administrator for financial matters, in the event that the person lacks capacity, and there is a need for a decision: s 12. Sections 62 to 65 of the Guardianship and Administration Act 2000 (Qld) deal with a health provider undertaking 'healthcare' (not 'special healthcare') without consent in situations in which the adult patient has lost their capacity to make a healthcare decision and the substitute decision is not available.

South Australia

A person with a mental incapacity is one who has 'an inability to look after his or her own health, safety and welfare or manage his or her own affairs' as a result of damage to themselves, illness, disorder, imperfect development, impairment or deterioration of the brain or mind or any physical illness or condition that renders the person unable to communicate their intention or wishes: s 3. The person may have a consent to treatment provided on their behalf by a relative, a person appointed under the Guardianship and Administration Act 1993 as a guardian or by the guardianship board itself. Only the board is empowered, under the legislation, to consent to 'prescribed' medical treatments and procedures such as the termination of a pregnancy and sterilisation.

Tasmania

The Guardianship and Administration Act 1995 states that a person may apply to the Guardianship and Administration Board (the board) for an order appointing a full or limited guardian in respect of a person with a disability who is of, or over, the age of 18 years. The term 'disability' is defined to mean 'any restriction or lack (resulting from any absence, loss or abnormality of mental, psychological, physiological or anatomical structure or function) of ability to perform an activity in a normal manner'. A guardian may be appointed under a guardianship order or as an enduring guardian in an instrument of appointment. Medical or dental treatment may only be given without consent if the medical practitioner or dentist considers the treatment is necessary as a matter of urgency to save the person's life, prevent serious damage to the person's health or, except in cases of 'special treatment', to prevent the person from suffering or continuing to suffer significant pain or distress: s 40. The board may consent to medical or dental treatment where it is satisfied the treatment is otherwise lawful, the person is incapable of giving consent and the medical or dental treatment is in the person's best interest. The consent of the board is required prior to undertaking 'special treatment' which is defined in s 3 as:

- treatment intended or reasonably likely to render the person permanently infertile
- termination of pregnancy
- removal of non-regenerative tissue for purposes of transplantation
- any other medical or dental treatment declared by regulations to be a special treatment.

Victoria

In Victoria, the Guardianship and Administration Act 1986 provides for the appointment of a guardian when an adult has a 'disability'. Disability is broadly defined and includes an intellectual impairment, mental illness, brain damage, physical disability or dementia. The legislation provides that a 'person responsible': s 37, may consent to treatment of a person who is not competent to do so if they are available, and willing to make the decision. The hierarchy of 'persons responsible' is as follows:

• a person appointed under s 5A of the Medical Treatment Act 1988
• a person appointed by the Victorian Civil and Administrative Tribunal
• a person appointed under a Guardianship Order
• a person appointed as the enduring guardian
• a patient's spouse or domestic partner
• a patient's primary carer
• a patient's nearest relative.

Consent to 'special procedures' is from an order of the Victorian Civil and Administrative Tribunal: s 39. 'Special procedures' are covered in Division 4 and are defined to include: procedures intended or reasonably likely to result in the person being permanently infertile, termination of a pregnancy, removal of tissue for the purpose of transplantation to another, and any other medical or dental treatment prescribed by the regulations.

Western Australia

Under the Guardianship and Administration Act 1990, the State Administrative Tribunal will appoint a guardian where it is satisfied that a person in respect of whom an order is sought has attained the age of 18 years, is incapable of looking after his or her own health and safety, is unable to make reasonable judgments relating to their person or are in need of oversight, care or control for their protection or the protection of others and is in need of a guardian: s 43. On declaring a person in need of a guardian the tribunal may appoint a 'plenary' or' limited' guardian. The authority of a plenary guardian is, subject to Division 3 to consent to any treatment of healthcare of the represented person: s 45. Section 119 which covers medical and dental treatment provides that where a person cannot give consent the person who can consent on their behalf is determined based on the following hierarchy:

• the guardian
• the spouse or de facto partner
• a person who, on a regular basis provides or arranges for domestic services or support to the person on an unpaid basis
• a person who is the nearest relative who maintains a close relationship with the person
• any other person who maintains a close relationship with the person.

If, in the opinion of a medical practitioner, a person is in need of urgent treatment, is incapable of consenting to the proposed treatment or is, at the time of presentation, a person for whom a guardian could be appointed, the medical practitioner may provide the treatment without consent.

Commonwealth

The Family Law Act 1975 (Cth) confers on the Family Court the power to make orders authorising a person to carry out medical treatment on an intellectually disabled person who is the 'child of a marriage' even where the treatment is not authorised by the state or territory guardianship Act.[26] This position is consistent with the Constitution (s 109) which serves to strike down state and territory legislation to the extent that it is inconsistent with federal legislation.

CHILDREN

General principles

As a general principle, a parent or legal guardian is capable of consenting to the medical and dental treatment of his or her child. Persons who are caring for children on a casual basis, however, such as babysitters, friends, relatives and schoolteachers, have no such authority. Where a parent or guardian is not able to be located and a child requires emergency treatment it may be given without a consent being obtained or, if it is only minor first aid which is required, the child will be legally capable of giving a valid consent to, for example, the application of a band aide on their foot. As will be discussed, the authority of the parent is not absolute and may be overridden by the courts or through legislative provisions.

Once persons have reached the age of 18 years, they are considered at law to have full legal capacity.[27] Prior to this age, particular legislation specifies the age at which the consent will be taken as valid at law. In a number of Australian jurisdictions, the legislation distinguishes between a child and a young person. In New South Wales, the Children and Young Persons (Care and Protection) Act 1998 defines a child (for purposes other than employment) as a person under the age of 16 years and a young person as being 16 to 18 years.[28] Similarly in the ACT, the Children and Young People Act 1999 defines a child as being under the age of 12 years and a young person as being aged 12 to 18 years.[29] In Tasmania the Children, Young Persons and their Families Act 1997 defines a young person as either 16 or 17 years of age. It is clear from the decision in *K v Minister for Youth and Community Services*,[30] litigated against the background of the Minors (Property and Contract) Act 1970 (NSW), that such legislation which stipulates the age for consenting to medical treatment operates to protect medical and dental practitioners treating persons who might, but for the Act, be considered minors. In this case, the protection was held to extend to the treatment of minors over the age of 14 years where their prior consent had been obtained. Under the age of 14 years, the consent of the parent or guardian is necessary. It is appropriate therefore to consider the *legislative and common law indicators of the age at which a child will be capable or legally competent to give a valid consent.*

The common law

The common law is silent on a specified age at which a child (also referred to as a minor) is competent to give a valid consent. The common law incorporates the notion of understanding and comprehension. Is the individual of sufficient intelligence and at an age where they are able to understand the consequences of their decision? Are they legally competent for the purposes of consent? This is referred to as 'Gillick competency' and is based on the English House of Lords decision in *Gillick v West Norfolk and Wisbech Area Health Authority*.[31] The case involved a 15-year-old female who had been prescribed contraceptives by the local medical practitioner without the consent of her parents. The issue for consideration was whether the contraceptive advice and treatment could be given lawfully to a girl under the age of 16 years without parental consent. The majority of the House of Lords held that the authority of the parent decreases, as the child becomes increasingly competent.[32] Lord Scarman stated:

> I would hold that as a matter of law the parental right to determine whether or not their minor child below the age of 16 will have medical treatment terminated if and when the child achieves a sufficient understanding and intelligence to enable him or her to understand fully what is proposed. It will be a question of fact whether a child seeking advice has sufficient understanding of what is involved to give a consent valid in law. Until the child achieves the capacity to consent, the parental right to make the decision continues save only in exceptional circumstances.[33]

The competence of the child to consent was therefore determined on the basis of the child's capacity to understand the nature of the treatment. The High Court of Australia approved the Gillick test as to capacity in *Secretary, Department of Health and Community Services v JWB and SMB (Marion's case)*.[34]

While the foregoing addresses the capacity of a person under 18 years to give a legally valid consent to medical and dental treatment, the *capacity of the child to refuse to consent* to treatment may be overridden by the court. In the case of *Re W (A Minor) (Medical Treatment)*,[35] it was held that even though *W* was 'Gillick competent', the inherent power of the court under the *parens patriae* jurisdiction enabled the overriding of the wishes of a person under the age of 18 years. In this case, the minor was suffering with anorexia nervosa. The court found that she had an understanding of her condition but nonetheless had refused to be treated at the time recommended by her medical practitioner. The court stated that *although there was authority for the right of a minor who had the requisite level of understanding to consent to treatment, this did not give a corresponding absolute right to refuse treatment.*

The decision of Johnson J in *R v M*[36] highlights the legal and ethical dilemmas associated with situations where minors refuse what would be considered as life-saving treatment or procedures. M was a 15-and-a-half-year-old girl who suffered from sudden onset heart failure requiring a heart transplant to save her life. Though M's mother consented to the transplant operation, M refused to consent to the surgery. As time was of the essence and no other treatment was capable of saving M's life, the hospital applied to the court for permission to carry out the operation despite her refusal. M's objection to the heart transplant was based on the following reasons:

- she felt depressed at the thought of having to take tablets for the rest of her life
- she preferred to die rather than undergo a transplant operation, and
- she did not want someone else's heart in her body.

Johnson J held that the hospital surgeons were authorised to transplant a donor heart into the body of M. The decision recognised the right of the court to override the refusal of treatment by even 'Gillick competent' minors. While the child's refusal was considered an important issue, it was held that the best interests of the child would be served by the decision that would save her life. Johnson J stated:[37]

> M will live with the consequences of my decision, in a very striking sense … There is the risk too that she will carry with her for the rest of her life resentment about what has been done to her.

Legislation

In all jurisdictions, legislation exists which authorises the emergency treatment of a child without the consent of their parent or guardian.[38] In most cases the legislation applies to treatment which is 'necessary to save the child's life' or required as 'a matter of urgency', or specifically applies to the transfusion of blood.

In **New South Wales**, the Minors (Property and Contract) Act 1970 states that a child 14 years and over can consent to medical and dental treatment. The effect of the consent is the same as if the child was an adult. The legislation also provides for emergency medical and dental treatment carried out where the doctor or dentist believes the treatment is necessary 'as a matter of urgency ... in order to save the child's life or prevent serious damage to the child's health'.[39] Section 175 of the Children and Young Persons (Care and Protection) Act 1998 requires that treatment identified as 'special medical treatment' may not be carried out by a medical practitioner unless the medical practitioner is of the opinion the treatment is necessary as a matter of urgency to save the child's life or to prevent serious damage to the child's health, or the Guardianship Tribunal gives consent. 'Special medical' treatments are identified in the legislation and within the Children and Young Persons (Care and Protection) Regulations 2000 as:

- treatment that results in permanent infertility
- administration of long acting injectable contraceptives
- administration of drugs of addiction (other than those administered for the purpose of treating cancer) over 10 days in any 30 days
- sterilisation
- any medical treatment that involves the administration of a psychotropic drug to a child in out-of-home care for the purpose of controlling his or her behaviour, and
- experimental procedures that are outside government guidelines.

A child under the age of 16 years may also undergo an examination without the consent of the parent or guardian where the medical practitioner is of the opinion that the child has been the victim of abuse.[40]

In **South Australia**, any person 16 years and over may consent to medical or dental treatment under s 12(b) of the Consent to Medical Treatment and Palliative Care Act 1995. If the child consents, the medical practitioner believes the child is able to 'understand the nature, consequences and risks of the treatment', the 'treatment is in the best interests of the child's health and wellbeing' and another medical practitioner has examined the child prior to the treatment and gives written support for the opinion, it will be a defence to a charge of assault and battery.

In the **Northern Territory**, there is no legislation that specifically addresses the rights of the minor to give consent or to refuse consent to treatment. The Medical Services Act (NT), however, provides that females under the age of 16 years will require the consent of a parent or guardian before the termination of a pregnancy will be carried out.[41]

Authority of the parent or guardian

Bennett notes that the child's capacity to consent does not mean that the parent has lost the power to refuse to consent.[42] In some circumstances, there may well be a disagreement between the parent and the child as to the treatment which the child is, or is not, going to undertake. In the event of conflict between parents or guardians and a child, the courts may exercise a general supervisory role to act to protect the best interests of the child: *Dalton v Skuthorpe*,[43] *Secretary, Department of Health and Community Services v JWB and SMB (Marion's case)*.[44]

In *Marion's case*, the parents of a 14-year-old intellectually disabled child applied to the Family Law Court for an order permitting a hysterectomy and ovariectomy to be carried out on their child or a declaration that they could lawfully consent to the surgical procedure. The issue before the court was whether the parents of the child had the legal authority to consent to their child's sterilisation.[45] The majority of the Full Court of the Family Court held that the parents could lawfully consent to the sterilisation of their child. However, on appeal to the High Court, the majority determined that the procedure required the authority of the court. The majority adopted the approach of Lord Scarman in the *Gillick* case and applied it to minors with intellectual disabilities:[46]

> [I]t is important to stress that it cannot be assumed that an intellectually disabled child is, by virtue of his or her disability, incapable of giving consent to treatment. The capacity of the child to give informed consent to medical treatment depends on the rate of development of each individual.

It is important to note that the High Court expressly stated that the performance of a sterilisation procedure was a 'special case' which took the decision outside what would be considered as the ordinary scope of a parent's authority to consent.[47]

This would also be the case in relation to other non-therapeutic medical interventions involving children; such as removal of bone marrow and gender reassignment. Where the type of medical intervention sought is non-therapeutic, it would be for the Supreme

Court in the individual jurisdiction, or the Family Court to make a decision as to consent.

Where the parents of a child are separated or divorced medical practitioners may assume that either of them can give a valid consent to the medical treatment of their child. This would be the case unless a Family Court order was in place which identified one parent as the decision-maker to the exclusion of the other. In such a situation the medical practitioner is required to sight the Family Court order and have a copy placed in the child's medical record. Similarly, where a child is under the care of the state, the medical practitioner must request a copy of the order to ensure the appropriate adult is consenting on the child's behalf. For example, a child may be the subject of a Child Protection Order giving custody of the child to the chief executive of the Department of Child Safety (or equivalent government department). Where the order is one giving custody only, the biological parent retains the legal authority to consent to the treatment of their child. If, however, the order identifies the chief executive as the guardian of the child, then the parent no longer has the legal authority to consent.

EMERGENCIES

When a patient requires emergency treatment, and is so incapacitated as to be incapable of giving a valid consent, the medical practitioner may initiate treatment which he or she honestly believes is reasonable and necessary in the circumstances, under the common law 'doctrine of emergency'. This may also be referred to as the 'doctrine of necessity' though it has been suggested that the 'necessity principle is separate from that of emergency and is wider in application'.[48] The doctrine effectively provides the medical practitioner with a defence to an action in assault and battery for the treatment given at the time. There are, however, important criteria which must be satisfied before such a defence is available. The first is that the situation must be an emergency. Though the term 'emergency' has not been defined at common law, it is described as a treatment necessary 'to save life' or to 'prevent serious injury to their health'.[49] As discussed in the case of *Murray v McMurchy*,[50] the circumstances must indicate that the treatment is necessary and not that it is merely convenient. The second requirement is that the medical practitioner takes only 'such steps as good medical practice demands'.[51]

In Queensland, the Northern Territory and South Australia, legislation applicable to emergency situations permits the treatment of patients by medical practitioners without their consent.[52] In some jurisdictions, the authorisation applies only to doctors, while in others it also covers a more diverse group of health professionals such as ambulance officers and honorary ambulance officers.

The lawful authority to treat children in an emergency is very similar to that which applies to adults. If the parent of the child, or the legally responsible adult, is not contactable and the treatment is necessary to save the child's life, or prevent serious harm, then the medical practitioner may proceed with the medical intervention without consent. There are also provisions which serve to override the refusal to consent by a parent when the treatment is necessary to save a child's life. Table 6.1 provides an overview of the legislative provisions authorising medical intervention for children and young people.

Table 6.1 Medical intervention for children and young people	
ACT	Transplantation and Anatomy Act 1978 s 23
NSW	Guardianship Act 1987 s 37, Children and Young Persons (Care and Protection) Act 1998 s 174
NT	Emergency Medical Operations Act 1973 ss 2, 3
Qld	Transplantation and Anatomy Act 1979 s 20
SA	Consent to Treatment and Palliative Care Act 1995 s 13
Tas	Human Tissue Act 1985 s 21
Vic	Human Tissue Act 1982 s 24
WA	Human Tissue and Transplantation Act 1982 s 21

Unconscious patients

Where a patient is in an unconscious state or due to his or her condition is incapable of consenting, the common law will deem a consent for the treatment given provided that it was necessary, reasonable and given in good faith.

Transfer to hospital

Where a patient has sustained significant injuries in an accident and requires an emergency transfer to a hospital, he or she is not required to provide a consent. This presumption of consent to obtain treatment immediately has been considered an exception to the general requirements.[53]

Refusal of treatment in an emergency

It is important to distinguish the legal position in an emergency situation where the patient is unconscious or not capable of consenting due to the severity of the injuries, from the situation where an adult person of sound mind refuses emergency treatment. Where the latter is the case, it is an assault to initiate or continue treatment once the person has refused to consent. In the case of *Malette v Shulman*,[54] the plaintiff was seriously injured and taken to hospital. Though unconscious and unable to communicate her wishes verbally, she was carrying an unsigned and unwitnessed card stating she was a Jehovah's Witness who refused blood transfusions. Her condition deteriorated significantly due to the large volume of blood loss from her injuries. The medical practitioner commenced a blood transfusion. Ms Malette sued the medical practitioner who defended the action claiming that as Ms Malette was unconscious and incapable of giving an informed refusal, he had proceeded with emergency treatment in the form of a blood transfusion under the doctrine of emergency or doctrine of necessity. The trial court found for the patient. On appeal, the court held that the card represented a valid restriction on the nature of treatment for which the plaintiff was willing to give her consent. The court held that it was not for the doctor to determine the reasonableness of the wishes of the patient, provided the wishes in the form of the refusal was legally valid.

The dilemma for medical practitioners highlighted in the *Malette* case is far from resolved. On the one hand, it is fundamental to the medical practitioner–patient relationship that the autonomy of the patient is respected and his or her decisions adhered to. However, there is also the countervailing argument that the treatment to which the patient objects may involve minimal clinical risk and would most probably save his or her life. This issue was raised in the Supreme Court of Victoria Court of Appeal decision, handed down in the matter of *Qumsieh v Guardianship and Administration Board*.[55]

An issue not yet raised in the Australian courts is the legal position when the adult refusing life-saving emergency treatment has young dependents or is pregnant. In the United States the decisions, grounded in the particular facts of each case, have not given any clear line of authority as to how the issue is to be resolved. In *Raleigh Fitkin-Paul Memorial Hospital v Anderson*,[56] the court held that the woman could not refuse a blood transfusion because she owed a duty to her unborn child. In the case of *Re S (Adult: Refusal of Medical Treatment)*,[57] the courts in the United Kingdom made a declaration that a woman in labour, who had refused a caesarean section on religious grounds, was to undergo the procedure and any consequential treatment. The reasoning of the court was based on the medical evidence that the procedure was necessary to save the lives of the mother and unborn child.

REFUSAL TO CONSENT

As stated, adults of sound mind have the legal capacity not only to consent to the treatment recommended by the health professional but also to withhold their consent. The patient has the legal right, even after giving a valid consent, to withdraw it and refuse to continue to undergo the procedure.[58] Provided the patient is competent, he or she has the right to refuse all treatment regardless of whether the refusal will result in permanent physical injury or death. (Refer to Chapter 7, End of life decisions.)

CONSENT BY RELATIVES

Though it is common for some institutions to require the consent from a spouse or next-of-kin in an emergency situation, as a general principle this has no legal foundation. Other than the situation where there are specific legislative provisions which authorise a substitute decision-maker, no person has the legal ability to consent to the treatment of another adult.

OBTAINING CONSENT

All health professionals need to obtain consent for procedures carried out by them on patients. In the vast majority of circumstances, consent to care by a patient is implied or oral (verbal). The health professional who is to undertake the procedure is responsible for obtaining the patient's consent. Thus, obtaining consent for medical treatment, including surgical procedures carried out by the medical practitioner, is a medical responsibility as the legal relationship or contract is set up between the medical practitioner and the patient.

All health professionals may witness the signing of the consent form by a patient. The health professional's signature, however, does not represent a validation of the process of obtaining the consent by the medical practitioner who is to carry out the procedure. It is evidence only that the health professional witnessed the patient providing their signature.

The patient is always free to alter the consent form prior to signing the form and obtaining the signature of the treating physician or surgeon. The impact of this is similar to altering the terms on any contract prior to the agreement by the parties bound by it. It is noteworthy that the medical practitioner may, once the patient has made alterations to the consent form, refuse to continue any further with that line of treatment. Such may be the case, for example, where the patient makes it clear to the surgeon that he or she will not consent to the transfusion of blood or blood products. At that point the surgeon is at liberty to suggest some other procedure or recommend the patient to another medical practitioner on the basis that he or she is unwilling to proceed under the terms or conditions established by the patient (usually in relation to denying a blood transfusion).

After the consent is completed the patient may, at any time, and without penalty, withdraw the consent. In this circumstance, any health professional made aware of the revocation of the consent should ensure all reasonable attempts are made to notify the medical practitioner of the withdrawal of the consent. The health professional initially notified, or the medical practitioner, should note the withdrawal of consent by the patient in the patient's records and indicate time, date, context and action taken. The immediate superior should be informed of the patient's decision and an entry made in the patient's records indicating this has been done and the action taken by his or her superior. If the medical practitioner or any other health professional is aware that a patient has withdrawn or not given consent for treatment, he or she should not participate in administering that treatment. A failure to do this may constitute a trespass to the patient.

CONSENT TO RESEARCH

Any research that requires contact with the subjects will necessitate the researcher obtaining the consent of the participants prior to the commencement of the study or project. Where research is conducted without a legally valid consent, it gives rise to the possibility of a subject suing in negligence or civil assault. While the courts have not considered the precise depth and extent of the information necessary to obtain a valid consent for research purposes, it is accepted that the extent of the information is greater than that required in the treatment situation.[59] In the Canadian case of *Halushka v Saskatchewan*,[60] the court held the researcher must give 'full and frank' disclosure. It is also important within the healthcare context that health professionals clearly identify and explain to patients the distinction between the role of clinician and that of researcher. That is, where health professionals are seeking participants in research projects from their patient and client load, they must identify prior to obtaining a consent that participation or non-participation will not alter the therapeutic relationship that already exists. The *National Statement on Ethical Conduct in Research Involving Humans* states:[61]

1 The ethical and legal requirements of consent have two aspects: the provision of information and the capacity to make the voluntary choice. So as to conform with ethical and legal requirements, obtaining consent should involve:

   a. provision to participants, at their level of comprehension, of information about the purpose, methods, demands, risks, inconveniences, discomforts, and possible outcomes of research (including the likelihood and form of publication of research results)

b. the exercise of voluntary choice to participate

c. where a participant lacks competence to consent, a person with lawful authority to decide for that participant must be provided with that information and exercise that choice.

2 A person my refuse to participate in a research project and need give no reasons nor justification for that decision.

3 Where consent to participate is required, research must be so designed that each participant's consent is clearly established, whether by a signed form, return of a survey, recorded agreement for interview or other significant means …

4 The consent of a person to participate in research must not be subject to any coercion, or to any inducement or influence which may impair its voluntary character.

FALSE IMPRISONMENT

All adults of sound mind have the right not to be unlawfully detained against their will. Where a patient alleges that a health professional has interfered with his or her freedom of movement, the action is referred to as false imprisonment. False imprisonment is defined as the unlawful, intentional and complete application of restraint upon a person which restricts his or her freedom to move from one place to another 'or causing them to be confined to a place against their will'.[62] No physical contact is required, it being sufficient if the patient fears some harm should he or she refuse to remain.

The *restriction on the freedom of movement must be total*. That is, there must be no means by which the patient can exit. This is a significant factor, in that the presence of an exit that is not known to the patient, or not reasonable for the patient to attempt to use, still amounts to a restraint on movement for which the patient will have a cause of action. *There is no need for the patient to know, at the time, that he or she has been detained*. Thus the decision in *Hart v Herron*[63] is of great significance for health professionals working in intensive care units or other high dependency areas. In this case a patient, who had undergone deep sleep therapy at the Chelmsford Hospital, initiated action in the New South Wales Supreme Court alleging that he had been falsely imprisoned during the time he had undergone the treatment for which he had not given his consent. The court held that the patient had been falsely imprisoned even though he had no recollection of his time in the hospital, or that he had been detained.

Therefore, any action of a health professional that *unlawfully restricts the freedom of movement of a patient and to which the patient does not consent*, clearly places the health professional at risk of defending a claim for damages. Such action may relate to preventing patients leaving their bed or ward areas or the hospital. It may also relate to simple acts such as applying wheelchair brakes to prevent a patient moving from one place to another or to the application of therapeutic devices such as intravenous fluid therapy, and the attendant machinery that goes with it, for no purpose other than to prevent the patient's freedom of movement. Actions to restrict the freedom of movement of patients may also include the administration of drugs prescribed deliberately to control and restrict the freedom of the patient. These include sedatives and tranquillisers prescribed outside recommended therapeutic guidelines and administered to restrict the patient's freedom of movement. Most hospitals and healthcare facilities have clear policies on the application of physical or chemical restraint on patients. These will include express requirements as to the ordering of the restraint of a patient, the review of that order and the management of a patient during the period of the restraint. Some important inclusions are that:

- The medical practitioner or health professionals designated by the policy to care for the patient authorise the application of a restraint. Prior to the ordering of a restraint, the health professional is obliged to carry out a full assessment of the patient to determine the cause of the patient's behaviour and ensure that restraint is the only option. This must be the case whether the patient is being physically or chemically restrained.
- The restraint of a patient occurs only in circumstances where he or she is a danger to himself or herself, other patients or the staff.
- The patient has regular and frequent observations to monitor his or her condition.
- The restraints, if physical, are released at regular intervals.
- The next-of-kin is notified of the application of physical, or initiation of chemical, restraint.
- The restraint decision be reviewed frequently and at pre-determined intervals. This review must include a full assessment of the patient.

The defences applicable within the hospital setting to an action of false imprisonment are available at common law and through the various provisions of legislation in each state and territory. The courts view the deprivation of any individual's freedom of movement as a very serious issue. The application of common law defences is, therefore, restricted to clearly defined circumstances. Decisions to apply restraints to a patient must be made in accordance with hospital guidelines and protocols. Legislation which makes provision for the legal detention of individuals includes crimes legislation permitting police powers of arrest and restraint, mental health legislation where a person can be made an 'involuntary patient', the Quarantine Act 1908 (Cth) and, in some instances, public health legislation.[64]

SCENARIO AND ACTIVITY

The medical student attending clinical practicum has been requested by the consultant to obtain a blood sample from the patient for the purpose of undertaking a pre-operative screening.

- What issues should the medical student consider in relation to obtaining the patient's consent?

REVIEW QUESTIONS

To ensure that you have identified and understood the key points of this chapter please answer the following questions.

1 How is an action assault distinct from an action in negligence?
2 What are the elements of a valid consent?
3 How much information is required for a consent to be valid? Is this different from an action based on the breach of the duty of care for failing to warn/disclose risks?
4 What are the types of consent?
5 Describe what you understand by the term 'autonomy' or autonomous decision of a patient.
6 How would a patient exercise his or her right to be autonomous?
7 Explain what you understand by 'Gillick competency' in relation to a child.
8 Describe the common law doctrine of emergency.
9 Identify within your own state or territory the criteria for 'capacity' in the context of making a healthcare decision.
10 Identify the legislation in your state or territory which provides the legal authority for a substitute decision-maker where the patient has lost capacity to give a valid consent to healthcare or treatment.
11 Define false imprisonment.
12 What are the legal requirements when restraining a patient becomes necessary?

Further reading

Bennett, B, *Law and Medicine*, LBC Information Services, Sydney, 1997.

Devereux, J, 'Competency to Consent to Treatment: An Introduction' in Freckelton, I, Peterson, K, (eds), *Controversies in Health Law*, The Federation Press, Sydney, 1999.

Devereux, J, Parker, M, 'Competency issues for young persons and older persons' in Freckelton, I and Peterson, K, (eds), *Disputes and Dilemmas in Healthcare*, The Federation Press, Sydney, 2006.

Hamblin, J, 'Blood transfusions and the limits of autonomy' (1999) 7(5) *The Australian Health Law Bulletin* 49–51.

Langslow, A, 'Safety and Physical Restraint' (1999) 17(2) *Australian Nursing Journal* 34.

Millbank, J, 'When is a Girl a Boy? *Re A (A child)*' (1995) 9 *Australian Journal of Family Law* 173.

Parkinson, P, 'Children's Rights and Doctors' Immunities: The Implications of the High Court Decision in *Re Marion*' (1992) 6 *Australian Journal of Family Law* 101.

Peterson, K A, 'Selective Treatment Decisions and the Legal Rights of Very Young Infants' (1994) 160 *Medical Journal of Australia* 377.

Retsas, A, Forrester, K, 'Consent: Implications for Healthcare Practitioners' (1995) 2 *JLM* 317.

Richman, D, 'To Restrain or Not to Restrain' (1998) July *RN* 55.

Rieth, C, Courtney Bennett, C, 'Restraint-free Care' (1998) 29(5) *Nursing Management* 36.

Shields, L, Nixon, J, 'The rights of children in hospital' (1997) *Health Law Bulletin* 6(1) 1.

Skene, L, *Law and Medical Practice: Rights, Duties, Claims and Defences*, 2nd edn, LexisNexis, Sydney, 2004.

Skene, L, Smallwoood, R, 'Informed consent: Lessons from Australia' (2002) 324 *British Medical Journal* 39–41.

Wallace, M, 'Restraint: Some Legal Implications' (1997) 4(2) *Collegian* 15.

Wallace, M, *Healthcare and the Law*, 3rd edn, Law Book Co, Sydney, 2001.

Endnotes

1 *Department of Health and Community Services (NT) v JWB (Marion's case)* (1992) 175 CLR 218.
2 *Malette v Shulman* (1990) 2 Med LR 162.
3 Retsas, A, Forrester, K, 'Consent: Implications for Healthcare Practitioners', (1995) 2 *JLM* 317.

4 (1914) 105 NE92 at 93.

5 *Good Medical Practice: A Code of Conduct for Doctors in Australia*, Australian Medical Council, Canberra, (2009), section 3.2.5.

6 Wallace, M, *Healthcare and the Law*, 3rd edn, Law Book Co, Sydney, 2001, p 67.

7 (1975) 12 SASR 174 at 177.

8 *Hart v Herron* (1984) Aust Torts Reports 80-201.

9 *Mohr v Williams* 104 NW 12 (1905).

10 *O'Brien v Cunard SS Co* 28 NE 266 (1891).

11 Above, n 8.

12 'Catch all' clauses are those which are so general they cannot be considered as covering any particular contingency. For example, the consent may state 'I consent to any adverse event which occurs during my period of hospitalisation and a result of which I sustain and injury'.

13 *Holland v Hardcastle* unreported, 16 December 1997, District Court of Western Australia, No 970403.

14 Above, n 3, Retsas & Forrester.

15 *Beausoleil v La Communaut'e des Soeurs de la Chatit'e de la Providence et al* (1964) 53 DLR 65.

16 [2003] ACTSC; [1949] 2 DLR 442.

17 District Court of New South Wales, No 1919/89, 22 December 1993.

18 *Rogers v Whitaker* (1992) 175 CLR 479.

19 Ibid.

20. Ibid at 490.

21 [1980] 3 WLR 1003 at 1014.

22 Guardianship Act 1987 (NSW) s 33(2); Guardianship and Administration Act 2000 (Qld) Schedule 3; Powers of Attorney Act 1998 (Qld) Schedule 3; Guardianship and Administration Act 1995 (Tas) s 36(2); Guardianship and Administration Act 1986 (Vic) s 36(2).

23 Defined under s 33 as, '(a) any treatment that is intended, or is reasonably likely, to have the effect of rendering permanently infertile the person on whom it is carried out, or (b) any new treatment that has not yet gained the support of a substantial number of medical practitioners or dentists specialising in the area of practice concerned, or (c) any other kind of treatment declared by the regulations to be special medical treatment for the purposes…'.

24 Defined under s 33 as: 'treatment that is not special treatment, major treatment or treatment in the course of a clinical trial. Major treatment means: treatment (other than special treatment or treatment in the course of a clinical trial)'.

25 *A Guide to the New Laws about Enduring Powers of Attorney*, Queensland Government, Department of Justice.

26 *P v P* (1994) FLC 92-462.

27 Age of Majority Act 1974 (Qld); Minors (Property and Contract) Act 1970 (NSW); Age of Majority (Reduction) Act 1970 (SA); Age of Majority Act 1973 (Tas); Age of Majority Act 1977 (Vic); Age of Majority Act 1973 (WA); Age of Majority Act 1974 (ACT); Age of Majority Act 1974 (NT).

28 Section 3.

29 Sections 7 and 8.

30 [1982] 1 NSWLR 311.

31 [1986] AC 112.

32 *Gillick v West Norfolk and Wisbech Area Health Authority* [1986] AC 112 (HL) per Lord Fraser at 171–2, per Lord Scarman at 188–9.

33 Ibid at 188–9 per Lord Scarman.

34 (1992) 175 CLR 218 at 238.

35 [1992] 4 All ER 627.

36 Unreported, Royal Courts of Justice, Family Division, United Kingdom, 15 July 1999.

37 Ibid.

38 Children (Care and Protection) Act 1987 (NSW); Human Tissue Act 1982 (Vic); Transplantation and Anatomy Act 1979 (Qld); Consent to Medical Treatment and Palliative Care Act 1995 (SA); Human Tissue and Transplant Act 1982 (WA); Human Tissue Transplant Act 1989 (NT), Emergency Medical Operations Act 1973 (NT); Transplantation and Anatomy Act 1978 (ACT).

39 Children and Young Persons (Care and Protection) Act 1998 (NSW) s 174.

40 Ibid at s 23.

41 Section 11.

42 Bennett, B, *Law and Medicine*, LBC Information Services, Sydney, 1997, p 25.

43 McLelland J, Supreme Court of NSW, 17 November 1989.

44 (1992) 175 CLR 218.

45 It should be noted that the preceding cases determined by the Family Law Court had not given a clear principle on the issue. In *Re a Teenager* (1989) FLC 92-006 and *Re S* (1990) FLC 92-124 the court held the parents of the respective children could give a valid consent. However, in *Re Jane* (1989) FLC 92-007 and *Re Elizabeth* (1989) FLC 92-023 the sterilisation of the child required a court order.

46 *Secretary, Department of Health and Community Services v JWB and SMB (Marion's case)* (1992) 175 CLR 218 per Mason CJ, Dawson, Toohey and Gaudron JJ.

47 Ibid at 249.

48 L Skene, *Law and Medical Practice: Rights, Duties, Claims and Defences*, Butterworths, Sydney, 1998, p 83.

49 Wallace, M, *Healthcare and the Law*, 3rd edn, Law Book Co, Sydney, 2001, p 79.

50 [1949] 2 DLR 442 (BC SC).

51 *T v T* [1988] FamD 2 WLR 189.

52 *Statute Law Revision (No 2)* 1995 (Qld) — Aid in Emergency s 15; Guardianship and Administration Act 2000 (Qld) ss 62, 63; Emergency Operations Act 1973 (NT) s 3(1); Consent to Medical Treatment and Palliative Care Act 1995 (SA) s 13(1).

53 *Collins v Wilcock* [1984] 1 WLR 1172.

54 (1990) 2 Med LR 162.

55 [1998] VSCA 45.

56 201 A 2d 537 (1964).

57 [1992] 4 All ER 671.

58 *Re T* (1992) 3 Med LR 306.

59 *Chatterton v Gerson* [1981] 1 All ER 257.

60 (1965) 53 DLR 436.

61 www.health.gov.au/nhmrc/publications/synopses/e72syn.htm (accessed 22 July 2010).

62 Laufer, S, *Law for the Nursing Profession and Allied Healthcare Professionals*, 2nd edn, CCH, Sydney, 1992, p 74.

63 (1984) Aust Torts Reports 80-201.

64 Above, n 3, Retsas & Forrester, at 325–6.

7

End of life decisions

LEARNING OBJECTIVES

This chapter aims to introduce you to the key areas relating to end of life decisions and substitute decision-makers. While reading this chapter you should focus on:

- distinguishing between withdrawal of treatment from competent and incompetent adults
- explaining the significance of the common law in end of life decisions
- identifying the statutory requirements and mechanisms which allow patients to make advance directives in Australian jurisdictions
- describing the requirements of a medical power of attorney
- discussing the role of guardianship in relation to patient decisions for treatment
- explaining the legal significance of a not for resuscitation order.

INTRODUCTION

There is often confusion associated with end of life decisions and withdrawal of medical treatment. The source of this confusion commonly relates to the context, where a patient refuses treatment, or is incompetent to make a decision, and the medical practitioner has limited knowledge of the existing legal framework. This area relies on the common law and two key areas of legislation: guardianship acts, and specific legislative frameworks which deal with advance directives and the appointment of substitute decision-makers. The importance of medical practitioners' understanding of the relevant legal principles cannot be overstressed as their criminal and civil liability is protected if they act in good faith and comply with the specific laws in their respective state or territory.

THE COMMON LAW
Competent adults

The common law of consent recognises that a competent adult patient has the right to consent to, accept, or refuse medical treatment including treatment that may be life-saving. In *Brightwater Care Group v Rossiter* (2009)[1] a competent male quadriplegic, with no ability to move, requested that his medical and health carers discontinue the provision of nutrition and hydration via his gastrostomy tube. The court held that provided Mr Rossiter was first given an explanation by a medical practitioner, including the consequences of ceasing such care, he could refuse the nutrition and hydration. Furthermore, the Brightwater healthcare facility would not be criminally responsible for any consequences to Mr Rossiter's life or health.

Incompetent adults

The leading case which has influenced Australian courts relating to withdrawal of treatment from incompetent patients is the English case of *Airedale NHS Trust v Bland* [1993].[2] Anthony Bland was a 17-year-old who suffered severe brain damage after being crushed in a football crowd accident. His cerebral cortex was destroyed, he was unable to see, hear or feel and, having no cognitive function, he was described as being in a persistent vegetative state. There was sufficient brain stem function which enabled him to breath without assistance, receiving artificial feeding via a nasogastric tube. The Airedale NHS Trust made an application to the court for a declaration to allow the nasogastric feeds and other treatment to be lawfully discontinued. The court accepted the principle that the sanctity of life is not absolute and *when a respectable body of medical opinion believes that the patient has no hope of recovery and that treatment is futile and of no benefit to the patient, then such treatment could be withheld.* It was considered that when treatment is futile the treatment is not in the 'best interests' of the patient. The principles established in this case have provided persuasive guidance and have been incorporated into the Australian courts' decisions.

Futility and disagreement by family members

Where the decision to withdraw treatment from an incompetent patient is made by practitioners on the grounds that treatment is futile and not in the best interests of the patient, family members do not always agree. There are Australian cases where such decisions have been tested. For example, in 2004 75-year-old Mr Messiha was admitted to hospital with severe brain hypoxia following a cardiac arrest. He had a history of severe lung disease and cardiac problems. Two days after his admission the hospital staff raised the possibility of withdrawing mechanical ventilation on the basis that there had been no improvement in his condition and there was no realistic prospect of recovery. Mr Messiha's family members disagreed and sought an order from the New South Wales Supreme Court to prevent the hospital staff from withdrawing treatment. The court declined to order continuance of the treatment and Mr Justice Howie commented that:

It seems to me that it would be an unusual case where the Court would act against what is unanimously held by medical experts as an appropriate treatment regime for the patient ... This is not to make any value judgment of the life of the patient in his present situation or to disregard the wishes of the family and beliefs they genuinely hold for his recovery. ... But it is principally a matter for the expertise of professional medical practitioners ...[3]

In *Herrington's case*[4] in 2007, an application was made to the Victorian Supreme Court by John Herrington seeking orders that medical treatment be given to his partner, Rosalie King. Ms King had been in a persistent vegetative state (PVS) for 4 months and was being hydrated and fed via a percutaneous endoscopic gastrostomy tube (PEG). The medical staff wished to cease feeding due to the danger of her vomiting and aspirating. The medical staff met with Mr Herrington and Ms King's family to discuss the change in treatment plan. Ms King's parents and partner, Mr Herrington, provided evidence in relation to Aboriginal culture which believes a sick person should be cared for and not left to die, and Ms King's beliefs that, if she could express an opinion, she would not agree with the ceasing of the PEG feeding. In addition, Mr Harrington believed that he had spent more time with Ms King than the medical staff and he firmly held to the view that she might improve if treatment continued. He also requested an independent assessment.

Mr Justice Williams indicated that he had taken into account all of the evidence put before the court. The medical evidence was of the universal opinion that treatment would be futile and could possibly hasten Ms King's inevitable death. The judge stated:

I recognise the concern and anguish of Ms King's partner and family and their desire for her to continue to live ... However, I can only act on the evidence before the Court. I am satisfied ... that it would not be in Ms King's interests to recommence any treatment involving the administration of fluids ... In my opinion, it would not be reasonable to administer treatment, even if it would prolong Ms King's life for a few days, when it would serve no therapeutic purpose.[5]

In the Northern Territory in *Melo v Superintendent of Royal Darwin Hospital* (2007)[6] the parents of a severely brain injured man sought an injunction to prevent the hospital withdrawing mechanical ventilation and the court provided further insight into relevant considerations. The court has jurisdiction to protect the right of an unconscious person to receive ordinary, reasonable and appropriate medical treatment, sustenance and support, as opposed to extraordinary, excessively burdensome, intrusive or futile treatment. What constitutes appropriate medical treatment in a given case is a medical matter in the first instance. However, where there is doubt or serious dispute in this regard, the court has the power to act to protect the life and welfare of the unconscious person. In this case the medical evidence indicated that there was not the slightest possibility that there was anything that could be done and the parents' request was refused.

ADVANCE CARE DIRECTIVES

Advance care planning allows patients to have their treatment wishes respected in the event that they become incompetent to communicate their wishes. Advance directives, sometimes called living wills, are documents that enable a competent patient to specify treatment of a future condition, including any limitations to life-threatening treatment. The states and territories legislative frameworks provide varying mechanisms which allow for advance directives and medical powers of attorney. The legislative frameworks of many states require the advance directive to be in a prescribed format and if this is not undertaken the directive may not be relied upon. It is imperative, therefore, that medical practitioners are familiar with the requirements in the states and territories in which they practice.

If the common law principles are consistent with the statutory requirements, the directive can be given verbally or in writing. It is advisable, for clarity and evidence, to have a written advance directive.[7] The elements to consider are threefold:

1 the patient must be competent at the time the directive is made
2 the directive must have been intended to apply to the circumstances that have arisen — broad and vague statements may provide little guidance to medical practitioners
3 there must be no evidence that the patient was unduly influenced at the time the directive was made.

COMPETENT ADULTS — LEGISLATIVE MECHANISMS
Medical powers of attorney

The power of attorney mechanism, traditionally utilised for business transactions, has been adopted to allow for decisions to be made in the healthcare environment. *A medical treatment power of attorney* (also referred to in some states as an enduring medical power of attorney) allows an individual (the donor/patient) to appoint another adult (the agent or attorney), to make decisions related to medical treatment when the donor is unable to do so. This is one form of substitute or proxy decision-making. This type of power of attorney is specific to medical treatment and does not extend to include decisions regarding business affairs. *The agent/attorney has the legal authority to make decisions regarding medical treatment on behalf of the incapacitated donor, including decisions at the end of life*, hence the importance when selecting the attorney. As with all powers of attorney, the donor can revoke the power at any time, provided he or she is legally competent. The need for witnesses applies to all powers of attorney and in most situations one witness must be eligible to sign a statutory declaration and the witnesses must not be the appointed agent. Should the agent (or any proxy decision-maker) be considered not to be acting in the best interests of the patient, and this is where health professionals may be involved, then the courts or guardianship boards may remove the agent/attorney.

State and territory legislative frameworks

Most states and territories have passed specific legislation which incorporate the appointment of a medical power of attorney and/or an advance directive. It is important to remember that this area of the law is an extension of the law of consent which fundamentally recognises the autonomy of the individual. The aim of establishing mechanisms to specify treatment wishes, or providing for the appointment of an agent, allows the patient to choose who will make decisions and what type of treatment decisions will be made on his or her behalf should he or she be incapacitated. For example, a patient who wishes a spouse to make decisions relating to medical treatment when the patient loses competence, or the Jehovah Witness patient who will not accept a blood transfusion as part of the treatment plan. Research demonstrates that medical practitioners working in acute care settings are not expecting patients to refuse therapy, or are unclear about the legal standing of relatives' input, when treatment decisions need to be made, with resultant dilemmas.[8] This requires knowledge of the existing legal frameworks.

Not every Australian jurisdiction has enacted legislation to deal with refusal of medical treatment, medical powers of attorney or advance directives. The following provides an overview of the differing requirements established in each state and territory.

Victoria

The Medical Treatment Act 1988 applies to competent adults and establishes two key mechanisms. The first mechanism, in Schedule 1 of the Act, allows a person to refuse treatment using a refusal of treatment certificate. The features related to this mechanism require the person to identify the 'specific' area of treatment (such as antibiotics or blood) he or she intends to refuse or, more broadly, treatment in 'general' may be refused. The patient's refusal of treatment should relate to treatment of a 'current condition' (diagnosis) that must be identified by a medical practitioner. The common law principles of consent have been incorporated into the certificate. Therefore, the patient's decision to refuse treatment must be made voluntarily and the patient must be competent, that is, of sound mind, and at least 18 years of age. The certificate requires the signature of two witnesses. One must be that of a medical practitioner and both witnesses must be satisfied that the aforementioned criteria are met. The Act is intended to allow individuals to clarify their wishes in relation to treatment and includes a section making it an offence for medical practitioners to continue to provide treatment once the certificate is signed. The sanction under the Act for non-compliance amounts to a fine. This penalty has never been invoked, and where a medical practitioner is acting in good faith, without the knowledge of the certificate, the conduct will not be subject to the fine.

The second mechanism allows a competent adult (the donor) to appoint an agent using a medical power of attorney (called an enduring power of attorney medical treatment; Schedule 2 of the Act). Two witnesses are required to sign this document; one must be eligible to witness a statutory declaration. It is important to note that neither witness should be named as the attorney, this must be a different individual.[9] To assist the agent in understanding the donor's views about possible medical treatment the Office of the Public Advocate suggests that donors write this information down and give it to the appointed agent. The agent's power extends to providing consent to treatment and refusing or withdrawing consent to medical treatment. (Schedule 3 of the Act allows an agent or guardian to refuse treatment on behalf of the incompetent patient.) The agent can only refuse treatment if the treatment would cause the donor unreasonable distress or the agent believes, on reasonable grounds, that the donor would not want the treatment to continue. A competent donor can cancel a medical enduring power of attorney at any time. If there is reason to believe that the agent is not making decisions as the donor intended or is abusing his or her power, the Guardianship and Administration Board may revoke or suspend the power of attorney.

Differentiating medical treatment from palliative care

The Victorian legislation allows adults to refuse 'medical treatment', but not 'palliative care'. The Act defines medical treatment as 'an operation, the administration of a drug or other like substance, or any other medical procedure'. Palliative care is defined as 'the provision of reasonable medical procedures for the relief of pain, suffering and discomfort or the reasonable provision of food and water'. There is some overlap between these definitions, providing confusion when healthcare decisions were to be made. This was clarified in the case of BWV[10] where the family of a woman suffering Pick's disease (a rare and progressive dementia) wished to have her percutaneous endoscopic gastrostomy (PEG) tube removed. The health facility where she resided refused the request. The PEG tube had been inserted some years earlier but she had deteriorated to the extent that she had no cognitive capacity and medical opinion agreed that she would not improve. There had been no appointment of an agent to articulate her wishes once she became incompetent.

The court decided that the use of a PEG, or any form of artificial feeding, constituted a medical procedure. Justice Morris reasoned that this was the case because 'artificial nutrition and hydration involves protocols, skills and care which draw from, and depend upon medical knowledge' and must be subject to regular medical and nursing supervision.[11] His Honour also noted that the Osmolite, the nutritional substance administered via the PEG, was 'intended to provide complete and balanced nutrition, without the need for any food whatsoever.'[12] The court considered whether the provision of artificial feeding in this manner also amounted to palliative care. The court held that palliative care, within the context of the Act, was to mean 'care, not to treat or cure a patient, but to alleviate pain or suffering when a patient is dying'.[13] His Honour reasoned that the administration of hydration and nutrition via a PEG could not amount to palliative care as this is a procedure 'to sustain life, it is not a procedure to manage the dying process, so that it [death] results in as little pain and suffering as possible'.[14] The court concluded that:

> the intention of Parliament, in excluding the provision of food and water from the concept of medical treatment was to ensure that a dying person would have food and water available for oral consumption, if the person wished to consume such food or water. It can hardly have been the parliament's intention that dying patients would be forced to consume food and water.[15]

The reference to the provision of food and water was intended to apply to the ordinary, non-medical provision of food and water.[16]

Northern Territory

The Natural Death Act 1988 in the Northern Territory allows legally competent adults who have a terminal illness to refuse 'extraordinary' measures. 'Extraordinary' treatment or procedures include medical or surgical measures which prolong life by supplanting or maintaining the operation of bodily functions that are temporarily or permanently incapable of independent operation. The regulations set out the prescribed format required to document an individual's wishes. The individual may refuse 'extraordinary' treatment and procedures generally or specify the particular 'extraordinary' treatment and procedures he or she wishes to refuse. Two witnesses must sign the certificate; neither may be the medical practitioner responsible for the treatment of that person. The Act specifies that the withdrawal of, or the non-application of, the 'extraordinary' measures to a person with a terminal illness does not constitute a cause of death when made in accordance with a direction of the patient.

South Australia

The Consent to Medical Treatment and Palliative Care Act 1995 allows legally competent adults to provide advance directives. The directions must relate to treatment given where the patient suffers a terminal illness or is in a permanent vegetative state, and where the patient is incapable of making decisions. The directive is required to conform to a prescribed format (Schedule 2 of the Act) and must be witnessed by an authorised person. The patient directions should define those circumstances or conditions regarding acceptable or non-acceptable medical treatment.

There is also provision in the South Australian Act to appoint an agent by a medical power of attorney. The requirements and scope of the agent's power are outlined in considerable detail in the legislation. The power of attorney includes the main features outlined in the section discussing Victoria, mentioned above. In addition, the agent must indicate acceptance of the appointment; this is evidenced by signing the document. The sole authorised witness also attests that both the donor and donee have signed voluntarily and appear to understand the effect of the power. A person is not eligible to be an agent if they are, in a professional or administrative capacity, directly or indirectly responsible for the medical care or treatment of the patient.

In relation to the provision of palliative care, the agent cannot refuse the natural provision or administration of food, water or drugs to relieve pain. This is similar to the Victorian requirement. The agent cannot refuse medical treatment that would result in the donor regaining capacity to make decisions. Lastly, if the donor has made anticipatory directions the agent must make decisions which are consistent with those directions.

Australian Capital Territory

The Medical Treatment Act 1994 permits competent adults to refuse medical treatment. The refusal may be communicated orally, in writing or in any other way the person is able to communicate.

When the refusal of treatment is not in writing, a direction must be witnessed by two adults, with one signatory being a medical practitioner. Provision is made in the Act for a person to provide a written direction. This must be in the prescribed format (Form 1 in the Schedule). The requirements are similar to those in the Victorian certificate in that the fundamental principles of consent are highlighted and the signatures of two witnesses are required. The specific directions to refuse treatment do not have to relate to a current condition, as is the requirement in Victoria, nor must the patient have a terminal illness, as in the South Australian legislation.

The Act defines palliative care in a similar manner to the Victorian legislation. However, instead of explicitly stating a patient cannot refuse palliative care, as in Victoria, the Act does not affect any right, power or duty to provide palliative care. Effectively, this would not allow a person to refuse the reasonable provision of medical and nursing procedures for the relief of pain and suffering, or the reasonable provision of food and fluid. Thus the provision of palliative care remains the responsibility of the medical practitioner.

The Act places the onus on the medical practitioner to take reasonable steps to ensure that the patient has been informed about the nature of the illness, alternative forms of treatment and the consequences of treatment, or of a failure to treat. The Act specifies that the medical practitioner should not follow a patient's direction to refuse or withdraw treatment unless the practitioner believes that the patient has understood the information regarding the illness and has weighed the options. Moreover, the medical practitioner is not to proceed if the professional believes the direction to withdraw or refuse treatment fails in any way to comply with the Act, or the patient has changed his or her mind. The Act allows for the granting of a medical power of attorney, as provided in Form 2. The requirements are similar to other medical powers of attorney.

Queensland

The Powers of Attorney Act 1998 allows for competent adults to give an advance directive regarding 'healthcare' and 'special healthcare', and appoint an enduring power of attorney (personal and/or financial). In relation to advance directives the patient must understand the nature and effect of each directive, which only operate while the patient is incompetent. 'Healthcare' is defined broadly to include treatment and procedures to diagnose and treat the patient's condition and includes the withholding or withdrawal of life-threatening measures. Healthcare excludes first aid treatment, the administering of non-prescription drugs and non-intrusive diagnostic examinations. 'Special healthcare' is defined to include more precise situations such as removal of organs for donation, sterilisation, termination of pregnancy and participation in research and experimental healthcare. A directive to withhold or withdraw life-threatening measures is dependent upon the application of specific conditions and criteria. An advance directive can only operate when the person:

1   has an illness that is incurable or irreversible and is likely to die within 12 months; or
2   is suffering a persistent vegetative state; or
3   is permanently unconscious; or
4   the person suffers an illness of such extreme severity that there is no chance of recovery.

In addition, the directive to withhold or withdraw life support must be considered good medical practice in the circumstances, and the person to whom it applies must have no reasonable prospect of regaining capacity. 'Good medical practice' is defined to have regard to recognised medical practices and ethical standards of the medical profession in Australia.

The Act provides for an adult of sound mind to appoint an enduring power of attorney (personal) to make decisions in relation to healthcare. The Act provides for the appointment of one or more attorneys, who may act jointly or severally. The attorney may make decisions, as in other jurisdictions, including the power to exercise an advance directive for healthcare in the event that the patient's directions are inadequate. However, the Act explicitly excludes an attorney's decision in the event that the advance directive is unclear and relates to 'special healthcare'. The Queensland Act also recognises lawful medical powers of attorney made in other jurisdictions.

In the absence of an advance directive or the appointment of an enduring power of attorney (personal) the right to consent to the treatment of the incompetent adult is deemed to vest in the non-paid primary carer. This person is referred to as the statutory health attorney. The Act refers to a spouse, an adult who has the care of the patient, a close relative or the adult guardian, as persons who may be eligible statutory health attorneys. Moreover, in the absence of a lawful agent or advance directive a medical practitioner is given authority without a consent to provide care that is minor and uncontroversial, provided it is necessary to promote the adult's health and wellbeing and the health professional is unaware of any objection to the contrary.

Western Australia

Legislation was introduced in 2008: the Acts Amendment (Consent to Medical Treatment) Act amends the existing Guardianship and Administration Act 1990. The legislation makes provision for advance health directives, in a prescribed form and the patient is advised to seek medical or legal advice, presumably for correctness and precision relating to the information and format. A treatment decision in an advance directive operates only in the circumstances specified in that directive. The legislation expressly indicates the matters to be considered in relation to the directive before it is acted on. These include the person's age at the time the advance directive was made at the period of time that has since elapsed. Other persons may be consulted regarding the directive, probably to confirm the person's wishes, from an enduring guardian, to the person's spouse or de facto, the primary carer or child, parent or sibling, in that order.

Individuals can appoint an enduring guardian (enduring power of guardianship) using a prescribed form, including the need for witness signatures at the time of the appointment. More than one individual can be appointed and they are called substitute enduring guardians. The enduring guardian can make decisions to consent to, or refuse consent to, medical or surgical treatment, including life-sustaining measures. The patient may record directions about how the enduring guardian is to perform any of his or her functions. As with other jurisdictions the Administrative Tribunal has the power to intervene, consider decisions and revoke the enduring guardian's power should decisions not be in the patient's best interests.

New South Wales and Tasmania

New South Wales and Tasmania rely on guidelines and the common law. The New South Wales Health Department has published guidelines for end of life care and decision-making.[17] The guidelines address a range of issues including the importance of collaboration between the patient and the treating healthcare team. When the patient is incompetent the guidelines recommend the treating team and family draw on existing knowledge of the patient's personal values and medical condition for shared decision-making. Palliative care should be continued throughout and this includes controlling pain and providing emotional and psychological support. The guidelines also highlight that accountability for decisions rests with the senior clinician regarding the reasonableness of the therapy plan. The guidelines deal with assessment, disclosure, discussion and consensus regarding treatment decisions and plan. There is also specific mention of artificial hydration and nutrition and not for resuscitation decisions, allowing these to be withheld. Children between the ages of 14–18 years should not solely make decisions limiting treatment; the guidelines state that this should be in conjunction with family and health professionals. The New South Wales Health Department recommends that health facilities develop policies in keeping with these guidelines.

The New South Wales guidelines recommend that before an advance directive has sufficient authority it must satisfy at least three criteria.

1   The directive must be *specific*; it must be clear that the direction applies to the clinical circumstances that arise and provide adequate guidance as to care.

2   The advance directive must be *current*, in so far as it must reflect the existing wishes of the patient. The guidelines state that the directive should be reviewed periodically, particularly after an illness or change in health status.

3   The person must be *competent* to make the directive, this includes appearing to comprehend, retain and weigh the relevant information. The guidelines suggest that it is not essential the document be witnessed, but recommend that this be undertaken. There is no precise format for a written advance directive, although the guidelines provide information of organisations where they can be obtained.

Tasmania does not have a separate legislative framework in relation to refusal of treatment decisions and advance directives, hence the common law applies. The guardianship legislation (discussed below) does, however, allow for the appointment of an enduring guardian who can make decisions regarding treatment when the patient is unable to participate by reason of disability.

PATIENTS' AUTONOMY RESPECTED WITH THE EXCEPTION OF UNLAWFUL TREATMENT

It is important to note that *regardless of the legislative or policy frameworks* within Australia *an individual patient can withdraw his or her refusal to treatment or change his or her mind at any time*. In addition, none of the mechanisms allow for care to be provided which is unlawful. For example, a patient could not provide an advance directive, or delegate power to an agent or attorney, that provided for the suffocation of that patient as soon as he loses competence, as this would amount to homicide. Patients and agents must operate within the boundaries of what is considered, in the particular circumstances, 'reasonable care' although this may well include the withdrawal of life support.

Know your state/territory framework and assist patients to plan

Medical practitioners must be able to identify the state legislative provisions and be familiar with the prescribed documents, as there are significant differences between the various Australian state and territory jurisdictions. Where no legislative framework exists, or the person has not completed the relevant documentation, then the common law of consent applies. Where a patient is competent it may be prudent to complete an advance directive or appoint a medical power of attorney.

The Respecting Patient Choices (RPC) program, initially established in Victoria, has been introduced into health facilities in a bid to encourage patients to discuss future therapy, including end of life care.[18] The program provides for the education of staff, who then assist patients to record advance care plans and appoint medical powers of attorney. Evaluation of the RPC program found that 70% of patients introduced to the RPC program went on to document preferences for future therapy and that these were easily located in patient files. Importantly, patients also wanted to discuss their illness and impending therapy options, but they expected medical practitioners to initiate the conversations with them.[19]

INCOMPETENT ADULTS — GUARDIANSHIP LAWS

When adult patients are incompetent due to disease, birth defects or injury, medical practitioners may be uncertain as to their role when providing treatment. Obtaining a consent or ascertaining patient wishes in these situations is generally not possible. If a patient has not made a relevant advance directive or appointed a medical power of attorney, then the issue of treatment direction and who may provide consent, or refuse treatment, is raised. The healthcare team may rely on the nearest next-of-kin. However, there is no clear judicial authority to support this practice, despite the fact that anecdotal evidence suggests that attending family members decide. Guardianship legislation has, therefore, been enacted in all states and territories with the primary purpose of protecting incompetent or disabled people. Moreover, in recent years a number of jurisdictions have identified specific categories of people who, it is considered, are likely to have a relationship with the incompetent patient and thus be suitably located to be involved in decisions. The guardianship legislation in New South Wales, Queensland (called a statutory health attorney), Victoria, Tasmania and Western Australia has been amended to identify appropriate individuals, provided they are available and willing to act. This individual is called the 'person responsible'. The legislation identifies a system where priority is given to a person responsible to make decisions. This person is identified from a list of potential decision-makers. For example, in Victoria, this includes: a person who is an agent under a medical power of attorney; a person appointed by the Victorian and Civil Administrative Tribunal; a spouse or domestic partner; a primary carer; or the nearest relative over 18 years of age.

Where there is no person responsible or difficult decisions must be made, the guardianship laws allow for another type of substitute decision-maker, a guardian. *Guardianship legislation has been enacted in all states and territories with the primary purpose of protecting incompetent or disabled people.* The legislation allows for the appointment of a guardian to act in the best interests of the disabled person, and to ensure general care is adequately provided; this includes healthcare and living arrangements.

Individuals who may attract guardianship laws

The group of individuals to whom the legislation in the various jurisdictions applies is similar but the definitions in each Act vary. For example, in New South Wales, individuals who may require a guardian include people with a disability. Section 3(2) of the Disabilities Services and Guardianship Act 1987 (NSW) defines a disabled person as one who is intellectually, physically, psychologically or sensorily disabled, or who is of advanced age, or who is a mentally ill person within the meaning of the Mental Health Act 1990, or who is otherwise disabled. In Victoria, a disabled person is defined in s 3 of the Guardianship and Administration Act 1986 to include adults who suffer an intellectual impairment, mental illness, brain damage, physical disability or senility. Clearly, these are very broad definitions which would apply to many patients. The South Australian and Western Australian definitions are also expansive. The remaining jurisdictions, the Australian Capital Territory, the Northern Territory, Queensland and Tasmania, have slightly more restrictive definitions in that they state 'disabled' relates to persons who are intellectually or mentally impaired.

The legislation differs slightly in relation to the terminology and scope of the type of guardian who may be appointed. Most jurisdictions allow for the appointment of a *full-time (plenary) guardian or limited (emergency) guardian*. The full-time guardian tends to have the same powers as a parent over a child such as to make decisions as to where the disabled person should live and consent to healthcare. The limited guardian usually has specific powers and/or time limits conferred by the guardianship board. Should a decision be required for a procedure at short notice, the limited guardianship order would most likely be used.

Appointing a guardian or financial manager

The criteria upon which a guardianship board decides that a guardian or financial manager should be appointed requires at least three issues to be addressed. The board must:
1 decide if the patient has a disability within the meaning of the legislation
2 determine whether the person is unable to make decisions or manage various aspects of his or her life as a result of that disability
3 consider whether there is a need to appoint a guardian.

The philosophy underpinning this legislation aims to ensure that the guardian takes the least restrictive approach when making decisions for a disabled or incompetent individual. *Wherever possible, the wishes of the disabled person are to be taken into account.* It is important to note that the guardian does not automatically handle the financial affairs of the individual. Most legislative frameworks allow for the appointment of a separate person, called an administrator or financial manager, to handle the disabled person's financial affairs. It is possible to be both a guardian and a financial manager but this would depend on the determination of the board.

When a board is making an order for the appointment of a guardian, there are a number of relevant considerations regarding the suitability of the individual proposed. The guardian:

- should not have a conflict of interest with the disabled person
- is obliged to advocate on their behalf and protect the disabled person from neglect and abuse
- should have a willingness to act in the best interests of the disabled person, taking into account their wishes wherever possible
- should encourage the disabled person to care for him or herself.

If there is no-one available to be appointed, then many jurisdictions allow for the appointment of a public advocate or public guardian. If the board is considering the appointment of an administrator, it may appoint an accountant or the State Trustee if the financial affairs of the disabled person require specific expertise.

Recent decisions regarding limiting or withdrawing treatment

The guardianship boards/tribunals and appointed guardians do not have the same broad powers as the superior courts, nonetheless they are frequently becoming involved in decisions to withdraw or refuse treatment. In *Re AG* [2007][20] an intellectually disabled woman, who lived alone, had been diagnosed with a renal tumour with lymphadenopathy in the abdomen and pelvis, and possible secondary brain tumours. Her prognosis was very poor and she had a history of refusing medical treatment. She accepted that she had cancer, but refused to acknowledge the renal tumour. The public guardian was asked to make a decision to refuse resuscitation and dialysis. The Guardianship Tribunal was approached for direction. The tribunal found that the guardian could provide consent or refuse care and this included palliative care. The tribunal stated that the weight of authority supported the notion that limiting treatment can promote a person's health and wellbeing if it prevented futile treatment. The tribunal also found that guardians involved in healthcare decisions could be involved in advance care planning.

In Queensland in *Re HG* [2006][21] the guardianship tribunal was asked to determine whether a man suffering from Wernicke's encephalopathy and Korsakoff's psychosis and who had suffered a brain stem stroke could have artificial hydration and feeding discontinued. The tribunal found that the medical evidence was sufficient to indicate that continuation of the feeding and hydration was inconsistent with good medical practice and that it should cease. The case also highlighted that a finding of good medical practice did not require unanimous support from all medical opinion.

In Western Australia in *BTO* [2004][22] the guardianship board, interpreting s 119 of the Guardianship and Administration Act 1990 which deals with consent to treatment, allowed the interpretation to be extended to include withdrawal of artificial nutrition and hydration. The board found that consent for withdrawal of treatment could be given, provided it was in the patient's best interest. In this case a man had suffered a severe stroke and was in a coma. The board interpreted the legislation to include consent to medical procedures and decisions to withdraw life-sustaining procedures. A guardian was appointed with the power to refuse artificial hydration and feeding.

Are guardians always required when patients are incompetent?

As mentioned above, there are times when the patient is unable to make decisions regarding treatment and there is no agent or guardian. In these situations, it is clear that patients receive treatment. Often the treating medical practitioner will discuss the treatment options with the next-of-kin and then treatment proceeds. There is English case law which suggests that a medical practitioner may act in the absence of the patient's consent where it is 'not practicable to communicate with the assisted person' and 'the action taken … such as a reasonable person would in all the circumstances take, acting in the best interests of the person'.[23] This view is far less clear in Australia as McHugh J states:

the approach of their Lordships [in *Re F*] transfers the issue [of what medical treatment is most appropriate for a patient] to the medical profession for determination … Whatever may be the position in England, the approach of their Lordships is not consistent with the common law of Australia.[24]

Thus, although the Australian judicial position remains unclear, treatment decisions need to be made daily regarding incompetent patients. In many jurisdictions, it is common medical practice to treat a patient when it can be asserted the treatment is in the *best interests* of the patient. Should there be any concerns expressed by the family, carers or members of the healthcare team regarding the nature, scope or need for the treatment, then the appointment of a guardian is most preferable.

In Victoria, the Guardianship and Administration (Amendment) Act 1997[25] has attempted to streamline decisions for incompetent adults. If there is a refusal of treatment certificate under the Medical Treatment Act 1988, the wishes of the patient prevail. If there is no certificate, and the medical practitioner considers treatment to be in the best interests of the patient, the practitioner may give notice to the public advocate and treatment will be given.[26] Treatment includes medical and dental care. If there is a 'person responsible' for the patient and that person does not agree to the proposed treatment then the medical practitioner must give a notice (called a 42M) to that person and the public advocate.[27] The notice states that there has been no consent provided by the 'person responsible' and unless there is an application to oppose the decision made to the Victorian Civil and Administrative Tribunal (VCAT) within 7 days, the practitioner may provide the treatment. If the 'person responsible' responds and makes an application to VCAT, then VCAT must make a ruling as to whether treatment will proceed or not. (See the guardianship and administration flowchart in the appendices at the end of the book.)

Enduring power of guardianship

The changes to the legislation in Victoria and Tasmania[28] have established the ability of a competent adult (the donor) to appoint a guardian. The guardian acts on behalf of the donor when the donor is no longer able to make reasonable decisions about matters including medical treatment, accommodation, access to services and other non-financial personal decisions. In Victoria, the guardian's scope of decision-making is wider than that of an enduring power of attorney medical treatment. Moreover, should a donor have appointed an agent and a guardian, both have the ability to make decisions in relation to medical treatment. The enduring guardian can also make lifestyle decisions. The legislation, however, has foreseen the potential for conflict. Should there be disagreement between the two appointed individuals, the decision of the agent, appointed pursuant to the enduring power of attorney medical treatment, will take priority.

DISTINGUISHING SUICIDE AND EUTHANASIA WITH REFUSAL OF TREATMENT AND END OF LIFE DECISIONS

There may be some confusion as to whether a patient's refusal decision can be considered suicide or amount to euthanasia. The common law elements of *suicide require that a person who intends to commit suicide must deliberately intend to kill himself/herself, and at the same time, must cause their own death.* Given that patients have a common law and statutory right in most jurisdictions to refuse treatment, it can be clearly argued that a patient who suffers a serious illness and makes a decision to refuse therapy is not committing suicide. Conversely, should a medical practitioner consider that a patient may attempt suicide, five jurisdictions have made provision in their crimes legislation relating to this area. The legislation provides that it is not an assault or battery to restrain or attempt to prevent a person from committing suicide.[29] The expected practice for health professionals in Australia is to provide emergency treatment to preserve life.

The word '*euthanasia' is not a word recognised in law*; there is no crime of euthanasia. The word loosely means 'good death' and while the definition of euthanasia can be broadly interpreted, the word has been described in varying contexts. Euthanasia has been used to describe the death of a person when disconnected from a life support machine (involuntary euthanasia). Conversely the term has been used where a competent patient wishes to be assisted to die (voluntary euthanasia). The term should also be distinguished from homicide. For example, where medical care is provided, such as the administration of large doses of morphine, the principle of 'double effect' has been accepted by the courts. The reasoning is as follows: while the large doses of analgesia may shorten the patient's life, the actions of the medical practitioner are to relieve the patient's pain and suffering, hence the 'double effect' of the practitioner's action. The courts recognise that it is the intention of the practitioner that must be distinguished and where it is to relieve pain and suffering it will not amount to the crime of homicide. The use of the word 'euthanasia' in the context of current healthcare practices should be avoided as it creates confusion.

NOT FOR RESUSCITATION ORDERS

Should a patient suffer collapse requiring cardio-pulmonary resuscitation the *not for resuscitation (NFR) order signifies that resuscitation will not be commenced* by the healthcare team. Not for resuscitation and do not resuscitate (DNR) or no-cardio-pulmonary resuscitation (No CPR) orders usually become relevant in situations in which a patient's condition is unlikely to improve and is considered to be clinically futile. This has traditionally been a decision made by the treating medical practitioners. However, with the existing recognition of advance directives the not for resuscitation decision can also be viewed as a patient or attorney's decision to refuse treatment. Therefore, the decision may be a medical one where the burden of resuscitation for the patient outweighs the benefits or likelihood of success, or it may be that the patient with a chronic or terminal illness wishes to address this decision as part of an advance directive. This requires the often difficult conversation with the patient or patient's proxy, regarding future care and expectations in order to reach some clear decision. Regardless of who generates the decision, *wherever possible it is desirable that a NFR order be based on a shared perception and understanding of what amounts to a benefit worth pursuing.*[30] When considering who is involved in making the decision, it follows that this should comply with the law of consent. Therefore, the patient or attorney should be involved in making the decision, or at least informed when the medical team believe that resuscitation is futile.

The following issues should be addressed and documented in the patient notes:

- a brief statement regarding competence or incompetence of the patient
- who was involved in the decision, that is, the patient or the patient's substituted decision-maker and any others included such as family and health team members
- a description of the discussion around the decision, including the reasons and wishes of the patient (wherever possible)
- where the patient or substitute decision-maker is not involved in the decision, the reason/s should be recorded
- the precise scope of the order.

Many healthcare facilities have criteria clearly listed and incorporated into policies and any order should be reviewed regularly. Covert practices such as abbreviations and symbols used to denote the order can create confusion and brevity can also be problematic. Australian jurisdictions that have enacted legislative frameworks in relation to advance directives provide some assistance to patients. It is considered that a NFR order is appropriate where it conforms with the patient's or substitute decision-maker's wishes. Table 7.1 provides a summary of the type of treatment an incompetent patient may require and the necessary considerations health professionals should address prior to providing treatment.

Table 7.1 Those who can provide consent for legally incompetent adults

Type of treatment	Consent considerations
Emergency/life-threatening Routine care, includes non-intrusive examination	No consent required.
All other care minor/ major	• Has the patient specified treatment according to the relevant legislative framework? Has an agent/guardian been appointed? • Are there any guidelines (e.g. NSW or Tasmanian Health Department)? • Does the guardianship board have a 'person responsible' list to guide health professionals? • If no next-of-kin or relatives in disagreement and healthcare team is uncertain then guardianship board.
*Controversial care, special care or where there is disagreement as to care by family and/or healthcare team.	Guardianship board or court.

*Special or controversial care could include any experimental procedures, sterilisation, termination of pregnancy, and any aversive treatment or withdrawal of life support. Disagreement between family or health carers may be in relation to *any* care provided.

SCENARIO AND ACTIVITY

A patient with a serious illness is admitted to your unit. Once an explanation of his therapy is provided the patient states that he will only provide consent for part of the treatment.

• How might you proceed and what considerations need to be addressed?

REVIEW QUESTIONS

To ensure that you have identified and understood the key points of this chapter please answer the following questions.

1 Does the common law allow patients to refuse treatment even if they might die?

2 Can treatment be withdrawn from incompetent patients? What considerations should be addressed?

3 Select and compare two legislative frameworks allowing patients to provide advance directives. Discuss which framework you find more accommodating from a clinician's viewpoint.

4 Is there a difference between palliative care and medical treatment?

5 Who may be a 'person responsible' and what role do they play in patient care?

6 What is the difference between suicide and euthanasia?

7 Outline the key issues necessary before a guardianship board can appoint a guardian and discuss the relevant considerations regarding the suitability of the potential guardian.

8 A decision has been made that a patient should be not for resuscitation. Describe the issues which should be addressed and documented in the patient file.

Further reading

Biegler, P, Cameron, S, Savuiescu, J, Skene, L, 'Determining the validity of advance directives' (2000) *Medical Journal of Australia* 172:545.

Cavell, R, 'Not for resuscitation orders: the medical, legal and ethical rationale behind letting patients die' (2008) 16 *Journal of Law and Medicine* 305.

Freckelton, I, 'Withdrawal of Life Support: The 'Persistent Vegetative State' Conundrum' (1993) 1 *Journal of Law and Medicine* 35.

Kerridge, I, Lowe, M, Stewart, C, *Ethics and law for health professions*, Federation Press, Sydney 2009.

Lanham, D, 'Withdrawal of artificial feeding from patients with PVS' (1994) 6(1) *Current Issues in Criminal Justice* 135.

Linden, S, 'Refusal of medical treatment — clarification of rights and responsibilities' (2003) 11(6) *Australian Health Law Bulletin* 61–4.

Manning, J, 'Autonomy and the Competent Patient's Right to Refuse Life-prolonging Medical Treatment — Again' (2002) 10 *Journal of Law and Medicine* 239.

Skene, L, 'When can doctors treat patients who cannot or will not consent?' (1997) 23(1) *Monash University Law* Review 77–91.

Stewart, C, 'Who decides when I can die? Problems concerning proxy decisions to forgo medical treatment' (1997) 4(4) *Journal of Law and Medicine* 386.

Thiagarajan, M Savalescu, J, Skene, L (2007) 'Deciding about life-support: A perspective on the ethical and legal framework in the United Kingdom and Australia' 14 *Journal of Law and Medicine* 583.

Winn, G 'Changes to the law of guardianship and administration' (2000) February, *Law Institute Journal of Victoria* 95.

Endnotes

1 (2009) WASC 229.
2 [1993] 1 All ER 821.
3 *Messiha v South East Health* [2004] NSWSC 1061 at 1072.
4 *In the Matter of an Application by John William Herrington for a Declaration concerning Rosalie Anne King and Austin Health* (2007) VSC, 151.
5 Ibid at 163.
6 (2007) 21 NTLR 197.
7 An example of the common law advance directive being incorporated into the legislation is seen in Victoria's Schedule One — Refusal of a Competent Person, Medical Treatment Act 1988. However, in Victoria because there is also a mechanism to appoint a medical power of attorney the Schedule One document appears to be valid only when the patient remains competent.
8 Griffiths, D, *Agreeing on a way forward: Management of patient refusal of treatment decisions in Victorian hospitals*, (2008) PhD Thesis, Victoria University, Melbourne.

9   *Qumsieh v Guardianship and Administration Board* [1998] VSCA
    45 Unreported 17 Sept, 1998. A 21-year-old Jehovah's Witness
    suffered a severe haemorrhage, becoming unconscious, following
    the delivery of her baby, her condition declined and she required
    blood transfusions. She had written an advance medical directive
    indicating her wish to refuse blood but had failed to comply
    with either mechanism of the Victorian legislation, in that she
    had not successfully appointed an agent or completed a refusal
    of treatment certificate. A guardian was subsequently appointed
    and she was given the transfusions. Following her recovery
    she sought to challenge the appointment and decisions of the
    guardian, however the court concentrated predominantly on
    whether the appointment by the guardianship board was within
    the meaning of the guardianship legislation. The court held that
    the appointment was lawful. The court did not address the fact
    that Mrs Qumsieh had indicated a refusal of blood products. This
    suggests that at the very least the legislative mechanisms must be
    utilised if patients wish them to be relied upon.
10 *Gardner. Re BWV* [2003] VSC 173 (29 May 2003).
11 Ibid at 76.
12 Ibid at 78.
13 Ibid at 80.
14 Ibid at 81.
15 Ibid at 85.
16 Ibid at 86.
17 NSW Health, *Guidelines for end-of-life care and decision making*
    (2005). Online. Available: www.cena.org.au/nsw/end_of_life_
    guidelines.pdf (accessed 22 July 2010).
18 Austin Health (2004). *Respecting Patient Choices Program.* Online.
    Available: www.austin.org.au/Content.aspx?topicID=416 (accessed
    15 June 2010).
19 Lee, M, Heland, M, Romios, P, Naksook, C, Silvester, W
    'Respecting patient choices: Advance planning to improve
    patient care at Austin health' (2003) *Health Issues*, 77, 23–6.
20 [2007] NSW GT 1.
21 [2006] QGAAT 26.
22 [2004] WAGAB 2.
23 Lord Goff in *Re F (Mental Patient: Sterilisation)* [1990] 2 AC 1 at 75.
24 *Department of Health and Community Services NT v JWB* (1992)
    175 CLR 218 at 246.

25 Commenced operation 1 January 2000.

26 Guardianship and Administration Act 1986 (Vic) s 42K.

27 Section 42m establishes the notice.

28 Guardianship and Administration (Amendment) Act 1997 (Vic); Guardian and Administration Act 1995 (Tas).

29 Crimes Act 1900 (ACT), s 18; Crimes Act 1900 (NSW); Criminal Code Amendment Act 1996 (NT), s 574B; Crimes Law Consolidation Act 1935 (SA), s 13(a); Crimes Act 1958 (Vic), s 463B.

30 Kerridge, I, Mitchell, K, Myser, C, 'The decision to withhold resuscitation in Australia: problems, hospital policy and legal uncertainty' (1994) 2 *Journal of Law and Medicine* 127.

8

Fertility and reproductive technology

LEARNING OBJECTIVES

This chapter aims to introduce you to the key areas relating to reproduction and fertility. While reading this chapter you should focus on:

- discussing the various foci of abortion law
- explaining the rights of the mother, father and foetus in the termination of pregnancy
- identifying when a medical practitioner may lawfully terminate a pregnancy
- differentiating between the laws designed to protect foetuses
- highlighting the Australian courts' approach to unwanted births and children born severely damaged as a result of misdiagnosis
- outlining how the laws in Australia deal with reproductive technology, including parentage and cloning
- explaining the legal implications of surrogacy for all parties involved.

INTRODUCTION

This chapter examines activities concerned with fertility and reproduction and highlights the diverse legal requirements associated with these areas. These areas of the law may not necessarily impact on the daily practice of medical practitioners, however, an overview of the current regulatory frameworks may assist in a general understanding. The chapter commences with the laws relating to abortion where historical underpinnings reveal a 19th century approach to regulation and the emergence of considerable differences between state and territory laws. Also included is an overview of wrongful life claims, and then a brief outline of the key areas involving reproductive technologies.

ABORTION

Medical abortions are obtainable throughout Australia, however until quite recently, in all jurisdictions, the criminal law has sought to regulate this area. An abortion can be defined as the untimely expulsion (or removal) of the foetus from the uterus. Abortion can be either *spontaneous*, commonly referred to as 'miscarriage', or it can be artificially induced, commonly referred to as '*a medical abortion*' or '*termination of pregnancy*'. It is the artificial intervention, using instruments or drugs, which gives rise to the involvement of the criminal law, when an abortion is considered to be 'unlawful'.

Pre-reform — early English law

Australian law was traditionally based on the English Acts, the first of which in 1803 made abortion after 'quickening' a crime.[1] 'Quickening' is the first movements of the foetus felt by the mother (from approximately 16 weeks gestation). The 1803 Act made it an offence for any person 'unlawfully to administer any noxious and destructive substance or thing with intent to procure the miscarriage of a woman quick with child'. The intention of this Act was to protect the as yet unborn foetus. The later 1929 Act made the intentional, wilful destruction of the life of a child, capable of being born alive, a felony.[2] This is known as the offence of *child destruction* which acts to protect the foetus during birth. These two offences potentially overlap. The 1929 Act also introduced justification for a termination of pregnancy for the purpose of preserving the life of the mother. Hence the differentiation of a lawful or unlawful abortion.

The significant case which established the principles governing abortion is the English case of *R v Bourne*.[3] MacNaghten J considered that the meaning of the word 'unlawful' in the legislation was of vital and decisive significance. His Honour was influenced by the defence of 'necessity', used in child destruction cases where the head of the foetus was collapsed to save the mother's life.[4] His reasoning was that to procure an abortion was defensible if it was necessary to save the life of the mother, 'the unborn child must not be destroyed except for the purpose of preserving the yet more precious life of the mother'.[5] When MacNaghten J considered the life of the mother, he went beyond the physical fact of life and included its quality. Thus, in this case the medical practitioner undertaking the abortion was acting 'lawfully' if he acted with an honest belief that the intervention was to preserve the life of the mother. Furthermore, the concept of 'life of the mother' included both the mental and physical health of the woman. The law clearly made the decision a medical one.

The Australian context

The laws in several states and territories are still based on the old English laws.[6] The framing of criminal legislation to make abortion unlawful led the courts to develop specific criteria in the late 1960s and early 70s to enable a '*lawful*' *abortion*. For example, in Victoria in *R v Davidson*[7] the court ruled that for an abortion to be lawful there were two criteria: first, the accused (the doctor) must have honestly believed on reasonable grounds, that the act was *necessary to preserve the woman from a serious danger to her life or physical or mental health* (not merely being the normal dangers of pregnancy and childbirth) and, second, in the circumstances *the termination was not out of proportion to the danger to be averted*. This decision was accepted and extended in the New South Wales case of *R v Wald*[8] where the court stated that it would be for the 'jury to decide whether there existed … any economic, social or medical grounds or reason … which an accused could honestly and reasonably believe would result in a serious danger to (the woman's) physical or mental health'.[9] Commentators suggest that the role of the law is to place obstacles in the way of women seeking an abortion, making doctors the key gatekeepers to decide the risks.[10]

In South Australia[11] and the Northern Territory[12] the legislation has given meaning to the word 'unlawful' by establishing the circumstances in which an abortion is lawful. In both jurisdictions, before an abortion can be undertaken, two doctors must have examined the woman and agreed that to continue with the pregnancy would involve greater risk to her physical or mental health than to terminate it, or that the child would suffer such physical or mental abnormalities so as to be seriously handicapped. When making the assessment the doctors may consider the mother's actual or reasonably foreseeable environment. In South Australia there is a requirement that the woman must have been a resident of that state for at least 2 months. The South Australian legislation also provides a maximum sentence of life imprisonment for the termination of a pregnancy where the foetus is capable of being born alive, set at 28 weeks gestation.[13] However, this provision does not apply when the abortion is necessary to save the life of the mother. Hence, the statutory requirements are not applicable in an emergency.

New South Wales relies on the ruling in *Wald's* case, mentioned above. The law was re-stated in *R v Sood* [2006],[14] a termination occurring between 22–24 weeks gestation. Dr Sood failed to physically examine the woman, ask the patient her reasons for wanting the abortion or discuss possible alternatives with the patient. The medical practitioner told the patient that bleeding more heavily, and for a longer period, were the only likely complications. The doctor inserted a prostaglandin tablet into the patient's vagina, provided her with further tablets and instructed her to take them orally. The patient was directed to return the next day for the procedure. The woman went into labour that night and gave birth to the child in the toilet. The court held that the person must honestly believe on reasonable grounds that the termination was necessary to protect the mother from a serious danger to her life. It was held that the medical practitioner had not made adequate enquiries as to the need for the abortion; had she done so, she would be able to form a reasonable belief about the associated risks. The medical practitioner was convicted for an unlawful abortion.

In the Northern Territory there is a time frame established, of no more than 14 weeks gestation, when an abortion may be undertaken. This time limit is extended to 23 weeks gestation if the doctor believes in good faith that an abortion is 'immediately necessary' to prevent grave injury to the woman's physical or mental health. Moreover, if the woman's life is in immediate danger, then no time limit applies. The Northern Territory is the only jurisdiction to impose a time limit on when a pregnancy may be terminated. Where the woman is under 16 years of age the consent of the guardian is required. The Northern Territory and South Australian legislation specifically allow a pregnancy to be terminated when the foetus has a serious hereditary disorder.[15]

In Queensland and Tasmania abortion will be permitted in particular circumstances. For example, in Tasmania the Criminal Code Act 1924 was amended in 2001; section 164 makes it clear that a 'legally justified' abortion is not a crime.[16] This section requires two tests to be satisfied: (1) two medical practitioners must certify in writing that the continuation of the pregnancy would involve greater risk of injury to the physical or mental health of the woman, than if the pregnancy were terminated; and (2) the woman must provide informed consent, unless it is impracticable to do so.

The Queensland Criminal Code 1899 provides that:

a person is not criminally responsible for performing in good faith and with reasonable care and skill, a surgical operation upon any person for his [or her] benefit, or upon any unborn child for the preservation of the mother's life .[17]

In *R v Bayliss and Cullen*[18] this section has been interpreted in accordance with the Menhennitt judgment in Victoria in the case of *R v Davidson* [1969] VR 667. However, section 282 of the Criminal Code considers the use of surgical intervention, and with the introduction of drugs to induce abortion, the law was arguably unclear. In 2009 in Queensland criminal charges were pursued against a young couple for obtaining the drug Misoprostol (a drug used in conjunction with RU486) to bring about a medical abortion. It was alleged that the woman performed an abortion by administering the drug to herself and that she was aided and assisted by her partner. This produced significant public debate regarding the abortion laws in Queensland. Section 282 of the Criminal Code was amended in 2009 to extend the exemption for doctors to perform terminations using abortion drugs. The revised section now reads:

> A person is not criminally responsible for performing or providing, in good faith and with reasonable care and skill a surgical operation on or medical treatment of:
>
> a) a person or unborn child for the patient's benefit; or
>
> b) a person or unborn child to preserve the mother's life;
>
> if performing the operation or providing the medical treatment is reasonable, having regard to the patient's state at the time and to all circumstances of the case.

In Western Australia abortion is illegal under the Criminal Code (WA), s 199, unless it is performed by a medical practitioner in accordance with s 334 of the Health Act 1911. It is not an offence if the medical practitioner carries out the abortion in good faith and where:

1 the woman has given consent; or

2 the woman will suffer serious personal, family or social consequences if the abortion is not performed; or

3 the woman will suffer serious physical or mental health problems if the abortion is not performed; or

4 the pregnancy is causing serious danger to her physical or mental health.

Wherever possible the woman must provide 'informed consent' unless, in the latter two situations (listed above), it is impractical for her to do so. Informed consent is defined as 'freely given consent' where a second medical practitioner has provided counselling regarding the medical risks of both termination and continuation of the pregnancy. If the gestation is more than 20 weeks then two doctors, specifically designated by the Health Minister, must agree that the mother or foetus has a severe medical condition justifying the termination. In addition, the procedure must be undertaken in an approved health facility. If the woman is less than 16 years of age, and therefore a minor, she has no legal capacity to provide an 'informed consent'. In this situation the woman's custodial parent must be informed and offered the opportunity to be included in the process.

Decriminalisation of the law

In 2002 the Australian Capital Territory introduced the Crimes (Abolition of Abortion) Act which removed the crime of abortion from the criminal law. The Health Act 1993 (ACT) requires that only a medical practitioner may carry out an abortion and that it must be carried out in an approved facility.[19] The Act also makes provision for a health professional to refrain from performing or assisting in the performance of an abortion.[20] Likewise, Victoria introduced the Abortion Law Reform Act 2008 which repeals abortion as a crime from the Crimes Act 1958. The new legislation allows a medical practitioner to perform an abortion on a woman who is not more than 24 weeks pregnant.[21] If the woman is more than 24 weeks pregnant the Act requires two criteria to be fulfilled: (1) the medical practitioner reasonably believes that the abortion is appropriate in all the circumstances; and (2) the medical practitioner has consulted at least one other medical practitioner who also reasonably believes the abortion appropriate. In considering whether the abortion is appropriate the doctors may consider all of the relevant circumstances and the woman's current and future physical, psychological and social attributes.[22] The Act also specifies the obligations of a health practitioner who has a conscientious objection.[23]

The foetus and father

Before a foetus is born alive it has no legal rights and is generally considered to be part of the mother's body. Legal recognition is granted when the foetus is 'born alive' which requires some indication of life, such as a pulse in the umbilical cord, movement, coughing or breathing. The child can still be attached to the umbilical cord and be considered alive. If the child is born alive but later dies from a prenatal injury the criminal law may be invoked against the person who caused the injury.[24]

In the case of *A-G (ex rel Kerr) v T*[25] the biological father sought a restraining injunction to prevent the woman with whom he had conceived a child from seeking an abortion. The court denied the injunction and applied the principles established in an English case,[26] using the guiding principles that the father and foetus have no identifiable rights.[27] The law is clear in relation to the rights of the foetus and the father. *There is no rule in common law or statute which gives the father the right to be consulted about a termination.* Furthermore, the courts distinguish the father's relationship in terms of biological and not marital status.

Child destruction (late termination of pregnancy)

The criminal offence of child destruction exists in most Australian jurisdictions. The offence *involves the deliberate destruction of the foetus that is capable of being born alive.* In the Northern Territory an offence exists for killing an unborn child, or for preventing a birth, where a person is about to be delivered of a child.[28] Western Australia, the Australian Capital Territory and the Queensland Criminal Code also make it an offence to 'stop the child being born alive'.[29] In South Australia the separate offence of 'child destruction' is committed when a person 'destroys the life of a child capable of being born alive, by any wilful act, or unlawfully causing such child to die'.[30] Tasmania and the Northern Territory also have legislation in this area.[31] New South Wales and Victoria do not have a specific offence of child destruction. There are no judicial rulings on child destruction cases in Australia.

The legislation emphasises the deliberate intention of the person undertaking the act of 'destruction'. The issue of a child capable of being 'born alive' is relevant. The presumption is that the gestational age of a foetus capable of being born alive is 28 weeks or more. There is no judicial interpretation in Australia hence the courts may refer to the English courts for guidance.[32] The issue of the precise age a foetus is capable of being born alive has not been resolved. As Skene[33] argues, the gestational age at which the death of a stillborn must be registered is a significant stage for the purposes of establishing the offence. In Victoria, for example, a medical practitioner must notify the Registrar of Births, Deaths and Marriages if a child dies after the 20th week of gestation or weighs 400 grams or more.[34]

Late term abortion

In the *Royal Women's Hospital v Medical Practitioners* Board (Vic)[35] medical practitioners became the *focus of professional misconduct allegations* after they were involved in a 31-week termination of a pregnancy. The woman was referred to the Women's Hospital after her foetus was diagnosed with skeletal dysplasia (dwarfism). This diagnosis was confirmed after further testing. Following counselling, a psychiatrist recommended that termination take place to preserve the health of the mother, several medical practitioners who had also been consulted, concurred. The board cleared the medical practitioners of unprofessional conduct and stated that it was not the role of the board to determine whether specific clinical decisions were appropriate, but whether the conduct of the medical practitioners in making that decision had been professional. No criminal charges were brought against the medical practitioners.

'Wrongful' conception, life and birth claims

Practices relating to the sterilisation, diagnosis and advice provided in relation to pregnancy and foetal abnormality, have led to three groups of actions in negligence (refer to Chapter 5, Negligence). The actions can be grouped as follows.

1 Wrongful conception — action by a parent or parents to recover damages for the birth of an unplanned child

This negligence action could occur, for example, with an unsuccessful sterilisation procedure. The High Court in the case of *Cattanach v Melchior*[36] settled the law in Australia regarding the rights of the parents to recover damages for the unintended birth of a healthy child. The medical practitioner applied a clip to the left fallopian tube, on the mistaken belief the patient had only one tube. The question the High Court was to determine was whether damages were reasonable for the past and future costs of raising the child, not for harm caused by the child's life. By a majority judgment the court held that the costs of raising a healthy, but unwanted child, were recoverable. Following the High Court's decision in this case Queensland, New South Wales and South Australia passed legislation to prevent damages being awarded for the costs of raising a healthy child.

2 Wrongful birth — action by the parent for failing to diagnose a pregnancy

In *CES v Superclinics Australia Pty Ltd*[37] the plaintiff, a single 21-year-old pregnant woman was not correctly diagnosed until she was 19 weeks pregnant, despite her repeated visits to the medical clinic. The woman gave birth to a healthy child and then sought damages for the depression, pain and suffering that the pregnancy and birth had caused, and for the financial loss caused by her confinement and the costs to be incurred of having to raise her child to adulthood. The New South Wales Court of Appeal found that the woman was owed a duty of care and that this had been breached. The majority of the court held that compensation should cover only the confinement, the birth and the costs associated with rearing the child to an age where adoption was possible. The fact the plaintiff had kept the child was her decision, and the defendants had not caused her to take on the child-rearing role to adulthood.[38] This decision was to be challenged in the High Court of Australia; however, the case settled and the chance for the High Court to make a ruling was lost.

3 Wrongful life — action by the child born with disability due to negligent care

The High Court has dismissed claims in two relatively recent cases. In *Harriton v Stephens*[39] the plaintiff claimed damages relating to the circumstances of her birth and life, where she was exposed to the rubella virus in utero. She was subsequently born with hearing and vision impairment, spasticity and mental retardation. It was accepted that the child's mother would have terminated the pregnancy had she been correctly advised of her rubella status and the probable effects on the foetus, and it would not have been unlawful for her to do so.[40] The court accepted that the medical practitioner had erred, but found that there was no duty of care to the foetus. The second case, *Waller v James; Waller v Hoolahan* [41] involved a child conceived using IVF technology, who was born with a genetic clotting disorder which led to the baby suffering a cerebral thrombosis, resulting in permanent brain damage. The High Court had to determine whether a wrongful life action should constitute a recognisable action. The contentious nature that wrongful life claims raise is clear in *Harriton*: how might we compare a rubella-affected existence with the only possible alternative — non-existence? Gleeson[42] argues that a majority of judges in *Harriton* were concerned about the effect a successful action would mean, or indicate, about the value of life with disability and the potential liability of mothers who produce children with disabilities.

REPRODUCTIVE TECHNOLOGY

There are many different procedures utilised by this technology[43] which raise questions relating to when life commences, parentage, experimentation on embryos and confidentiality issues. The following outline provides an overview of the current legal frameworks and, readers will note, ethical guidelines also provide guidance.

Legislative frameworks

Four states have legislated to address the areas of reproductive technologies — South Australia, Western Australia, Victoria and New South Wales. There are similarities in that each state Act has established an authority or an equivalent entity to grant licences to those scientists and medical practitioners wishing to undertake this work. The established authority advises the relevant Minister on matters relating to the various practices including experimental procedures. The requirements and prohibitions for the regulation of fertilisation are incorporated into each states' legislation and associated regulations. For example, in South Australia the Reproductive Technology (Code of Clinical Practice) Regulations 1995 deal with issues of consent, storage, disposal, eligibility criteria and record-keeping. The Code prohibits mixing gametes from different sources or culturing or maintaining an embryo outside the body.

Where there is no legislative framework or the technology falls outside the state legislation the National Health and Medical Research Council (NHMRC) ethical guidelines are utilised. The guidelines address a number of areas affecting practice, including the need for approval of all procedures by an institutional ethics committee and the requirements include the maintenance of registers with data relating to success or failure of procedures, parentage and attempted pregnancies. There should be no commercial component such as the selling of embryos. The Fertility Society of Australia's Reproductive Accreditation Committee also have a code of practice.[44] It is important to note that guidelines and codes of practice may well be examined by the courts but do not have the same status as legislation.

Artificial insemination (AI)

The common law recognises the procedure of donor sperm being introduced into the woman's reproductive system. The regulation focuses on approved or licensed personnel and premises where the procedure occurs. The states with legislation include:

- South Australia — AI services provided free are not regulated. When a fee is involved, the medical practitioner must be registered according to the legislation and must abide by the Code of Ethical Clinical Practice contained in the associated regulations in that state.
- New South Wales — a person providing this service must be registered with the Director-General in that state.
- Victoria — regulates the AI of a woman with sperm that is not from her husband and the procedure must be carried out on licensed premises by an approved medical practitioner.
- Western Australia — as with the other states, a person offering AI services must have a license (or approval) and there is a requirement to comply with the Code of Practice of the Human Reproductive Technology Council.

Cloning

The federal government passed legislation in 2002 relating to human cloning. The Research Involving Embryos Act and the Prohibition of Human Cloning Act were passed to ban human cloning. The Lockhart Committee was appointed in 2005 to consider the legislation and made 54 recommendations, including overturning the ban. Somatic cell nuclear transfer (SCNT), also called 'therapeutic cloning', for research purposes is now permitted in Australia subject to licence from the NHMRC.[45]

Parentage

A woman who gives birth to a child as a result of reproductive procedures is the legal mother of that child. This is regardless of whether donor gametes were used. The woman's husband or de facto is the legal father assuming he is a consenting party. The converse is that those individuals who donated gametes will remain anonymous unless, for example, the infertile couple have family members donating gametes. Regardless of whether the donors are known they will normally have no legal connection with the child.

In *Re Patrick*[46] a mother and her lesbian partner applied to remove orders for contact between a child and his sperm donor father. The court placed significant emphasis on the discussions between the parties prior to conception. The sperm donor argued that he had been intended to be known to the child as a father figure. The court was influenced by the donor's commitment to the conception, there were 27 attempts, and to his ongoing involvement with the child. While it was recognised that their agreement was not binding, Justice Guest stated 'He has at all times ... demonstrated by both sacrifice and concession a sensitive tolerance of a secondary role to the mother and co-parent'.[47] The court ordered that the child continue to have contact with the donor father and that this should increase to include every second week end and half of all school holidays. The court's decision reflected acceptance that the sperm donor was the child's father but was not a parent.

Gametes from a dead parent
This can occur where either parent dies after gametes have been previously taken and frozen, or both parents die when there are pre-existing embryos, or when gamete tissue is taken from a dead parent (e.g. when on life support). Early cases demonstrate the courts have been less inclined to allow removal.[48] In 2005 a woman's application was rejected by a Victorian court to remove sperm with the purpose of becoming pregnant.[49] However, she was successful in having her dead husband's sperm removed and transported to another state, where it was legal to implant.[50] The NHMRC ethical guidelines outline the necessary considerations, indicating that gametes should not be used unless:

- there is clear direction as to use of the gametes
- there is witnessed consent from the donor
- the prospective parent receives counselling about the consequences of such use
- the use of the gametes does not diminish the fulfilment of the rights of any child born.[51]

Surrogacy
Surrogacy occurs when a woman agrees to be inseminated, either artificially or naturally, with the intention the child will be given up, usually to the sperm donor and his partner. The laws regulating

surrogacy have been incorporated into the legislation of those states with reproductive legislation; the remaining states and territories have enacted specific legislation. Commercial surrogacy agreements have been outlawed in the Australian Capital Territory, New South Wales, Queensland, South Australia, Tasmania and Victoria. The Queensland and South Australian legislation also specify that gratuitous surrogacy agreements are illegal.

SCENARIO AND ACTIVITY

Case example – A woman of 31 weeks gestation threatens to kill herself if she does not have an abortion because her foetus has a serious genetic disorder.

- Will this amount to child destruction or possibly an unlawful abortion?

REVIEW QUESTIONS

1 Of the differing laws relating to abortion, which approach do you consider most appropriate and why?

2 What is the role of the medical practitioner and should the law focus on other parties when the decision is made to terminate a pregnancy?

3 What is the difference between the wrongful life claims and should medical practitioners ever be held responsible?

4 How would you approach a homosexual couple who seek your advice, wishing to proceed with a pregnancy from the donated sperm of a friend?

5 What advice can you provide to a couple wishing to engage in a surrogacy agreement?

Further reading

Campbell, J, 'Hatching, unmatching and parental responsibility' (2002) 10(10) *Australian Health Law Bulletin* 101–6.

Chalmers, D, 'Can the law keep up with changes in medical technology and cloning?' (2007) 19(2) LEGALDATE 4-6.

De Crepigny, L. & Savulescu, J, 'Abortion: time to clarify Australia's confusing laws' (2004) *Medical Journal of Australia*, 181(4), 201–3.

Faunce, T, 'The Carhart case and late-term abortions — What's next in Australia?' (2007) 15(1) *Journal of Law and Medicine* 23–31.

Fertility Society of Australia, *Code of Practice for Assisted Reproductive Technology Units*, Reproductive Accreditation Committee, 2008. Online. Available: www.fsa.au.com (accessed 12 January 2010).

Forrester, K, Griffiths, D, *Essentials of Law for Health Professionals*. Elsevier, Sydney, 2010, Chaps 8, 9.

Gleeson, K, 'Bracket creep in Australian abortion indications: When did rubella arrive?' (2007) *Journal of Law and Medicine* 15, 424.

National Health and Medical Research Council (NHMRC), *Ethical Guidelines on the use of Assisted Reproductive Technology in Clinical Practice and Research*, NHMRC 2007. Online. Available: www.nhmrc.gov.au/PUBLICATIONS/synopses/e78syn.htm (accessed 20 January 2010).

Nemes, I, 'Therapeutic cloning in Australia: One small stem from man, one giant leap for mankind' (2008) 16 *Journal of Law and Medicine* 139–60.

Endnotes

1 Miscarriage of Women Act 1803 (UK) and the Infant Life (Preservation) Act 1929 (UK).
2 Infant Life (Preservation) Act 1929 (UK).
3 [1938] 1 KB 687.
4 Ibid at 691.
5 Ibid.
6 Yet the UK Abortion Act 1967 repealed and replaced its antiquated laws. Online. Available: www.btinternet.com/~DEvans_23/legislat.htm (accessed February, 2009).
7 [1969] VR 667.
8 (1971) 3 DCR (NSW) 25.
9 Ibid at 29.
10 De Crepigny, L, Savulescu, J 'Abortion: time to clarify Australia's confusing laws' *Medical Journal of Australia* (2004) 181(4), 201–3.
11 Criminal Law Consolidation Act 1935 (SA) s 82.
12 Criminal Code Act 1983 (NT) s 174.
13 Section 82(1).
14 [2006] NSWSC 1141.
15 Criminal Code Act 1983 (NT), s 174 and the Criminal Law Consolidation Act 1935 (SA) s 82A.

16 Rankin, M, 'Recent developments in Australian abortion law: Tasmania and the Australian capital Territory' (2003) *Monash University Law Review*, 29(2) 316–35.

17 Section 282.

18 (1986) 9 Qld LR 8 at 45.

19 Health Act 1993 (ACT), ss 8, 82.

20 Section 84.

21 Abortion Reform Act 2008 (Vic) s 4.

22 Section 5.

23 Section 8.

24 In *R v F* (1993) 40 NSWLR 245. A child was born prematurely and subsequently died after its mother was involved in a car accident caused by the defendant. The court had to decide whether the child was a 'person' within the meaning of the Crimes Act 1900 (NSW). Justice Grove stated 'the common law has long recognised that where an unborn child receives injuries, is born alive but dies of those antenatal injuries, the perpetrator may suffer criminal liability for homicide …'.

25 [1982] 1 NSWLR 311.

26 *Paton v Trustees of the EPAS* [1978] 2 All ER 987.

27 The same reasoning was applied in *F v F* where the judge considered that to grant an injunction would force the wife to carry and give birth to a baby she clearly did not want. The court pointed out that the fact the foetus would grow in the wife's body and not the husband's, was a relevant factor and should not be overlooked.

28 Criminal Code Act 1983 (NT) s 170.

29 Criminal Code 1913, s 29 (WA); Crimes Act 1900, s 42 (ACT); Criminal Code Act 1995 s 109 (Qld); Criminal Code Act 1899 s 313 (Qld).

30 Criminal Law Consolidation Act 1935 (SA), s 82A.

31 Criminal Code Act 1924 (Tas), s 290 and Criminal Code Act 1983 (NT), s 170.

32 For example, in *C v S* [1987] 1 All ER 1230 the English Court of Appeal held that a foetus born between 18 and 21 weeks' gestation was not capable of being born alive based on the medical advice that the foetus at this stage could not breathe naturally or without the use of artificial ventilation.

33 Skene, L, *Law and Medical Practice*, 2nd edn, LexisNexis Butterworths, Sydney, 2004 at 364.

34 Registration of Births, Deaths and Marriages Act 1996 (Vic) s 4.

35 [2006] VSCA 85.

36 [2003] HCA 38 (16 July 2003).

37 (1995) 38 NSWLR 47.

38 Ibid at 83.

39 (2006) 226 CLR 52.

40 Ibid at 190.

41 (2006) 226 ALR 457.

42 Gleeson, K, 'Bracket creep in Australian abortion indications: When did rubella arrive?' *Journal of Law and Medicine* (2007) 15, 424.

43 These include artificial insemination by donor (AID), in vitro fertilisation (IVF), embryo transfer, gamete intrafallopian transfer (GIFT) and pro-nuclear stage ovum transfer (PROST).

44 Fertility Society of Australia, *Code of Practice for Assisted Reproductive Technology Units*, Reproductive Accreditation Committee, 2008. Online. Available: www.fsa.au.com (accessed 12 January 2010).

45 Prohibition of Human Cloning for Reproduction and the Regulation of Human Embryo Research Amendment Act 2006 (Cth).

46 (2002) 28 Fam LR 579.

47 Ibid at para [275].

48 *MAW v WAHS* (2000) 49 NSWLR 231 and *In the matter of Gray* (2000) QSC 390.

49 [2005] VSC 180.

50 *YZ v Infertility Treatment Authority (General)* [2005] VCAT 2655, 20 December 2005.

51 National Health and Medical research Council (NHMRC) *Ethical Guidelines on the use of Assisted Reproductive Technology in Clinical Practice and Research*, NHMRC, 2007. Online. Available: www.nhmrc.gov.au/PUBLICATIONS/synopses/e78syn.htm (accessed 20 January 2010).

9

Drugs and poisons

LEARNING OBJECTIVES

This chapter aims to introduce you to the key areas regulating the therapeutic use of drugs and poisons. While reading this chapter you should focus on:
- describing the focus of the legislation at the federal level
- explaining the manner in which drugs and poisons are scheduled
- discussing the requirements the state and territory legislation has on the practice of medical practitioners
- identifying the role of medical practitioners in relation to the incorporation of complimentary medicine.

INTRODUCTION

Due to the significant development and involvement of pharmaceuticals in the delivery of healthcare since the 1940s, successive governments have sought to control access to certain medicines by members of the broader community. The manufacture and supply of pharmaceuticals is a multi-billion dollar industry which is heavily regulated in Australia. Legislation and policy exist at federal, state and territory spheres and serve to control and influence access, cost and use of medicines, and therefore the practice requirements of medical practitioners.

FEDERAL INFLUENCE AND REGULATION

Several controls exist at the federal level of government designed to organise and manage the use of drugs and poisons in the community, including their use in the delivery of healthcare. An overview of the policy frameworks is necessary to understand the policy and legislative provisions in place in Australia.

Policy background

In the 1990s a review of medication use and waste led to the formulation of the National Medicines Policy (NMP) in 2000.[1] The NMP is administered within the Commonwealth Department of

Health and Ageing to meet medication and related service needs and has four central objectives, including:

1   timely access to medicines that are both required and affordable
2   medicines that meet appropriate standards of quality, safety and efficacy
3   quality use of medicines (QUM)
4   maintaining a responsible and viable medicines industry.

The aim of the policy is to meet the medicine needs of the Australian population, focusing on health outcomes and the financial costs.

The Australian Pharmaceutical Advisory Council (APAC), established in 1991, comprises representatives of key professional groups including members drawn from medicine, nursing and pharmacy, and members from the pharmaceutical industry and consumer organisations. APAC is responsible for identifying and considering issues and advising the federal government on a range of pharmaceutical policy matters in association with the implementation of the NMP. In addition, the Pharmaceutical Health and Rational Use of Medicines (PHARM) Committee is a multi-disciplinary group that is responsible for reviewing the implementation of QUM in Australia. The national strategy for QUM emerged in 2002 to compliment the NMP.

Legislation

The Therapeutics Goods Act 1989 establishes the Therapeutic Goods Administration (TGA) which regulates the licensing, manufacture and distribution of therapeutic substances. The TGA engages in a range of assessment and monitoring activities to ensure that therapeutic substances and goods available in Australia are of an acceptable standard. A substance for which a therapeutic claim is made must be entered on the Australian Register of Therapeutic Goods (ARTG) before it can be supplied in Australia. 'Therapeutic substances' include any product used in the prevention, diagnosis, cure and alleviation of disease. The Act also embraces vitamins, minerals and herbal remedies. Substances that are 'registered' on the ARTG, including prescription medicines, must have a demonstrated quality and safety. Substances classed as 'listed' goods, includes vitamins and must also have demonstrated quality and safety. Complimentary medicines can be either 'registered' or 'listed', this is dependant on the medicines constituents. The Act imposes standards on corporations manufacturing therapeutic goods, including those who export, import and manufacture therapeutic goods. This is achieved by the provision of licences. Licensed companies are monitored to ensure their operations comply with international standards in the

manufacture of the products; hence the premises and actual process
of manufacture are strictly regulated.

The Therapeutic Goods Regulations 1990 (Cth) set out provisions
for providing medication information to patients, called Consumer
Medication Information (CMI). The information is manufacturer
produced and provides a useful reference for practitioners when
discussing medication. Pharmacists are paid for the provision of
CMIs and there are guidelines directed at pharmacists, detailing these
requirements.[2]

National Drugs and Poisons Schedule Committee (NDPSC)

In 1999, the federal government established the National Drugs and
Poisons Schedule Committee (NDPSC), pursuant to section 52B of
the Therapeutics Goods Act 1989 (Cth). The NDPSC consists of state
and territory government members and other persons appointed by the
Health Minister such as technical experts and representatives of various
sectional interests. The function of the committee is to classify substances
(drugs and poisons) into schedules and to provide advice to all Australian
governments in relation to policies affecting the advertising, labelling and
packaging of substances. *Factors the committee must consider when classifying
and scheduling substances include the potential danger, toxicity of the drug, and
the risks or benefit of each substance.* All state and territory legislation now
adopts the committee's decisions into their individual jurisdictions,
although most state and territory legislation has the ability to vary
a scheduling classification for any poison should the relevant Health
Minister decide not to adopt a recommendation of the committee.[3]
Medicines scheduled as 2 and 3 are evaluated as low-risk medication
and those scheduled as 4, 8 or 9 are considered high-risk medication.
The schedules and some additional comments follow.

Schedule 1 — **poisons of plant origin** of such danger to life
 as to warrant supply only from medical practitioners, nurse
 practitioners authorised under s 23(2)(e), pharmaceutical
 chemists, or veterinary surgeons. There are currently no
 scheduled poisons in this category.

Schedule 2 — **poisons for therapeutic use that should be
 available to the public** from pharmacies, or if there is no
 pharmacy service available from persons licensed to sell Schedule 2
 poisons. These drugs do not require a prescription and are often sold
 direct to the public. Examples include paracetamol and aspirin in
 tablet form.

Schedule 3 — **poisons for therapeutic use that are dangerous
 or are so liable to abuse** as to warrant their availability to

the public being restricted to supply by medical practitioners, pharmaceutical chemists, dentists or veterinary surgeons. This group of poisons may be required for use urgently so their supply only on prescription from a limited group of prescribers may cause hardship. Hence, pharmacists can supply these poisons without a prescription. Examples include salbutamol aerosol inhalers and insulin.

Schedule 4 — **poisons that should, in the public interest, be restricted to prescription** or supply by a medical practitioner, nurse practitioner authorised under s 23(2)(e), dentist or veterinary surgeon together with substances intended for therapeutic use, the safety or efficacy of which requires further evaluation. The majority of medications administered to patients in the healthcare arena belong to this schedule. For example, drugs including antibiotics, anaesthetics, some antidepressants, anticonvulsants, antihypertensives and chemotherapeutic drugs are included in this schedule.

Schedule 5 — **poisons of a hazardous nature** which are available to the public, but which are **potentially dangerous and require caution** in handling, storage and use. This group includes many domestic poisons such as kerosene, methylated spirits and ammonia.

Schedule 6 — **poisons that are available to the public but are more hazardous or poisonous in nature than those in schedule 5**. Poisons in this schedule are generally used for agricultural and industrial purposes and include formaldehyde and cyanide.

Schedule 7 — **poisons which require special precautions** in their manufacture, handling, storage or use, or require special individual regulations regarding labelling or availability. Substances such as arsenic, strychnine and thalidomide are included in this group.

Schedule 8 — **poisons to which the restrictions recommended for drugs of dependence** by the 1980 Australian Royal Commission of Inquiry into Drugs should apply. This group includes drugs which are addiction-producing or potentially addiction-producing. The more common drugs include cocaine, codeine (except when it is in a different form and included in another schedule such as Schedule 2 or Schedule 4), methadone, morphine and pethidine.

Schedule 9 — **poisons which are drugs of abuse**, the manufacture, possession, sale or use of which should be prohibited by law except for amounts which may be necessary for educational, experimental or research purpose conducted with the approval of the Commonwealth or state/territory authorities.

PHARMACEUTICAL BENEFITS SCHEME (PBS)

The PBS is a significant federally funded scheme to enable patients to access low-priced medication, where the federal government subsidises the cost of numerous medicines. The scheme has been in existence for more than 60 years, when medicines were mass produced post World War II and governments embraced the notion that such substances should be available to all patients, not just those who had the ability to pay. Current provisions governing the operations of the PBS are embodied in Part VII of the National Health Act 1953 together with the National Health (Pharmaceutical Benefits) Regulations 1960 made under the Act. The scheme provides for approximately 80% of prescriptions dispensed in Australia. If a medication is not listed on the PBS, patients bear the total cost of the drug. As the type and variety of new medication has continued to expand, the cost of the PBS has been escalating in recent years. From 1 January 2010, patients pay up to $33.30 for most PBS medicines or $5.40 if they have a concession card. The PBS covered around 181 million prescriptions in the year to June 2009. This represents about eight prescriptions per person in Australia for the year. The cost of the PBS is currently around $7.7 billion per year.[4] The Pharmaceutical Benefits Advisory Committee advises the Federal Minister for Health and Ageing which medications should be subsidised by the PBS. This has generated debate regarding the ability and desire of the federal government to continue to fund the PBS in its current form.

STATE AND TERRITORY REGULATION

Policy

In addition to policy initiatives at the federal level, the requirements of practice are sometimes guided by the respective state and territory health departments, who administer the legislation. Policies will be taken into account should a medical practitioner injure a patient as a result of adverse drug use. Most professional organisations and regulatory authorities also have guiding policy statements in relation to drug administration. It is the responsibility of the medical practitioner to be aware of the guiding policies. At times, the policies are more prescriptively written than the law demands, particularly employer policies. For example, in many jurisdictions, Schedule 2 medicines do not require a written prescription although many hospital policies will require all medicines to be ordered by a medical practitioner and a record kept. This enables verification of all medicines given to the patient while in hospital. By recording all Schedule 2 medicines, the hospital can keep track of precisely when and where the Schedule 2 medicines are used.

Legislation

Legislation exists in all states and territories and it is this legislation which influences the daily practice of the health professionals. The legislation in each state and territory varies; however, there are some basic similarities. The Acts set out broad expectations including labelling requirements, identification of who may prescribe, and those professional groups who may legally supply and administer specified drugs, wholesaling requirements and the criminal aspects of drug misuse. The regulations generally deal in more detail with the day-to-day requirements of drug control such as administration, requirements of a valid prescription, storage requirements and the keeping of records. Definitions appear in both the Acts and the regulations. Table 9.1 identifies the relevant legislation in each jurisdiction.

Table 9.1 State and territory poisons legislation		
State or territory	**Act**	**Regulation**
Australian Capital Territory	Medicines, Poisons and Therapeutics Goods Act 2008	Medicines, Poisons and Therapeutics Goods Regulation 2008
New South Wales	Poisons and Therapeutics Goods Act 1996	Poisons and Therapeutics Goods Regulation 2008
Northern Territory	Poisons and Dangerous Drugs Act 1983	Poisons and Dangerous Drugs Regulations 1985
Queensland	Health Act 1937	Health (Drugs and Poisons) Regulation 1996
South Australia	Controlled Substances Act 1984	Controlled Substances (Poisons) Regulations 1996
Tasmania	Poisons Act 1971	Poisons Regulations 2002
Victoria	Drug Poisons and Controlled Substances Act 1981	Drug Poisons and Controlled Substances Regulations 2006
Western Australia	Poisons Act 1964	Poisons Regulation 1965

Definitions

The legislation in all jurisdictions provides a number of definitions to assist in the interpretation of the obligations of various health professionals. The definitions vary in each jurisdiction although the focus is associated with the criminal aspects of the legislation as well as facets of healthcare delivery. Hence, the words '*possession*', '*procure*' and '*supply*' have particular meanings. 'Possession' of a substance includes custody or control over the substance and 'supply' means to provide, give or deliver, whether or not for payment or reward. To 'supply' a substance in the Australian Capital Territory, Queensland, Victoria and Western Australia does not include the administration of the substance, while in New South Wales, the Northern Territory and Tasmania it does. The South Australian legislative definition of 'supply' includes provide, distribute, barter or exchange a substance. The definitions can delineate practice which is legal and illegal and for this reason practitioners must be aware of the meanings pertinent to their particular jurisdiction. The poisons legislation can be located on every state and territory government website.

There can be a *mistaken belief that the legislation is detailed* with respect to the specific requirements of drug administration, standing orders and protocols. These areas, by and large, are not addressed in all of the legislative frameworks, but rather by policy. The legislation authorises medical practitioners to possess, administer and, in some situations, provide a supply of a drug.

Prescribing

It is clear that to authorise the use of many scheduled medicines, one must belong to a particular professional group. Prescribing pertains to writing a medication order, either in a prescription notepad or on a patient's medication chart. The prescription specifically relates to the individual patient. The legislation in each jurisdiction identifies which professional groups may prescribe and the legal requirements for a valid prescription. Medical practitioners, dentists and veterinary surgeons are the most common professional groups identified in all jurisdictions, with the widest prescribing authority. They may prescribe a variety of medications, including Schedule 3, 4 and 8 drugs. Other professional groups with limited prescribing rights include nurse practitioners, chiropodists, optometrists and dental therapists. The drugs the latter group are authorised to prescribe relate specifically to their areas of expertise. Self-administration or self-prescribing of medication is not permitted.

It is the responsibility of the medical practitioner to determine the therapeutic need for any prescribed medication. For example, s 8 of the Drugs Poisons and Controlled Substances Regulations 2006 in Victoria states:

(1) A registered medical practitioner must not administer, prescribe, sell or supply a drug of dependence or Schedule 8 poison unless –

    (a) that drug or poison is for the medical treatment of a person under his or her care; and

    (b) he or she has taken all reasonable steps to ascertain the identity of that person; and

    (c) he or she has taken all reasonable steps to ensure a therapeutic need exists for that drug or poison.

(2) A registered medical practitioner must not administer, prescribe, sell or supply a Schedule 4 poison unless –

    (a) that poison is for the medical treatment of a person under his or her care; and

    (b) he or she has taken all reasonable steps to ensure a therapeutic need exists for that poison.

Elements of a valid prescription

The requirements of a valid prescription are specified in most jurisdictions and generally include the following:

- identifying prescriber information including name and address; the prescriber's address is not included on in-patient medication charts
- the patient's name and address; usually the patient's address is modified to an identifying number when a medication chart is used
- the date of the prescription
- the drug, either as a generic or trade name — the PBS authorises pharmacists to dispense a cheaper version of a drug when the trade name is used
- other drug details including the dose, route and frequency; in some jurisdictions, where an unusual dose is ordered, it should be underlined and initialled
- the prescription should be legible (it is a clear requirement in some jurisdictions e.g. Victoria), and computer-generated prescriptions are valid; most commonly a handwritten signature is required.

Verbal orders — a particular type of prescribing

There is more than one method of prescribing medication. Medical practitioners in all jurisdictions can provide verbal orders. In some jurisdictions, the verbal order is specifically contextualised and refers to telephone orders, orders given in an emergency, orders by facsimile or any 'approved' manner. 'Approval' must come from an authorised person; for example, in New South Wales, it is the Director-General. In clinical practice the most common example of verbal orders occurs when the medical practitioner is requested by other health professionals (commonly nurses) to prescribe a medication for that practitioner's patient. The assumption is that the medical practitioner has some knowledge or relevant details of the patient concerned.

In four jurisdictions, the Australian Capital Territory, New South Wales, Tasmania and Victoria, a verbal order must relate to an emergency situation. It is relevant to note that an emergency is not defined in the statutes or regulations. Presumably it remains the decision of the prescriber whether any given situation is in fact an emergency. In some jurisdictions, including the Australian Capital Territory, New South Wales, Queensland and Tasmania, the medical practitioner must record the verbal order within 24 hours. In Western Australia, if the patient is in a hospital, the doctor is required to endorse the patient's medication chart within 24 hours. The New South Wales regulation does not permit the verbal order to be ongoing but rather a 'one off' dose.

In the Australian Capital Territory, New South Wales and Queensland, responsibility rests with the registered nurse to report or follow up if the written order is not forthcoming from the medical practitioner. In Victoria and the Northern Territory, the order must be written up 'as soon as practicable' after the verbal order has been given. This allows for more realistic time frames and attendances on the part of the prescriber. Moreover, the Australian Capital Territory legislation requires the prescriber to inform the nurse or pharmacist that a particular verbal order is an unusual dose.

The South Australian and Tasmanian legislation allows for the registered practitioner to continue to administer the drug; in South Australia for 10 days and in Tasmania, if in the opinion of the registered practitioner it is necessary for the patient's wellbeing. In Queensland, several categories exist. A registered nurse or midwife may possess and administer Schedule 4 and 8 medications on a verbal order. Both a registered nurse or midwife in isolated practice can supply medications on an oral instruction to an outpatient or discharged patient. Isolated practice is defined as more than 25 kilometres from a pharmacy. In rural areas (defined according to specific location), the Director of Nursing or nominee can supply medication to an outpatient or discharged patient where there is no employed pharmacist or the pharmacist is not on duty. In Western Australia, a registered nurse working in a designated remote area can supply Schedule 4 medication for up to 3 days for the treatment of an acute medical condition on the instructions of the medical practitioner.

Medication error

The most commonly used definition of medication error was formulated by the American Society of Hospital Pharmacists in 1993. The definition emphasises the practice of the 'five rights', highlighting mistakes where a wrong dose, patient, route, drug or time occurs. The definition has been construed to largely focus on incidents or errors at the end point, the patient.[5] Regardless of the practice environment, medication error is a reality. Courts, employers, regulatory authorities and health professionals have historically blamed the individual practitioner for the error. This often results in a punitive response to the problem. While this may appear reasonable, the research demonstrates that it is unlikely to change the actual error rate occurring in the clinical environment.[6] Any system of reporting which leads to punishment has had the effect of deterring the reporting of medication error.[7] This is not to condone and disregard drug errors. Patients have every right to complain and resort to the legal system should they be harmed.

Contemporary approaches, based on research, transfer the focus from the individual to the systems of prescribing, dispensing and administrating medicines. All medication incidents can be regarded as potential errors, having their origin in the system, so that incidents or errors are grouped with other adverse events, such as allergies. Effectively, there is a shift from failure of the individual, to a failure of the system. Leape[8] argues the delivery of a single drug to a patient is the result of a long and complicated process and all elements of the process should be examined. This is now the current approach to medication error in many healthcare settings and has several effects on health professionals. First, they are encouraged to report events, not from the perspective of the 'defective' professional, but as a source of information to be used for improving the system. Second, when the entire system is addressed, errors which are discovered at the point of administration can be traced back to the point in the system where the failure commenced. Third, to remove a punitive approach is to encourage self-reporting. Moreover, many institutions are encouraging maximum patient involvement where possible. Patients are encouraged to self-medicate and in many healthcare environments medication is stored in lockable drawers beside the patient's bed.

Research in Australia demonstrates that medication incidents in acute care settings remain the second most frequent incident reported, with falls being the predominant incident. *Omission and overdose are the most common type of medication incident*, with failure to read, or misreading the medication chart and failing to follow protocol or guidelines, the most commonly cited causes.[9] One study in Queensland examining prescribing errors by hospital interns found that many factors were identified. The study highlighted four key areas of causation:

1 environmental factors, including the level of staffing, workloads and managerial support
2 team factors, including issues such as communication and supervision
3 individual factors, including knowledge, skills, motivation and individual health
4 task factors, including issues related to medication chart design, protocols and availability of pathology results.[10]

Storage

The legislative requirements relating to storage vary. In some jurisdictions, there is a requirement to store Schedule 4 drugs in a locked cupboard or equivalent, while in other jurisdictions no such requirement exists. There are, however, clear directions in relation to Schedule 8 medication. In all jurisdictions, they are to be stored in a locked cupboard and remain separate from other drugs. The legislation in some states and territories nominates the precise specifications of the cupboard, including the thickness of the steel plate. The keys of the drug cupboard are to be kept on the person of the individual in charge of the unit or facility.

All agencies with or without pharmacies are obliged to keep a register to record the details of Schedule 8 drugs. The information recorded includes the patient's name, the prescribed drug and dose, the medical practitioner's name, date and time of administration and the balance of the ampoules or tablets. Usually a witness checks this information with the practitioner who is to administer the drug. The health professional giving the drug must be authorised to administer it; this includes a medical practitioner or nurse in the hospital environment. The witness may be another health professional.

The balance of the Schedule 8 drugs remaining in the drug cupboard is recorded at regular intervals. The regularity of the record-keeping depends on the practice setting and the frequency of use of the Schedule 8 medication. For example, the acute care environment will require checking and recording at the completion of each shift, whereas an aged care facility may check the balance only once every 24 hours. When a discrepancy in the record is identified, there is a responsibility to report it, normally to the pharmacist, senior medical officer or the director of nursing. The police drug squad may become involved if there is tampering with Schedule 8 drugs, which is a reminder of the criminal focus of the legislation. This situation may be suggestive of a staff member with an addictive illness. Whenever ampoules are damaged or destroyed, this must also be reported. If the drug is discarded or destroyed, policy often dictates that it is done in the presence of a witness.

RELEVANCE OF THE COMMON LAW

The legislation in each of the Australian states and territories generally does not address the precise details of actually administering medications to patients. The common law cases provide the basis for many of the principles expected in clinical practice. For example, medical practitioners may be familiar with the term the '5 rights' in relation to medication administration. In everyday clinical practice patients suffer harm from incorrectly administered medication. Hence, an action in negligence might arise and be considered a breach of a duty of care when any of the '5 rights' has been contravened. This can occur when there is a failure to administer the *right* drug, in the *right* dose to the *right* patient at the *right* time via the *right* route.

COMPLIMENTARY AND ALTERNATIVE MEDICINES (CAM)

The Australian Medical Association (AMA) acknowledges the increasing use of complimentary medicines and therapies by the Australian population. The term complimentary refers to a wide range of non-prescription products with health claims such as herbal medicines, homoeopathic medicines and nutritional substances. Well-known therapies include acupuncture, chiropractic, osteopathy, naturopathy and meditation. Other alternative therapies include reflexology, iridology, kinesiology and the Alexander technique.[11] With the increase in CAMs there has also been growth in the education and training courses available for both medical and non-medical students. There has been an associated rise in the number of professional associations and bodies including peak bodies for medical practitioners associated with CAMS.

A study in 2004 revealed that nearly 40% of Australians are taking self-prescribed vitamins, more than 20% are taking herbal medicines, and 13.6% of people take mineral supplements. Interestingly, 11.2% of people use aromatherapy. A chiropractor was the CAM therapist most likely to be seen by an Australian (16.7% of Australians undertaking treatment), while naturopaths (5.7%) and acupuncturists (2.1%) were the next most likely to be visited. The study also shows that users of CAMs are mistakenly thinking that their alternative medicines and therapies are independently tested for safety by bodies such as the

Therapeutic Goods Administration (TGA), when it is not the case. People are often using CAMs without their doctor's knowledge.[12]

The TGA has established an Office of Complimentary Medicine which provides regulation over the safety and quality of manufactured complimentary medicines. The TGA provides information regarding the safety, quality and efficacy of the products it tests.[13] However, the AMA highlights concerns about the absence of quality controls over the importation and use of raw herbs, which is a state and territory responsibility.

With the significant use of CAM in Australia, medical practitioners should be careful to acknowledge the requirements and any restrictions on the use of specific complementary medicines. The legal requirements are the same as for the provision of any care and treatment, where patients have the right to be informed, given options and be included in the decision-making process. This includes some knowledge of the benefits and risks, including potential interactions between scheduled medications and those utilised in CAMs. Even where a medical practitioner does not engage in the use of CAMs, for safe patient treatment and outcomes, patients should be encouraged to disclose and discuss any alternative therapy undertaken when also receiving conventional care.[14]

The degree of knowledge a practitioner will be expected to have will be guided by the practitioner's area of practice or specialty and the extent to which the practitioner uses CAM as part of usual practice. This is because of the frequency with which patients consume both prescription medication and CAMs, the lack of clear understanding of the possible effects this may have on treatment, the opaque distinctions made by patients between complimentary and conventional medicines, and the increasing research into the efficacy of CAM.[15] It is necessary to highlight that while the substance may not be subject to the various state and territory poisons legislation, medical practitioners should work within their employer policies or guidelines to avoid potential problems. The AMA highlight that the medical profession must be an integral part of a systematic approach to information about adverse events. There is an increasing trend to incorporate evidence-based CAMs.[16]

MEDICAL PRACTITIONERS AND THE PHARMACEUTICAL INDUSTRY

The widespread use of medicines brings medical practitioners into close contact with members of the pharmaceutical industry. Kerridge, Lowe and McPhee[17] argue that medical practitioners generally perceive that their practice is determined by knowledge and evidence, however the commercial influences on therapeutic decisions and the subtle and pervasive effects of pharmaceutical promotion can be overlooked.

There is evidence that advertising does influence clinical decision-making. For example, one study found that contact with drug company representatives leads to the use and prescription of their drugs.[18]

The AMA state that despite the Code of Ethics there are occasions where additional guidance in relation to practice is necessary. Hence, the position statement on Doctors' Relationships with Industry — 2010.[19] Medical practitioners have a responsibility to ensure that their participation in any collaboration with the pharmaceutical industry is consistent with their duties towards patients and the broader community. The overwhelming advice is that *professional interactions between medical practitioners and members of the pharmaceutical industry should be at arms length* — a clear delineation should be kept at all times. Relationships between the two groups will be appropriate only insofar as they do not intrude into or distort the practitioner's primary obligation; that is, patient welfare. Accepting evaluation packages or samples from pharmaceutical representatives should allow practitioners to evaluate the clinical performance of the medications and should not involve any form of material gain, either personally or for the practice.

In *Medical Board of Queensland v Raddatz*[20] a medical practitioner used products from a company called Mannatach. The products were considered by the tribunal to be 'complimentary, alternative and unconventional in nature'. A complaint was made to the Queensland Medical Board that when treating a diabetic patient, Dr Raddatz had substituted insulin for a Mannatach product. Nevertheless, Dr Raddatz was a keen supporter and despite being investigated and counselled to desist from promoting and selling substances that were not scientifically validated, the practitioner continued. He denied any fault and indicated that he would continue to use the products and his wife would continue to sell them. Dr Raddatz had developed an association with the Mannatach Group through the use of a family trust. The tribunal found that the practitioner had a conflict of interest and his registration was cancelled for 2 years. Furthermore, the tribunal placed a condition on Dr Raddatz's re-application for registration; he could only re-apply if he truly resolved to abide by all ethical standards, policies and practices provided by the Medical Board.

Further reading

Australian Medical Association, 'Position Statement — Complimentary Medicine' (2002). Online. Available: www.ama.com.au/policy/positionstatements (accessed 4 May 2010).

Australian Medical Association (AMA), 'Position Statement — Doctors' Relationships with Industry' (2010). Online. Available: www.ama.com.au/policy/positionstatements (accessed 4 May 2010).

Kerridge, I, Lowe, M, McPhee, J, *Ethics and Law for the Health Professions*, 3rd edn, Federation Press, Sydney 2009.

Low, J, Hattingh, L, Forrester, K, *Australian Pharmacy Law and Practice*, Elsevier, Sydney 2010.

MacLennan, A, Myers, S, Taylor, A, 'The continuing use of complimentary and alternative medicines in South Australia: costs and beliefs in 2004' (2005) 184(1) *Medical Journal of Australia* 27–31.

Raftery, J, 'Paying for costly pharmaceuticals: regulation of new drugs in Australia, England and New Zealand' (2008) 188(1) *Medical Journal of Australia* 26–8.

Therapeutic Goods Administration, *The Regulation of Complimentary Medicines in Australia — An Overview* (2006). Online. Available: www.tga.gov.au/cm/cmreg-aust.htm (accessed 1 June 2009).

Endnotes

1 Australian Government, *National Medicines Policy* (2000). Canberra. Online. Available: www.health.gov.au/internet/main/publishing. nsf/Content/nmp-objectives-policy.htm-copy2 (accessed 26 March 2010).

2 Low, J, Hattingh, L, Forrester, K, *Australian Pharmacy Law and Practice*, Elsevier, Sydney, 2010 at 48.

3 Ibid at 187.

4 Pharmaceutical Benefits Scheme (PBS). Australian Government. Online. Available: www.health.gov.au/internet/main/publishing. nsf/Content/health-pbs-general-aboutus.htm-copy2 (accessed 26 March 2010).

5 Baker, H, 'Medication Error — Where does the fault lie?' in Hunt, S, Parkes, R, (eds), *Nursing and the Quality Use of Medicines*, Allen and Unwin, Sydney, 1999 at 73.

6 Baker, H, *Nurses, medications and medication errors: An ethnomethodological study*, (1994) Unpublished PhD Thesis, Central Queensland University.

7 Ibid.

8 Leape, L, 'Out of the darkness: hospitals begin to take mistakes seriously' (1996) 29:6 *Health Systems Review* 21.

9 Roughead, L, Semple, S, *Literature Review: Medication Safety in Acute Care in Australia* (2008). Online. Available: www.safetyandquality. gov.au/internet/safety/publishing.nsf/Content/com-pubs_ MedSafety (accessed 28 June 2009).

10 Ibid at 12.

11 Australian Medical Association (AMA) *Complimentary Medicine*. AMA, Canberra 2002.

12 MacLennan, A, Myers, S, Taylor, A 'The continuing use of complimentary and alternative medicines in South Australia: costs and beliefs in 2004' (2005) 184(1) *Medical Journal of Australia* 27–31.

13 Information can be obtained from the TGA website. Available: www.tga.gov.au/cm/cm.htm (accessed 10 July 2010).

14 Weir, M 'Obligation to advise of options for treatment — medical doctors and complimentary and alternative medicine practitioners' (2003) 10(3) *Journal of Law and Medicine* 296–307.

15 Kerridge, I, Lowe, M, McPhee, J *Ethics and Law for the Health Professions*, 3rd edn, Federation Press, Sydney 2009.

16 See the Cochrane Collaboration, which includes several systematic reviews of CAMs. Online. Available: www.cochrane.org (accessed 17 June 2010).

17 Above, n 14.

18 Peay, M, Peay, E, 'The role of commercial sources in the adoption of a new drug' (1998) 26 *Social Sciences Medicine* 1183–9.

19 Australian Medical Association (AMA), *Position Statement: Doctors' Relationships with Industry — 2010*. Online. Available: www.ama.com.au/node/5421 (accessed 10 July 2010).

20 Queensland Health Practitioner Tribunal. (unreported No. D 2392 of 2000), as cited in Kerridge, I, Lowe, M, McPhee, J *Ethics and Law for the Health Professions*, 3rd edn, Federation Press, Sydney 2009.

10

Mental health

LEARNING OBJECTIVES

This chapter aims to introduce you to the key areas relating to mental illness and the responsibilities of medical practitioners. While reading this chapter you should focus on:

- describing the legislative definitions of 'mental illness'
- discussing the specific behaviours which are excluded from the definition of mental illness
- explaining what is meant by 'voluntary' and 'involuntary' admission
- outlining the general considerations to be addressed for patients to be involuntarily admitted
- identifying the type of treatment banned or restricted by the legislation
- discussing the safeguards established for mentally ill patients.

INTRODUCTION

Individuals suffering a mental illness have traditionally received treatment and care which have raised questions regarding the appropriateness and suitability of the therapy. In part, this has been related to the stigma and lack of understanding of psychiatric disorders and because a diagnosis of mental illness can have a dramatic effect on patient's lives. Kerridge, Lowe and Stewart[1] highlight that a diagnostic label has a social function — the diagnosis of psychiatric illness validates patient's symptoms and has allowed people to avoid the military draft and escape punishment for certain crimes. A psychiatric diagnosis can also have a negative effect where it may be used to suppress political dissent.[2] People suffering from mental illness have been routinely institutionalised despite the fact that one in five Australian adults has, or will develop, some form of mental disorder.[3] This is an area which is now regulated by detailed legislative provisions about the type of care provided and how patients are to be treated. This is partly because patients who have psychiatric disorders are sometimes treated against their will, allowing a considerable relationship imbalance between patient and professional which is accentuated more than that evident for patients suffering other illnesses.

A NATIONAL APPROACH

Significant change in Australia can be traced to the federal government's participation and contribution in the development of the United Nations' Principles for the Protection of Persons with Mental Health Care (1991). These principles were adopted in the National Mental Health Plan (1992). The principles highlight, among other things, the importance of mentally ill individuals being free from discrimination, determination of mental illness to be made in accordance with internationally accepted principles, treatment to be individualised and discussed with the individual, detention should involve the least restrictive measures for the least necessary time, and include clearly established legislative procedures. The initial strategy provided a 5-year plan to reform mental health services, so that all Australian jurisdictions enacted legislation creating review mechanisms. There have been further reports culminating in 2006, when the federal government released *A National Approach to Mental Health — From Crisis to Community*.[4]. The recommendations relate to funding for mental health services, consistency of mental health legislation across the jurisdictions and increasing the number of community health and treatment facilities.

Mental health legislation exists in all states and territories (see Table 10.1).

The aim of the legislation in every jurisdiction is to ensure that patient rights are balanced with the need to provide care. This ensures that mentally

Table 10.1 Mental health legislation	
Jurisdiction	**Legislation**
Australian Capital Territory	Mental Health (Treatment and Care) Act 1994
New South Wales	Mental Health Act 2007
Northern Territory	Mental Health & Related Services Act 1998
Queensland	Mental Health Act 2000
South Australia	Mental Health Act 1993
Tasmania	Mental Health Act 1996
Victoria	Mental Health Act 1986
Western Australia	Mental Health Act 1996

ill individuals are not detained without reasonable justification. The strategy also advocates a change in modalities of treatment from a single psychiatric institution, to the use of a combination of treatment settings, including general hospitals, residential settings and community support services.

WHAT IS MENTAL ILLNESS?

There has always been some difficulty in providing a clear legislative definition of what constitutes a mental illness. The most recent legislation uses symptoms displayed by the patient as a method of defining mental illness. The mental health legislation varies in relation to the distinction made between those individuals with a mental illness and those who are intellectually or developmentally disabled. In New South Wales and Victoria, there is separate legislation,[5] whereas in South Australia, Western Australia and Tasmania, intellectual disability and psychiatric illness are dealt with under the mental health legislation. For example, the Tasmanian legislation deals with intellectual disability, anti-social personality disorders, patients with mental symptoms caused by organic disease, including senility, and psychiatric illness. In the Australian Capital Territory, Queensland and the Northern Territory, there is no clear distinction made between intellectual disability and psychiatric conditions.

In the New South Wales legislation s 14 of the Act defines 'mental illness' as:

… a condition which seriously impairs, either temporarily or permanently, the mental functioning of a person and is characterised by the presence in the person of any one or more of the following symptoms:

(a) delusions;

(b) hallucinations;

(c) serious disorder of thought;

(d) a severe disturbance of mood;

(e) sustained or repeated irrational behaviour indicating the presence of any one or more of the symptoms referred to in paragraphs (a)–(d).

A 'mentally ill person' is also defined as:

(1) A person is a mentally ill person if the person is suffering from mental illness and owing, to that illness, there are reasonable grounds for believing that care, treatment or control of the person is necessary:

(a) for the person's own protection from serious harm;

(b) for the protection of others from serious harm.

(2) In considering whether a person is a mentally ill person, the continuing condition of the person, including any likely deterioration in the person's condition and the likely effects of any such deterioration are to be taken into account.[6]

The New South Wales legislation introduced a new category to address situations in which individuals are not necessarily mentally ill but are temporarily irrational and a danger to themselves or others. An example would include a person who suffered from acute suicidal tendencies. The category of 'mentally disordered persons' allows for the individual to be detained if the person's behaviour is so irrational to justify a conclusion, on reasonable grounds, that temporary care, treatment, or control of the person, is necessary.[7]

While there is some degree of consistency in the terms used in the remaining jurisdictions, each definition does vary as every word must be considered when the sections are actually interpreted. The Australian Capital Territory and the Northern Territory legislative definitions have similar wording to that expressed in the New South Wales legislation. In the Australian Capital Territory, s 4 of the relevant Act defines mental illness as:

a condition that seriously impairs (either temporarily or permanently) the mental functioning of a person and is characterised by (a) delusions, (b) hallucinations, (c) serious disorder of thought form, (d) severe disturbance of mood, or (e) sustained or repeated irrational behaviour indicating the presence of the symptoms referred to in (a), (b) (c) or (d).[8]

The definitions appear to be relatively straight forward however, when interpreted by a court the importance of highlighting the actual symptoms or frequency of symptoms, as per the definition, become apparent. In *Burnett v Mental Health Tribunal* [1997][9] Ms Burnett retired from the public service for 'psychiatric reasons' in the early 1990s and since that time had been involved in a series of disputes with her neighbours. The police had been involved on occasion and she had been taken into custody and admitted at least 5 times to the psychiatric unit. In 1997 she assaulted a neighbour and caused some property damage, for which she was admitted to hospital again. The Mental Health Review Tribunal found Ms Burnett to be suffering from a psychiatric illness and she was ordered to be detained for 28 days, during which psychiatric treatment was to be given. Ms Burnett appealed the tribunal's decision to the ACT Supreme Court. The court acknowledged that there was much to suggest that Ms Burnett's behaviour was irrational on a number of occasions. The paucity of evidence, however, made it difficult to determine whether her behaviour could be viewed as 'sustained or repeated' as stated in the definition. To fulfil the definition of 'sustained or repeated' the court wanted evidence of the behaviour occurring more than once — 'it should refer to a pattern of irrational behaviour which occurs with a degree of frequency' — however, the court found this was not sufficiently made out. The judge went on to express concern that it was even more difficult to determine whether Ms Burnett's behaviour was indicative of the presence of delusions or other symptoms referred to in the definition. The court overturned the tribunal's decision.

The Northern Territory legislation considers mental illness is a condition that seriously impairs, either temporarily or permanently, the mental functioning of a person in one or more of the areas of thought, mood, volition, perception or orientation of memory, demonstrated by a list of symptoms including delusions, disorders of thought or mood.[10] The legislation also specifies that any determination must be:

in accordance with internationally accepted clinical standards and concordant with the current edition of the World Health Organization, International Classification of Mental and Behavioural Disorders, Clinical Descriptions and Diagnostic Guidelines or the American Psychiatric Association Diagnostic and Statistical Manual of Mental Disorders.[11]

In Victoria, mental illness is defined as 'a medical condition that is characterised by a significant disturbance of thought, mood, perception or memory'.[12] Moreover, 'serious temporary or permanent physiological, biochemical or psychological effects of drug or alcohol taking can be regarded as an indication that a person is mentally ill'.[13] The Queensland legislation is similar to Victoria, where mental illness is defined as 'a condition characterised by a clinically significant disturbance of thought, mood, perception or memory'.[14] In Western Australia, the Act states that a person has a mental illness if 'the person suffers from a disturbance of thought, mood, volition, perception, orientation or memory that impairs judgment or behaviour to a significant extent'.[15] The Tasmanian Act uses similar language. Mental illness is described as 'a mental condition resulting in a serious distortion of perception or thought, or serious impairment, or disturbance of the capacity for rational thought, or a serious mood disorder, or involuntary behaviour or serious impairment to control behaviour'.[16] South Australia is distinctive as the definition is very broad. Section 3 of the Mental Health Act 1993 states that a mental illness merely includes 'any illness or disorder of the mind'.

Behaviour excluded under the definition of mental illness

A number of mental health acts specify behaviour or beliefs which are expressly excluded as amounting to a mental illness. For example, people who hold particular religious beliefs, political views or philosophies, or express particular sexual preferences, or engage in immoral or anti-social conduct, are not considered as necessarily suffering a mental illness according to the legislation. For example, sexual preferences, certain beliefs and opinions are excluded in the Australian Capital Territory, New South Wales, Western Australia, Queensland, Northern Territory and Victoria.[17]

The Victorian Act is detailed with regard to the exclusion criteria of what does not constitute a mental illness. Section 8(2) states:

A person is not to be considered to be mentally ill by reason only of any one or more of the following –

  a) that the person expresses or refuses or fails to express a particular political opinion or belief;

  b) that the person expresses or refuses or fails to express a particular religious opinion or belief;

  c) that the person expresses or refuses or fails to express a particular philosophy;

  d) that the person expresses or refuses or fails to express a particular sexual preference or sexual orientation;

  e) that the person engages in or refuses or fails to engage in a particular political activity;

  f) that the person engages in or refuses or fails to engage in a particular religious activity;

  g) that the person engages in sexual promiscuity;

  h) that the person engages in immoral conduct;

  i) that the person engages in illegal conduct;

  j) that the person is intellectually disabled;

  k) that the person takes drugs or alcohol;

  l) that the person has an antisocial personality;

  m) that the person has a particular economic or social status or is a member of a particular cultural or racial group.

The difficulty of defining and excluding behaviour not considered to amount to a mental illness became evident in the *Gary David* case in Victoria.[18] Mr David was a convicted murderer and during his prison sentence he began to self mutilate, threaten prison staff and make threats against the broader public. He was certified as an involuntary patient under the Mental Health Act 1986 to detain and treat him, but he appealed to the Mental Health Review Tribunal, who ruled that he suffered a personality disorder, not a mental illness, and could therefore not be committed. In response, the government enacted the Community Protection Act 1990 'to provide for the safety of members of the public and for the care or treatment of Gary David'.[19] This legislation allowed the government to detain Mr David for 12 month periods, after an application was made to the Supreme Court and the court was satisfied that he was a serious risk to the safety of a member of the public and was likely to commit an act of violence against someone. Regular reports were required to be made to the government and in 1993 Mr David died as a result of his self-inflicted wounds.

Voluntary and involuntary admission

Voluntary admission

A vast number of patients with mental illness will agree to treatment and, should they require hospitalisation, agree to be admitted voluntarily (often referred to as 'voluntary' patients). From a legal perspective, *such patients have the same rights as any other patient; to provide their own consent to treatment* and involvement in treatment decisions and plans of therapy. While all states and territories provide for involuntary admission only four jurisdictions detail specific regulation to voluntary patients: New South Wales, Northern Territory, South Australia and Tasmania.

Involuntary admission

There are times when the *mental illness renders the patient a danger to themselves or others*. Patients with mental illness can sometimes lack insight into their mental state and will not agree to voluntary admission for treatment. When patients require admission in this situation, it is referred to as an involuntary admission or detention.

Admission procedures, care and conditions relating to involuntary admission are outlined in the relevant legislation in each jurisdiction. Individuals with mental illness can be apprehended, detained, examined and treated without their consent, in limited circumstances.[20] Forcing a person into an institution and then into a particular form of treatment is, understandably, contrary to the general rule of patient consent and this issue is clearly highlighted in the principles formulated by the United Nations in 1991. Where a patient requires involuntary admission his or her right to self-determination is abrogated, and the legislation attempts to balance this right with the need for detention and treatment. This is an extremely difficult balancing issue and the legislation has included checks and balances to try and avoid problems associated with long-term, unnecessary detention. Individuals may require involuntary admission when there is a risk of self harm, or harm to others, or in some jurisdictions where there are obvious signs of deterioration in their mental illness. The following points broadly distinguish the process of involuntary admission.

- There must be a request for admission, either from a relative, friend or authorised person, and this request must be supported by an assessment of a medical practitioner. For example, in Queensland a request for assessment must be 'made by someone who is an adult, and who reasonably believes the person has a mental illness ... and has observed the person within 3 days before making the request'.[21]

- Once admitted, the patient must be examined by a qualified psychiatrist, usually within the first 24 hours. This is to confirm that the patient does suffer from a mental illness and requires detention. In Western Australia, once the person arrives at the hospital, they must be examined within 24 hours by a psychiatrist.[22]

- In an emergency a person may be detained by police or health professionals and taken to a treatment facility. For example, in the Australian Capital Territory if 'a police officer has reasonable grounds for believing that a person is mentally dysfunctional or ill ... or has attempted to commit suicide or is likely to attempt suicide or to inflict serious harm on himself or another person, the police officer may apprehend the person and take him or her to an approved health facility'.[23]

- The assessment and decision to detain must be recent and adequately documented. In Tasmania, as in other jurisdictions, the legislation requires the person to be examined within 24 hours after which a continuing order can be made by two medical practitioners.[24]

- The recommendation for detention has a limited time frame, usually only days, after which time an order may be made to continue the detention. For example, in the Northern Territory, a mentally ill person may be detained for psychiatric assessment for 24 hours or up to 7 days if the person who made the recommendation was an authorised psychiatric practitioner.[25] It is important to observe the detention period in each jurisdiction as it is unlawful to continue treatment when the detention period has expired.

- A formal review of the patient and the decision regarding the need to continue involuntary detention is to occur within days of the initial admission.

- There are appeal processes available to patients should they wish to oppose the decision to detain them involuntarily.

PRESCRIBED TREATMENTS

There are a number of treatments that are prohibited or closely regulated. Sterilisation as treatment for mental illness is banned in the Northern Territory.[26] Deep sleep therapy is prohibited in New South Wales, Northern Territory, Queensland and Western Australia.[27] Psychosurgery, (where intracerebral electrodes are used to create a lesion in the brain with the intention of permanently altering the thoughts, emotions or behaviour of the patient), has been banned in New South Wales and the Northern Territory and is highly regulated in the remaining jurisdictions. For example, psychosurgery requires approval from a board or tribunal in the Australian Capital Territory, Queensland, Victoria and Western Australia, and in South Australia by two psychiatrists and with the patient's informed consent. The use of electroconvulsive therapy (ECT) is strictly regulated, requiring the patient's consent or approval from a mental health tribunal with supporting evidence, usually from a second psychiatrist.

Seclusion and restraint can also be utilised in the care of the mentally ill, however, there are limits and guidelines imposed. For example, in Queensland seclusion must not be authorised unless the medical practitioner or nurse is reasonably satisfied that 'it is necessary to protect the patient or other persons from imminent physical harm and there is no less restrictive way of ensuring safety of the patient or others'.[28] In addition, mechanical restraint can be authorised by a medical practitioner to be used on an involuntary patient 'only if the medical practitioner is satisfied it is the most clinically appropriate way of preventing injury to the patient or someone else'.[29]

Community treatment orders (CTO)

The preference to de-institutionalise mentally ill patients has resulted in a less restrictive treatment option which is in keeping with both modern psychiatric treatment trends and the national strategy. As discussed above, involuntary admission and detention usually occur in situations of acute psychiatric illness when patients may inflict harm on themselves or others, or where they may undergo a serious deterioration in their condition. There are also *patients who require supervision but are not considered to be a risk to others or to themselves.* This group of mentally ill patients are now encouraged to live in the community under ongoing supervision. Usually 'supervision' entails continued administration of medication. Tasmania, Western Australia, Queensland, the Australian Capital Territory, New South Wales and Victoria have legislative provisions which permit patients, who are classified as 'involuntary', to live in community care programs. Other jurisdictions rely on leave of absence provisions.

In the Australian Capital Territory, the legislation specifies that as far as possible patients should be encouraged to care for themselves in the community. The Mental Health Tribunal makes community care orders and may specify the type of care and at which agency this will occur.[30] Likewise in Queensland, Tasmania, Victoria, New South Wales and Western Australia, authorised personnel can make community treatment orders. The specifications of the orders vary but may include the type of treatment and care to be given, the treating medical practitioner, where the treatment will take place, the duration of the order and how the medical practitioner will make progress reports.

In New South Wales, the Act establishes community care agencies which have psychiatric case managers who monitor the patients under community treatment orders (CTOs). The CTO, made by a magistrate or the Mental Health Tribunal, can be issued while a person is either in a mental health facility or living in the community. The order may require a patient to attend a specified healthcare facility for treatment, which is usually counselling and medication. A CTO remains in force for up to 12 months. Should the patient refuse to comply with the order, he or she is given a warning that any further refusal will result in a return to hospital.

STATUTORY SAFEGUARDS

To avoid substandard care and provide recognition of patients' rights, the legislation embodies certain principles. For example, in the Australian Capital Territory, New South Wales, South Australia and Victoria, patients are to be handed a written statement of their legal rights. If a patient is not capable of understanding the statement, another explanation must be provided no later than 24 hours prior to an inquiry held before a magistrate. If English is not the patient's first language, there is a requirement that an explanation should be provided in a language understood by the patient.

Other safeguards include access to information regarding detention and the rights of patients to communicate with people outside the institution, both verbally and in a written form. The right to another psychiatric opinion and the right to complain are also included in many jurisdictions. The right to legal representation, when the patient appears before a magistrate or a mental health review board or tribunal, exists in several jurisdictions.

Provision is made in most jurisdictions for the appointment of officials, often called 'community visitors', 'authorised officers' or 'approved officers'.[31] They are required to visit health services to ensure that the level of care and the health facilities are maintained to a requisite standard. For example, in Western Australia 'official visitors' are appointed from the community and are required to visit each authorised hospital at least once each month. Involuntarily detained patients may request to see an 'official visitor' if they have a complaint about their care or treatment. It is the function of the visitor to ensure that the patient is made aware of his or her rights and that these rights are adhered to.[32] In South Australia and the Northern Territory, there is no equivalent to community visitors or authorised officers. Instead, in the Northern Territory, the chief health officer has the powers of a guardian in relation to the observation, care and control of a mentally ill patient who is unable to manage his or her affairs.[33] In South Australia, the Public Advocate appears to assume this role.[34]

PATIENT CONSENT

Patients generally have *the right to consent to treatment even when they are detained involuntarily*. Mental health legislation in all jurisdictions attempts to determine what treatment can be given and by whom, when patients are unable to provide consent for themselves. *Decisions regarding patient treatment are encouraged to be transparent* in that the decision must be justifiable, based on the patient's condition and need for treatment. There has been a shift away from providing a sole medical practitioner with unquestionable authority to order invasive treatment, such as psychosurgery or ECT, with boards and tribunals involved. The precise requirements of consent are outlined and this is particularly evident when invasive therapy is to be utilised. For example, s 53B in the Victorian Act sets out the requirements for obtaining 'informed consent' before invasive procedures are undertaken:

(1) ... a person is to be taken to have given informed consent to the performance on him or her of treatment only if the person gives written consent to that treatment after –

(a) the person has been given a clear explanation containing sufficient information to enable him or her to make a balanced judgment; and

(b) the person has been given an adequate description of benefits, discomforts and risks without exaggeration or concealment; and

(c) the person has been advised of any beneficial alternative treatments; and

(d) any relevant questions asked by the person have been answered and the answers have been understood by the person; and

(e) a full disclosure has been made of any financial relationship between the person seeking informed consent or the registered medical practitioner who proposes to perform the treatment, or both, and the service, hospital or clinic in which it is proposed to perform the treatment; and

(f) subsections (2) and (3) have been complied with.

(2) The person on whom the treatment is to be performed must be given the appropriate prescribed printed statement –

(a) advising the person as to his or her legal rights and other entitlements including –

(i) the right to obtain legal and medical advice (including a second psychiatric opinion) and to be represented before giving consent; and

(ii) the right to refuse or withdraw his or her consent and to discontinue all or any part of the treatment at any time; and

(b) containing any other information relating to the treatment that the Department considers relevant.

(3) In addition to the statement, the person must be given an oral explanation of the information contained in the statement and, if he or she appears not to have understood, or to be incapable of understanding, the information contained in the statement, arrangements must be made to convey the information to the person in the language, mode of communication or terms which he or she is most likely to understand.

(4) The statement may be printed in different languages so that, whenever possible, a person can be given a copy of the statement in a language with which he or she is familiar.

(5) It is the duty of the authorised psychiatrist to ensure that this section is complied with in the approved mental health service.

Where the patient is incapable of providing consent to ECT s 73(3) of the Victorian legislation identifies when the ECT may be performed:

(a) the authorised psychiatrist has authorised the ECT proposed to be performed after being satisfied that –

(i) the ECT has clinical merit and is appropriate; and

(ii) having regard to any benefits, discomforts or risks the ECT should be performed; and

    (iii)   any beneficial alternative treatments have been considered; and

    (iv)   unless the ECT is performed, the patient is likely to suffer a significant deterioration in his or her physical or mental condition; and

  (b) all reasonable efforts have been made to notify the person's guardian or primary carer of the proposed performance of the ECT.

MENTAL HEALTH REVIEW BOARDS OR TRIBUNALS

The mental health legislation in most jurisdictions establishes boards or tribunals to carry out a number of functions.[35] The functions of each are set out in the legislation.

There is some variation, however, the general review process in relation to detained patients is consistent. The boards or tribunals have the responsibility of hearing and determining appeals from a magistrate and periodically review all patients who have been detained; for example, informal patients who have been detained for a period of 12 months or longer. They also make determinations in relation to detained patients, when there is disagreement between the patient and the treating doctor as to treatment or category of admission or detention. Moreover, appeals against CTOs and counselling orders made by a magistrate can be heard and determined by the boards and tribunals. They may hear reports relating to restraint and seclusion and the non-psychiatric treatment of a patient.

In South Australia, there is a close relationship between the mental health legislation and the Guardianship Board, which has the power to review consent issues and detention orders.[36] The only appeal and review mechanism in the Northern Territory against a decision of a magistrate is an application to the Supreme Court to review the order.[37]

DUTY AND STANDARDS OF CARE OWED TO MENTALLY ILL PERSONS

The standard of care expected by certain classes of individuals raises questions as to the duty, and the scope of that duty, owed to people who may be suffering from a mental illness or in circumstances where a mentally ill person commits a serious crime. The following two cases involve examination of mental health legislation in two distinct cases.

The mental health legislation in some jurisdictions allows for certain classes of individuals to intervene and detain a person who is suicidal. A recent High Court case, *Stuart v Kirkland-Veenstra* [2009][38] examined the extent of that responsibility. The Victorian mental health legislation provides police officers with the statutory power to apprehend a mentally ill person 'if they reasonably believe that person has recently attempted suicide … or is likely to attempt suicide'.[39] The case involved two police officers who found a man, Mr Veenstra, in his car at a beachside car park with a hose leading from the exhaust pipe to the interior of his vehicle. The car engine was turned off and Mr Veenstra was sitting in the car with the window down. The officers spoke with him for some 15 minutes and offered him assistance, which he declined. Mr Veenstra stated that he had been contemplating 'doing something stupid', but had changed his mind and informed the officers that he would return home and talk to his wife. Later that same day at his home, Mr Veenstra committed suicide.

The court was required to consider whether the police officers were in breach of their duty and should have apprehended Mr Veenstra at the car park. The High Court observed that the mental health legislation required two conditions to be satisfied. Firstly, the person must 'appear to be mentally ill' — the definition of mental illness is characterised as a 'significant disturbance of thought, mood, perception or memory'.[40] The statutory power required the police officers to make an assessment in the circumstances, but they were not required to exercise clinical judgment. The court found that the officers' observation and interactions were sufficient for them to determine that Mr Veenstra was not mentally ill. The court also highlighted that there is no proposition at common law that attempted suicide or suicide gives rise to a presumption of mental illness. The second condition necessary before the power to apprehend would be satisfied focuses on the officers' belief that Mr Veenstra was likely to attempt suicide. The court noted Mr Veenstra's responses to the officers, that he was rational and cooperative, and this supported the officers' belief that he was not likely to attempt suicide in the near future. The court held that neither of the two conditions were satisfied and the officers were not obliged to exercise the statutory power provided. The situation for health professionals in providing care to a person who is suicidal might be distinguished from the actions of the police in this case.

The second case, *Presland v Hunter Area Health Service & Anor* [2003][41] involved a decision by the New South Wales Supreme Court where a mentally ill person committed a crime. Mr Presland suffered from delusional behaviour and, following a delusional episode, he was engaged in a violent incident with a work mate and his family. He was subsequently transported to hospital. It was noted that Mr Presland suffered head injuries and yet he appeared to understand that he required psychiatric assessment and treatment. He agreed to be transported to a psychiatric hospital. The following morning his brother arrived with some clothes for him and after a brief interview with the on-duty registrar, Mr Presland was discharged. There was some considerable confusion and debate as to the circumstances surrounding his departure from the hospital, the registrar stating that the patient wanted to leave, and Mr Presland's brother denied that this was the case. Nevertheless, the registrar formed the view that Mr Presland was not mentally ill and discharged him into his brother's care. A short time after his release Mr Presland, in a psychotic state, killed his brother's fiancé. He was tried for murder and acquitted, but detained in a psychiatric unit in Long Bay gaol.

When Mr Presland was released some 2 years later he sued the health service on the grounds that the service had breached its duty of care to him, in failing to recognise his mental illness and for failing to detain him as an involuntary patient. He argued that had he been detained he would have been treated and would not have subsequently committed the murder. The judge was critical of the fact that the registrar did not have a complete record of circumstances involving the admission and failed to adequately assess him.[42] The court discussed the role of the mental health legislation and reasoned that there were responsibilities owed by the medical profession to provide the best possible care. The court awarded him damages, however, this decision was overturned by the Court of Appeal in *Hunter Area Health Service & Anor v Presland* [2005].[43] The critical issue for the Court of Appeal was the scope of the duty of care, particularly whether it extended to encompass the effects of unlawful conduct. The court found that a duty was owed to Mr Presland yet his acts were unlawful, and public policy was against awarding damages in these circumstances. Moreover, to impose a duty could bias decisions made under the mental health legislation towards favouring detention. It is noteworthy that one judge, Spigelman J held:

> The doctor who made the decision not to detain him failed to conduct a proper inquiry into the Respondent's (Presland's) mental state … Furthermore, the records available to that doctor did not, by reason of defective record keeping, contain the full range of information available to the hospital, particularly the information conveyed by the police and ambulance officers who brought the Respondent to the hospital.[44]

After this case the New South Wales government amended the Civil Liability Act 2002 to prevent the recovery of damages for loss resulting from a serious offence (resulting in death, damage or serious injury to a person), committed by a mentally ill person.[45] The Mental Health Act was also amended to exclude personal civil liability of police officers, paramedics and other health professionals for *functions* exercised under the Act. The effect of this section does not exempt medical practitioners from liability in the provision of medical *treatment* within the meaning of the mental health act.[46] In other words, medical practitioners still have a responsibility to exercise a reasonable standard of care when *treating* under the Mental Health Act, because treatment is distinguished from those functions imposed on the police and health professionals generally.

SCENARIO AND ACTIVITY

A psychiatrist believes that he has developed a unique therapy for treating patients suffering a particular mental illness. The psychiatrist admits several patients for treatment into a psychiatric ward and commences his 'new' therapy on Eric, a voluntary patient, who after 3 days complains to you that he is not satisfied with the therapy and has 'no idea what the psychiatrist thinks he is doing'.

- What options does Eric have and how can you assist him?

REVIEW QUESTIONS

1 Discuss the statutory definitions of mental illness and consider challenging patient behaviour that may be difficult to include within the definitions.

2 Is it unusual that a therapy such as psychosurgery is banned in some jurisdictions and not in others? Does this provide insight into the difficulties and approaches of clinical practice?

3 Explain the necessary requirements for obtaining informed consent from an involuntary patient before invasive treatment is given.

4 Should a government have the right to pass legislation designed to detain a single person who displays challenging behaviour? Is there a more appropriate way to approach this situation?

Further reading

Australian Government, *A National Approach to Mental Health — From Crisis to Community*, First Report (30/3/06) and Final Report (28/4/06). Online. Available: www.aph.gov.au/senate/committee/mentalhealth_ctte/ (accessed 10 September 2009).

Diesfeld, K, Freckelton, I, 'Mental health law and therapeutic jurisprudence', in Freckelton, I, Peterson, K, (eds). *Disputes & Dilemmas in Health Law*. The Federation Press, Sydney 2006.

Kerridge, I, Lowe, M, Stewart, C, *Ethics and Law for the Health Professions*, 3rd edn, The Federation Press, Sydney 2009.

Mai, Q, D'Arcy, C, Holman, J, Sanfilippo, F, Emery, J, Stewart, L, 'Do users of mental health services lack access to general practitioner services?' (2010) 192 (9) *Medical Journal of Australia* 501–6.

McIlwraith, J, Madden, B, *Healthcare and the Law*, 4th edn, The Federation Press, Sydney, 2006.

Stewart, C, Kerridge, I, Parker, M, *The Australian Medico-Legal Handbook*, Elsevier, Sydney 2008.

Endnotes

1 Kerridge, I, Lowe, M, Stewart, C, *Ethics and law for the health professions*, 3rd edn, The Federation Press, Sydney, 2009.

2 Ibid at 500–1.

3 Edginton, J, *Law for the Nursing Profession*, 3rd edn, CCH Australia Ltd, Sydney 1995.

4 See First Report (30/3/06) and Final Report (28/4/06). Online. Available: www.aph.gov.au/senate/committee/mentalhealth_ctte (accessed 10 September 2009).

5 The Guardianship legislation in these states specifically deals with intellectual disability.

6 Mental Health Act 2007 (NSW), s 14.

7 Mental Health Act 2007 (NSW), s 15.

8 Mental Health (Treatment and Care) Act 1994 (ACT), see dictionary within the Act.

9 [1997] ACTSC 94.

10 Mental Health & Related Services Act 1998 (NT), s 6(1).

11 Section 6(2).

12 Mental Health Act 1986 (Vic), s 8(1A).

13 Section 8(3).

14 Mental Health Act 2000 (Qld), s 12.

15 Mental Health Act 1996 (WA), s 4.

16 Mental Health Act 1996 (Tas), s 4.

17 Mental Health (Treatment and Care) Act 1994 (ACT), s 5; Mental Health Act 1990 (NSW), s 11; Mental Health Act 1996 (WA), s 4(2); Mental Health Act 2000 (Qld), s 12; Mental Health and Related Services Act 1998 (NT), s 6; Mental Health Act 1986 (Vic), s 8(2).

18 As discussed in Kerridge I, Lowe M, Stewart C, *Ethics and Law for the Health Professions* (3rd ed), The Federation Press, Sydney 2009.

19 Ibid, pp 513–14.
20 Stewart, C, Kerridge, I, Parker, M, *The Australian Medico-Legal Handbook*, Elsevier, Sydney 2008.
21 Mental Health Act 2000, s 17.
22 Mental Health Act 1996, s36(1)(b).
23 Mental Health (Treatment & Care) Act 1994 (ACT), s. 37(1).
24 Mental Health Act 1996 (Tas), ss 26(4), 29(1).
25 Mental Health and Related Services Act 1998 (NT), s 39(1).
26 Mental Health and Related Services Act 1998 (NT), s 58.
27 Mental Health Act 2007 (NSW), s 83; Mental Health and Related Services Act 1998 (NT), s 59; Mental Health Act 2000 (Qld), s 162; Mental Health Act 1996 (WA), s 99.
28 Mental Health Act 2000 (Qld), s 151.
29 Section 143.
30 Mental Health (Treatment and Care) Act 1994 (ACT), ss 8, 25, 26, 28, 29.
31 Mental Health Act 2007 (NSW), s 129; Mental Health Act 1986 (Vic), ss 109, 112, 115, 116, 116A; Mental Health Act 1996 (Tas), ss 73–81; Mental Health (Treatment and Care) Act 1994 (ACT), ss 19, 34, 45, 121–122B; Mental Health Act 2000 (Qld), ss 531–532.
32 Mental Health Act 1996 (WA), ss 177, 179, 186–90.
33 Mental Health Act 1979 (NT), s 38.
34 Guardianship and Administration Act 1993 (SA), ss 21, 29, 35.
35 In New South Wales and Tasmania, there is the Mental Health Review Tribunal and the Mental Health Tribunal in the Australian Capital Territory. In Victoria and Western Australia, it is called the Mental Health Review Board.
36 Mental Health Act 1993 (SA), ss 24–26.
37 Mental Health Act 1979 (NT) s 34.
38 [2009] HCA 15.
39 Mental Health Act 1986 (Vic), s.10.
40 Mental Health Act 1986 (Vic), s 8(1A).
41 [2003] NSWSC 754.
42 Ibid at para 158.
43 [2005] NSWCA 33.
44 [2005] NSWCA 33 at para 5.
45 Section 54A.
46 Mental Health Act 2007 (NSW), ss 191(1), 191(2).

Professional regulation and discipline

This chapter aims to introduce you to the legal issues relevant to the registration and regulation of medical practitioners and the importance of regulatory legislation and disciplinary processes to medical students. While reading this chapter you should focus on:

- understanding the legal significance of registration of medical practitioners
- identifying the framework for national registration of all health practitioners in Australia operative on 1 July 2010
- identifying the requirements for registration
- identifying the legislation relevant to the regulation of medical practitioners
- identifying conduct that would provide the grounds for disciplinary action
- understanding the disciplinary process and possible outcomes of disciplinary hearings.

INTRODUCTION

Both regulated and unregulated workers and professionals undertake the delivery of healthcare services within Australia. Unregulated health workers and professionals are those not registrable or registered with a professional regulatory authority. That is, they are not required to have a practising licence, conferred by a regulatory authority, in order to work within the healthcare system. Examples of unregulated health workers or professionals include personal care attendants, dieticians and social workers. Regulated health professionals, such as nurses, pharmacists and medical practitioners must, however, possess a licence or practising certificate conferred by a professional regulatory authority in order to work in their chosen professions. The status of registration thereby restricts those who may practice in an identified profession to only those who hold a practising licence or certificate. Registration also confers on those professionals the legal authority to use an identified title (such as doctor, medical practitioner, or pharmacist) and undertake certain tasks; for example, prescribing narcotics or carrying out a specific procedure such as surgery. The objectives of registration and regulation of medical practitioners in Australia is to protect the public and maintain professional standards of practice. These objectives are met through the registration and regulation processes which require that each medical practitioner possesses the requisite educational qualifications, is fit to practice in their chosen profession and maintain a standard of conduct which is consistent with that expected by their peers and the public.

At the time of writing, the registration and regulation of medical practitioners is governed by the relevant state and territory Acts which establish medical boards in each of the individual jurisdictions. There are currently in excess of eighty health practitioner registration boards across Australia.[1] By 1 July 2010, however, a national registration and accreditation scheme will be in place which aims to standardise the regulation and disciplinary procedures across all the regulated health professionals. This chapter will provide an overview of the structures and broad principles relevant to the registration and regulation of those health professionals, including medical practitioners, who will be included under the national scheme. The chapter will also outline the professional disciplinary issues and procedures, and the codes of ethics and conduct, relevant to the regulation of medical practitioners.

BACKGROUND TO NATIONAL REGISTRATION

In 2005 the Commonwealth government requested that the Productivity Commission conduct a study into:

> issues impacting on the health workforce including the supply of, and demand for, health workforce professionals and propose solutions to ensure the continued delivery of quality healthcare over the next 10 years.[2]

In 2006 the Council of Australian Governments (COAG) supported the recommendations as contained in the Productivity Commission Research Report titled *Australia's Health Workforce*, and agreed to establish both a single national registration board and a single national accreditation board for the registration, eduction and training of health professionals. In 2008 COAG, under an intergovernmental agreement, agreed to establish a single national scheme 'to create nationally consistent, rigorous registration and accreditation arrangements and improve public protection'.[3]

[T]o establish a single national scheme, with a single national agency encompassing both registration and accreditation functions. The national registration and accreditation scheme will consist of a Ministerial Council, an independent Australian Health Workforce Advisory Council, a national agency with an agency management committee, national profession specific boards, committees of the boards, a national office to support the operations of the scheme and at least one local presence in each State and Territory.[4]

The objectives of the scheme were to:[5]

- provide for the protection of the public by ensuring that only practitioners who were suitably trained and qualified to practise in a competent and ethical manner are registered
- facilitate workforce mobility across Australia and reduce red tape for practitioners
- facilitate the provision of high quality education and training and rigorous and responsive assessment of overseas trained practitioners
- have regard to the public interest in promoting access to health services
- have regard to the need to enable the continuous development of a flexible, responsive and sustainable Australian workforce and enable innovation in education and service delivery.

Queensland was the state chosen to initially enact the substantive legislation giving effect to the national scheme. The national legislation was enacted in Queensland in two stages. The first stage, covering the provisions of the COAG Agreement, was introduced into the Queensland Parliament in October 2008[6] and the second stage in August 2009. The second stage included details for the arrangements required for registration, accreditation, complaints and enforcement, privacy and information sharing.[7] Extensive consultation, involving the professions and the public, was conducted as part of the process.[8] The other states and territories have followed the Queensland lead using their 'best endeavours' to repeal their existing regulatory legislation in relation to the health professionals included under the new scheme.

The legislative framework was introduced in such a way, and at a pace, so as to facilitate the development of entities and administrative arrangements necessary to implement the new national scheme. The following is an overview of the stages and legislation establishing the National Law:[9]

- First stage: Health Practitioner Regulation (Administrative Arrangements) National Law Act 2008, which commenced on 25 November 2008 and remains in force until 1 July 2010.[10] This Act gives effect to the administrative requirements to establish a National Registration and Accreditation Scheme.
- Second stage: Health Practitioner Regulation National Law Act 2009, with the Health Practitioner Regulation National Law (the National Law) contained in the Schedule effective on 1 July 2010.
- Third stage: Each state and territory introduced a Bill to adopt the National Law. As Queensland passed the Act in 2009 there is no requirement in that state for further legislation.[11]

Table 11.1 provides an overview of the implementation of the national scheme across the jurisdictions.

From 1 July 2010 the national registration and accreditation scheme covers the ten health professions to be initially included in the national scheme: chiropractors; dental (including dentists, dental hygienists, dental prosthetists and dental therapists); medical practitioners; nurses and midwives; optometrists; osteopaths; pharmacists; physiotherapists; podiatrists; and psychologists. From 1 July 2012 the scheme will be expanded to include Aboriginal and Torres Strait Islander health practitioners, Chinese medicine practitioners, and medical radiation practitioners.[12]

STRUCTURE AND FUNCTION OF THE NATIONAL SCHEME

In November 2008 the Health Practitioner Regulation (Administrative Arrangements) National Law Act (Qld) was enacted to establish the structure of the national registration and accreditation scheme and empower the bodies identified under the Act to develop and implement the scheme. The Act established the Ministerial Council, Australian Health Workforce Advisory Council, National Agency (the affairs of which are to be conducted by the Agency Management Committee) and the National Boards for each of the health professions covered by the scheme.[13] In relation to medical practitioners, the Medical Board of Australia was established under the Act. There will also be a local presence for each of the professional disciplines in each state and territory. Section 3 of the Health Practitioner Regulation (Administrative Arrangements) National Law Act 2008 (Qld) ('the Act') states the object of the legislation:

(1) ... is to facilitate the development and implementation of the national registration and accreditation scheme for health practitioners.

Table 11.1 Legislative basis for introduction of the National Law	
Jurisdiction	**Progress**
ACT	The Health Practitioner Regulation National Law (ACT) Bill. Adoption Law passed 16.3.2010
Commonwealth	Health Practitioner Regulation (Consequential Amendments) Bill 2010 introduced into the House of Representatives 24.2.2010 awaiting debate
New South Wales	Health Practitioner Regulation Act 2009. Adoption Law passes 11.11.2009
Northern Territory	Health Practitioner Regulation (National Uniform Legislation) Bill 2010. Adoption Law passed 17.3.2010
Queensland	Health Practitioner Regulation National Law Bill 2009. Adoption Law passed 3.11.2009
South Australia	Health Practitioner Regulation National Law (South Australia) Bill 2010. Consultation on draft Bill commenced
Tasmania	Health Practitioner Regulation National Law (Tasmania) Bill 2009. Passed by House of Assembly 17.11.2009 and awaiting debate in Tasmanian Legislative Council
Victoria	Health Practitioner National Law (Victoria) Act 2009. Statute Act Amendment (National Health Practitioner Regulation) Bill introduced into the Victorian Legislative Assembly 24.2.2010

(Source: Australian Health Practitioner Regulation Agency (AHPRA). Online. Available: www.ahpra.gov.au/legislative_framework.php [accessed 29 March 2010])

(2) A person or body that has functions under this Law is to exercise those functions having regard to the objectives of the national registration and accreditation scheme, as set out in the COAG Agreement.[14]

The Ministerial Council, comprising the Ministers of government in the participating jurisdictions of the Commonwealth with portfolios responsibile for health, must take into account concerns and advice from the Australian Health Workforce Advisory Council (Advisory Council). In anticipation of the commencement of the national registration and accreditation scheme, the Ministerial Council may also approve 'health profession standards'[15] for any health profession provided it has been approved by the National Board established

for that particular discipline of health professionals. In addition, the
Ministerial Council is empowered to request that a particular National
Board review a health profession standard, and approve or revoke
amendments to an existing health profession standard. That is, the
Ministerial Council may request the Medical Board of Australia to
review, approve, revoke or amend professional standards for medical
practitioners in Australia.

The Advisory Council is established under Part 3 of the Act
as an independent body which provides advice to the Ministerial
Council on:[16]

- any matter relating to the scheme referred to it by the
  Ministerial Council, including those matters upon which the
  Ministerial Council is not able to reach a decision
- any other matters relating to the scheme that the Advisory
  Council considers appropriate.

Part 4 of the Act provides for the Australian Health Practitioners
Regulation Agency and, under s 18, the National Agency. The
principle functions of the National Agency are set out in section
20(1) as follows:

  (a) to establish general requirements for the development of
      health profession standards for the purpose of ensuring
      the scheme operates in accordance with good regulatory
      practice;
  (b) in consultation with National Boards, to develop
      procedures for the purpose of ensuring the efficient and
      effective operation of the National Boards;
  (c) to provide administrative assistance to the National Boards
      and their committees;
  (d) to negotiate in good faith with, and attempt to come to
      agreement with, each National Board on the terms of a
      health profession agreement for the health professional for
      which the Board is established;
  (e) to provide advice to the Ministerial Council in
      connection with the development and
      implementation of the national registration and
      accreditation scheme;
  (f) when requested by the Ministerial Council to give any
      assistance or information reasonably required by the
      Ministerial Council in connection with the development
      and implementation of the national registration and
      accreditation scheme;

(g) in anticipation of the commencement of the national registration and accreditation scheme, to do anything else that is necessary or convenient for the purpose of preparing and enabling the National Agency to exercise any other functions the COAG Agreement provides will be conferred on the National Agency under the scheme.

The National Agency is required to establish a national office and at least one office in each participating state and territory.

The Agency Management Committee is established to conduct the affairs of the National Agency and is subject to the direction of the Ministerial Council. It is the role of the Agency Management Committee to determine the policies of the National Agency and ensure the National Agency performs its functions 'in a proper, effective and efficient way'.[17]

The National Agency is required to establish National Boards[18] for each discipline of health professions covered by the scheme. Under the Health Practitioner Regulation National Law Act (2009) the functions of the National Boards are to include:

- registering suitably qualified and competent persons and, if necessary, imposing conditions on their registration;
- determining the requirements for registration or endorsement, including arrangements for supervised practice;
- developing or approving standards, codes and guidelines for health professionals;
- approving accredited programs of study as providing qualifications for registration;
- overseeing the assessment of knowledge and clinical skills of overseas trained applicants for registration;
- negotiating in good faith with the National Agency on the terms of a health profession agreement;
- overseeing the receipt, assessment and investigation of notifications about persons who were or are registrants or students in the health profession;
- establishing a panel to conduct hearings about health, performance and professional standards;
- referring matters about health practitioners who are or were registered to responsible tribunals;
- overseeing the management of health practitioners and students registered in the health profession, including monitoring conditions, undertakings and suspensions imposed on registration;

- making recommendations, giving advice, assistance or information to the Ministerial Council;
- in conjunction with the National Agency keeping up-to-date publicly accessible national registers;
- providing financial or other support for health programs for registered health practitioners and students;
- doing anything else that is necessary or convenient for the effective or efficient operation of the national registration and accreditation scheme;
- any other function given to the board by or under this law.

On 8 May 2009 the Australian Workforce Ministerial Council issued a communiqué on the design of the national registration and accreditation scheme. In this communiqué the Australian Workforce Ministerial Council agreed that the function of accreditation was to be independent of government with accreditation standards developed by independent accrediting bodies or accreditation committees of the professional boards. The final decision as to whether 'the accredited standards, courses and training programs are approved for the purposes of registration is the responsibility of the National Board'.[19] It is noted, however, that the Ministerial Council has retained the power to act where changes to accreditation standards, such as clinical placement hours or workplace or work practices, would 'have a significantly negative effect'.[20] The national accreditation standards that currently exist are to continue until replaced by new standards. Bodies such as the Australian Medical Council and the Australian Pharmacy Council will continue in their current roles. In addition, the communiqué outlined the following:

- there will be both general and specialist registers where the Ministers agree there is a requirement for specialist registration
- there will be a requirement that registrants participate in continuing professional development programs approved by the national professional boards as a pre-requisite to registration renewal
- the introduction of mandatory reporting of registrants who place 'the public at risk of harm'[21]
- mandatory criminal history and identity checks of all health professionals registering for the first time, with all other registrants making an annual declaration upon application for renewal of registration; the National Boards will have the power to conduct ad hoc criminal history and identity checks of registrants
- simplified complaints processes with a flexible model of administrative arrangements for handling complaints

- registration of students enrolled in the health disciplines through a deeming process based on student lists supplied to the boards by educational providers
- the prescribing of cosmetic lenses to be restricted to optometrists and medical practitioners.

National Medical Board (Medical Board Of Australia)[22]

As stated above, the Medical Board of Australia was established under the Health Practitioner Regulation (Administrative Arrangement) Act 2008 and, from 1 July 2010 the Medical Board will operate under the Health Practitioner Regulation National Law (the National Law) in jurisdictions where it had been adopted. The first meeting of the Medical Board of Australia took place on 20 September 2009. To the time of writing, the board has:

> focused on its priorities in preparing for the introduction of the national registration and accreditation scheme and on preparatory work to enable it to fulfil its statutory functions from 1 July 2010.[23]

This has included consideration of the structure and delegation to state and territory boards, establishing a specialist register, development, adoption and re-issuing of codes and guidelines, registration standards, medical courses and specialist qualifications, mandatory reporting, advertising guidelines, scheduled medicine endorsements and decisions about the publication of conditions, undertakings and reprimands in the register.[24]

Transition from state- and territory-based to national-based registration

The Medical Board of Australia has determined that while it will, in addition to its other functions, assume the responsibility for developing and approving registration standards, codes and guidelines and approving accreditation standards, the state and territory boards, such as the Queensland Board of the Medical Board of Australia (and its equivalent in the other jurisdictions), will be delegated the responsibility of dealing with matters related to individual practitioners. This will include making the day-to-day decisions about applications for registration and investigations of notifications about health practitioners. The state- and territory-based boards will be assisted by a number of committees which are likely to include:

- Registrations Committee
- Assessment Committee

- Health Committee
- Performance and Professional Standards Committee.[25]

Registration

Registration of a medical practitioner is a prerequisite to practising medicine. From 1 July 2010 medical practitioners in all states and territories will need to be registered with the Medical Board of Australia under the Health Practitioner Regulation National Law Act 2009. The types of registration for medical practitioners by the board are: general registration, specialist registration, limited registration (includes the sub-types of post graduate training or supervised practice, area of need, teaching and research and in the public interest), provisional registration and non-practising registration. Specialists will be required to have both general and specialist registration.[26] Those medical practitioners with existing registration by state and territory medical registration boards will go through transition to registration under the National Law. Unlike the previous system, the requirements for registration will be the same regardless of which state or territory the medical practitioner intends to practise. There is therefore no need for the mutual recognition legislation in the individual Australian jurisdictions. A medical practitioner registered in one state or territory will have registration across all Australian states and territories. The National Law does not, however, affect the operation of the Trans-Tasman mutual recognition legislation in relation to registration to practise in New Zealand.[27]

Under the National Law an individual is eligible for general registration in a health profession if they:[28]

- are qualified for general registration in the health profession,[29] and
- have successfully completed the period of supervised practice in the health profession that is required by the approved registration standard for the health profession, or any examination or assessment required by an approved registration standard to assess the individual's ability to competently and safely practise the profession, and
- are a suitable person to hold general registration in the health profession, and
- are not disqualified from applying for registration or being registered as a health professional, and
- meet the other requirements of registration stated in an approved registration standard.

As previously stated, the National Boards must develop registration standards for their particular discipline.[30] The Medical Board of Australia has therefore developed registration standards that have been approved by the Ministerial Council. The approved registration standards for registration as a medical practitioner are as follows:[31]

- criminal history registration standard
- English language skills standard
- professional indemnity insurance standard
- continuing professional development standard
- recency of practice standard
- list of specialities, fields of specialty practice and related specialist title
- limited registration for area of need registration standard
- limited registration for post graduate training or supervised practice registration standard.

Criminal history registration

This standard applies to all regulated health practitioners whether they are applicants for registration or registered practitioners applying for renewal of their practising licence. To decide whether a health practitioner's criminal history is relevant the board will consider ten prescribed factors set out in the standards:

1. the nature and gravity of the offence, or the alleged offence, and its relevance to health practice;
2. the period of time since the health practitioner committed, or allegedly committed, the offence;
3. whether a finding of guilt or a conviction was recorded … or charge for the offence is still pending;
4. the sentence imposed for the offence;
5. the age of the health practitioner, and any victim at the time the health practitioner committed, or allegedly committed, the offence;
6. whether the conduct that constituted the offence or to which the charge relates has been decriminalised;
7. the health practitioner's behaviour since he or she committed, or allegedly committed, the offence;
8. the likelihood of future threat to a patient of the health practitioner;
9. any information given by the health practitioner;
10. any matter the board considers relevant.

For the purpose of the National Law, 'criminal history' is defined as:[32]

every conviction of the person for an offence, in a participating jurisdiction or elsewhere, and whether before or after the commencement of the Law ...

every plea of guilty or finding of guilt by a court of the person for an offence, in a participating jurisdiction or elsewhere, and whether before or after the commencement of this Law and whether or not a conviction is recorded for an offence ... every charge made against the person for an offence, in a participating jurisdiction or elsewhere, and whether before or after the commencement of this Law.

English language skills

The standards require that all internationally qualified applicants for registration or applicants who qualified for registration in Australia without completing their secondary education in English must demonstrate the necessary English language skills at International English Language Testing System (IELTS) academic level 7 or the equivalent.

Professional indemnity insurance

All medical practitioners who undertake any form of medical practice are required to have professional indemnity insurance or an alternative form of indemnity cover (as an example, salaried medical officers within the public sector will be indemnified as an employee under the government insurance scheme). The initial application for registration and the annual renewal process will require a declaration that the medical practitioner is insured for all areas of their medical practice for the duration of their licence (12 months).

Continuing professional development

Medical practitioners will be required to make an annual declaration that they have met the continuing professional development (CPD) standard as set by the board. Each practitioner is required to ensure that their CPD activities are recorded and available for audit and investigation purposes. It is important to note that a failure of a health practitioner of any discipline to comply with the CPD requirements is considered as a breach of the legal requirements for registration. The CPD requirements for any individual practitioner will be dependent upon the category of their registration. For example, Members or Fellows of medical colleges, accredited by the Australian Medical Council, must meet the standards for CPD as set by their college, and medical practitioners who hold provisional registration (interns), or limited registration for post graduate training or supervised practice must participate in the supervised training and education programs associated with their position.

Recency of practice

The periods of time to meet the requirements for recency of practice are dependent on the field of practice, the level of experience of the individual practitioner and the length of time they have been absent from their field of practice.[33] As an example, for practitioners returning to practice within their previous field, provided they have at least 2 years previous experience prior to their absence if they return within 1 year there are no specific requirements before they can recommence their practice. If the absence is for between 1 and 3 years, the person is required to complete a minimum of 1 year pro rata CPD activities that are relevant to their intended scope of practice and designed to update and maintain their knowledge and clinical skill prior to recommencement. If the length of the absence is greater than 3 years, the person is required to provide a professional development plan for re-entry to practice to the board for their consideration and approval.

List of specialties, fields of specialty practice and related specialist titles

The board has developed a specialist register which includes those fields of practice that closely align to the Australian Medical Council's specialist list. Of note is the inclusion of general practitioners with vocational registration on the specialist register.

Limited registration for area of need registration standard

This standard applies to international medical graduates (IMGs) who do not qualify for general or specialist registration.

Limited registration for post graduate training or supervised practice registration standard

This standard also applies to IMGs who are applying for limited registration for post graduate training or supervised practice.

Subject to the requirements in relation to the accreditation standards, the Medical Board of Australia may also develop and recommend standards about the physical and mental health of an applicant for registration or a registered medical practitioner or medical student, the scope of practice of a registered medical practitioner and any other issues relevant to the eligibility of an individual for registration.

Applications for registration must be in the form approved by the Medical Board of Australia, accompanied by the relevant fee, proof of identity and any other information reasonably required by the board.[34] The applicant must also provide a declaration as to their residential or practising address and their address for correspondence with the board. Students undertaking an approved program of study for the health profession may be registered as determined by the National Board for the profession. Registration under the National Law is granted for a period of not more than 12 months.

Recognition and registration as a specialist is significant for the purposes of obtaining a rebate under the Medicare Australia scheme. Before applying for recognition as a specialist[35] under the Health Insurance Act 1973 (Cth) the medical practitioner must be registered to practise as a specialist in his/her specialty. Alternatively, they may have an Australasian Specialist Medical College Fellowship and status as a Fellow of an Australasian Specialist Medical College in relation to the specialty. Recognition as a specialist under the Health Insurance Act 1973 (Cth) enables Medicare benefits to be paid at the higher rate and, in addition to the higher rebate attendance items, there are other items in the Medicare Benefit Schedule which are only available to those medical practitioners with specialist recognition.

DISCIPLINARY ISSUES

Where a medical practitioner practices in a manner which is considered below a standard acceptable to the profession, it is likely that disciplinary proceedings will be initiated. Broadly speaking, activities which warrant the imposition of disciplinary action for those practising as medical practitioners can be categorised as unsatisfactory professional conduct, professional misconduct; suspected mental or physical incapacity; alcohol or drug addiction; conviction for a serious offence; making a fraudulent or misleading statement to acquire registration; failing to comply with the lawful requirements of the board; committing an offence against the legislation; and cancellation of registration.

The terms 'unsatisfactory professional conduct' or 'professional misconduct', also referred to as 'misconduct', 'unprofessional conduct' or 'unethical conduct', have often been used as broad terms to encompass the grounds upon which medical practitioners have been disciplined for a breach of the relevant regulatory legislation in the states or territories in which they work. What constitutes unsatisfactory professional conduct of a sufficiently serious nature to justify removal of the health professional's name from the register may vary between individuals, the experience a medical practitioner has in a particular clinical area, and the subjective circumstances surrounding the incident. Is it unsatisfactory professional conduct or misconduct if it is the result of a mistake? Is it unsatisfactory professional conduct or misconduct if the patient sustains no injury?

Section 5 of the Health Practitioner Regulation National Law Act (2009) (National Law) defines 'professional misconduct of a registered health practitioner' to include:

(a) unprofessional conduct by the practitioner that amounts to conduct that is substantially below the standard reasonably expected of a registered health practitioner of an equivalent level of training or experience; and

(b) more than one instance of unprofessional conduct that, when considered together, amounts to conduct that is substantially below the standard reasonably expected of a registered health practitioner of an equivalent level of training or experience; and

(c) conduct of the practitioner, whether occurring in connection with the practice of the health practitioner's profession or not, that is inconsistent with the practitioner being a fit and proper person to hold registration in the profession.

Section 5 of the Act defines 'unprofessional conduct of a registered practitioner' to mean professional conduct that is of a lesser standard than that which might reasonably be expected of the health practitioner by the public or the practitioner's professional peers, and includes:

(a) a contravention by the practitioner of this Law, whether or not the practitioner has been prosecuted for, or convicted of, an offence in relation to the contravention; and

(b) a contravention by the practitioner of –
    (i) a condition to which the practitioner's registration was subject; or
    (ii) an undertaking given by the practitioner to the National Board that registers the practitioner; and

(c) the conviction of the practitioner for an offence under the Act, the nature of which may affect the practitioner's suitability to continue to practise the profession; and

(d) providing a person with health services of a kind that are excessive, unnecessary or otherwise not reasonably required for the person's wellbeing; and

(e) influencing or attempting to influence, the conduct of another registered health practitioner in a way that may compromise patient care; and

(f) accepting a benefit as inducement, consideration or reward for referring another person to a health service provider or recommending another person use or consult with a health service provider; and

(g) offering or giving a person a benefit, consideration or reward in return for the person referring another person to the practitioner or recommending to another person that the person use a health service provided by the practitioner; and

(h) referring a person to, or recommending that a person use or consult, another health service provider, health service or health product if the practitioner has a pecuniary interest in giving that referral or recommendation, unless the practitioner discloses the nature of that interest to the person before or at the time of giving the referral or recommendation.

'Unsatisfactory professional performance of a registered health practitioner' is defined under s 5 of the Act as meaning the knowledge, skill or judgment possessed, or care exercised by, the practitioner in the practice of the health profession in which the practitioner is registered is below the standard reasonably expected of a health practitioner of an equivalent level of training or experience.

In addition to the definitions of conduct which warrant a disciplinary response, the National Law imposes on all health practitioners, employers and education providers a *mandatory notification obligation*. Section 141 provides that a registered health practitioner:

who, in the course of practising [their] profession, ... form a reasonable belief that –

(a) another registered health practitioner ... has behaved in a way that constitutes notifiable conduct; or

(b) a student has an impairment that, in the course of the student undertaking clinical training, may place the public at substantial risk of harm.

... must, as soon as practicable after forming the reasonable belief, notify the National Agency of the ... notifiable conduct or the student's impairment.

'Notifiable conduct in relation to a registered health practitioner' is defined to mean the practitioner has:

practised while intoxicated by alcohol or drugs, or engaged in sexual misconduct in connection with the practice of the practitioner's profession, or placed the public at risk of substantial harm ... because the practitioner has an impairment; or ... placed the public at risk of harm because the practitioner practised the profession in a way that constitutes a significant departure from accepted professional standards.[36]

'Impairment' is defined as:[37]

> ... a physical or mental impairment, disability, condition or disorder (including substance abuse or dependence) that detrimentally affects or is likely to detrimentally affect the person's capacity to practice the profession.

The impact of the mandatory notification provisions extend across all disciplines of health professionals regulated by the National Law. That is, if a medical practitioner in the course of practising medicine forms a reasonable belief that any other health practitioner, regardless of their discipline, has conducted themselves in a manner that constitutes notifiable conduct, or a student of a health discipline is impaired to an extent that poses a substantial risk of harm, there is an obligation to notify the National Agency. While a notification can be made about an impaired student there is no mandatory obligation imposed on students to make a notification.

Where a *health practitioner in 'good faith' makes a notification or supplies information about the conduct of another health practitioner or student they are protected from civil, criminal and administrative liability including defamation.* It is important to note that the making of a notification in 'good faith' by a health practitioner, employer or education provider does not constitute a breach of professional etiquette or ethics or a departure from accepted standards of professional conduct.[38] The legislation does not provide a penalty for the failure by a health practitioner to make a notification, however, such a failure may provide the basis for conduct or performance action by the board. In relation to employers, a failure to notify may result in a written report to the Health Minister and a subsequent notification to the relevant health complaints entity or licensing authority. Under the Health Practitioner Regulation National Law Act there are provisions for:

- establishing Health Panels[39]
- establishing Performance and Professional Standards Panels[40]
- the National Board to refer matters to responsible tribunals in the appropriate jurisdiction.[41]

A 'responsible tribunal' within the respective states or territories, exercising disciplinary powers in a matter involving a medical practitioner, may:

- find there is no case to answer
- make a finding the medical practitioner behaved in a way that constituted unsatisfactory professional performance
- find the behaviour constituted unprofessional conduct
- find the behaviour constituted professional misconduct

- find the practitioner has an impairment
- find the practitioner's registration was obtained improperly ... based on false or misleading information.[42]

The outcome imposed by the 'responsible tribunal' may include a caution or reprimand of the medical practitioner, the imposition of conditions on the practitioner's registration, the order for payment of a fine, suspension or cancellation of the medical practitioner's registration.

Disciplinary case law

Under the National Law, the grounds for disciplinary proceedings against a medical practitioner, being 'professional misconduct', 'unprofessional conduct' and 'unsatisfactory professional performance', are defined within the Act. It is to be assumed that the introduction of the National Scheme in 2010 will result in a consistency in interpretation of the given meanings in each of the states and territories.

Professional misconduct, unprofessional conduct or unsatisfactory professional performance may present in many forms and it may be of assistance to consider some categories of conduct by medical practitioners that have historically resulted in disciplinary proceedings. In the case of *Qidwai v Brown*, [43] which involved a medical practitioner performing an appendicectomy in his private consulting room on a day surgery basis, the court found the practice to amount to professional misconduct. Priestley J proposed that the appropriate test for determining misconduct in a professional respect in relation to a medical practitioners was:[44]

> whether the practitioner was in such breach of the written and unwritten rules of the profession as would reasonably incur a strong reprobation from professional brethren of good reputation and competence.

Sexual misconduct

In the *Medical Board of Queensland v Alroe*[45] the psychiatrist established and maintained a social and sexual relationship with a 52-year-old patient who had a long history of depression and psychiatric illness. The relationship between the psychiatrist and his patient commenced shortly after the termination of the professional relationship. The Queensland Health Practitioner Tribunal found that, given the history of the patient and the strong possibility that her mental illness would reoccur or she would have a relapse, the registrant had an added responsibility to maintain professional boundaries. His conduct, the tribunal concluded, could 'only be described as predatory and exploitive'.[46] Such a relationship as existed between the registrant and his former patient was clearly contrary to the Royal Austration and New Zealand College of Psychiatrists (RANZCP)

Code of Ethics. The registrant was found guilty of unsatisfactory professional conduct. His registration was cancelled for 4 years with the cancellation to remain on the Board Register for 6 years. The registrant was ordered to pay the board's costs.

Disciplinary processes

In all Australian jurisdictions the disciplinary process is complaint driven, requiring a written complaint to initiate an investigation. The specific processes of the lodging of a complaint, investigation of the complaint and hearing of a charge are set out in the National Law and the legislation empowering the responsible tribunal in the particular states or territories. In all jurisdictions the standard of proof required for findings will be the civil standard. That is, the allegations must be made out on 'the balance of probabilities'. However, the 'clarity' of the proof required to discharge the burden must reflect the seriousness of the charge: *Briginshaw v Briginshaw*.[47] In all jurisdictions certain complaints about health professionals are simultaneously referred to the relevant state or territory complaints units or commissions which attempt to resolve complaints about healthcare professionals through conciliation and mediation. (For an overview of the complaint mechanisms in the states and territories refer to Chapter 2, Safety and quality in health.)

Natural justice

All disciplinary tribunals are bound by the requirement of recognising the right to natural justice. They are, as a general rule, not bound by the rules of practice about evidence and may inform themselves on any matter as the committee or tribunal considers appropriate. Western Australian legislative provisions as they apply to disciplinary tribunals are, however, bound by the rules of evidence 'though otherwise may proceed in a manner it [the Board] thinks fit subject to the rules of natural justice'. Forbes suggests that most 'applications for review of disciplinary decisions are based upon a claim that natural justice has been denied'.[48] Natural justice was held in *Byrne v Kinematograph Renters' Society*[49] per Harman J as:

> ... the person accused should know the nature of a accusation made; secondly he should be given an opportunity to state his case; and thirdly of course that the tribunal should act in good faith. I do not think that there is really anything more.

Reception of evidence

Forbes states that the 'common law allows these bodies (tribunals) to obtain information in any way they think fit'.[50] In the circumstances that are presented before disciplinary tribunals and committees, alleging misconduct by health professionals, it is suggested that evidential rules providing boundaries based on relevance, probative value and prejudicial effect are cast aside at the peril of the disciplinary body. As Evatt J said in *R v War Pensions Entitlement Appeal Tribunal; Ex parte Bott:*[51]

> After all, (the rules of evidence) represent the attempt made, through many generations, to evolve a method of inquiry best calculated to prevent error and elicit truth. No tribunal can, without grave danger of injustice, set them on one side and resort to methods of inquiry which necessarily advantage one party and necessarily disadvantage the opposing party.

Codes and guidelines

The Health Practitioner Regulation National Law Act 2009 empowers the Medical Board of Australia (as a National Board) to develop and approve codes and guidelines for the purpose of providing guidance to the medical practitioners it registers, and information about matters relevant to its functions.[52] The *Good Medical Practice: A Code of Conduct for Doctors in Australia*[53] was developed by a working party of the Australian Medical Council on behalf of the Medical Boards of the Australian states and territories in 2009. In preparation for the transition to the National Scheme the Medical Board of Australia has decided to reissue this code with minor editing to reflect the National Law. The board has also approved guidelines in relation to advertising and the new mandatory reporting obligations. It is the intention of the board to develop specific guidelines in relation to:

- professional boundaries;
- sexual misconduct;
- medical practitioners and medical students with blood-borne infectious diseases; and
- unconventional medical practices.[54]

Codes of ethics

Codes of ethics are distinct from, but complementary to, professional codes of conduct. As described by Freckelton they are:

> a means to an end ... [T]hrough the process of moral deliberation thereby engendered, they may operate as the catalyst for ethical conduct both by heightening awareness of ethical proprieties

and by providing guidance from experienced professionals for the resolution of ethical conundra encountered at a practical level by practitioners.[55]

The medical profession is but one group working within the healthcare context that has formulated quite a detailed code of ethics to guide the practice of their members in the care and treatment of patients and clients and their relationship with the community. The code therefore has become part of the regulatory armoury by which the National Medical Board and state entities will benchmark conduct. The code is part of a set of criteria for assessing professional standards of practice, the breach of which will result in disciplinary proceedings. In the unreported decision of *Childs v Walton*[56] the New South Wales Medical Tribunal found the charges of sexual misconduct, and breach of confidence proven against the practitioner. In the Court of Appeal Samuels JA, with whom Priestley and Meagher JJA agreed, held that 'professional misconduct' incorporated 'unethical conduct'. The courts have also indicated that the breach of the code of ethics by a doctor was relevant to determining whether there had been a breach of his duty of care. In the case of *Furniss v Fitchett*[57] the medical practitioner was found guilty in negligence after he had provided the husband of one of his patients with a summary of the wife's mental status. The couple were, at the time, involved in proceedings for separation and divorce. The solicitor for the husband tendered the documents as part of the case. In awarding damages to Mrs Fitchett the court held:

> the British Medical Association's code of ethics is evidence of the general professional standards of which a reasonably careful, skilled and informed professional would conform. I think it was admissible for that purpose and it, therefore became necessary to decide whether the law, as distinct from the ethical code of the British Medical Association, permitted any departure from those standards.[58]

The AMA Code of Ethics, editorially revised in 2006, has its origins in a history which extends back to the Hippocratic Oath. The AMA, in accepting the responsibility to set the standards for ethical behaviour expected of doctors, recognises the obligations of doctors to their patients, the profession and society.[59]

SCENARIO AND ACTIVITY

You are working as an intern in a metropolitan teaching hospital and have been there for the last 6 months. You have been rostered on the night shift frequently over the last 4 months. It has come to your attention that a registrar, with whom you work during the night, has been arriving late for the shift and is frequently unable to be contacted or does not respond when paged. On a number of occasions you have become aware that the registrar has failed to appropriately examine a patient, has failed to identify significant patient signs and symptoms, has made errors in the medical records and prescribed incorrect doses of medications. Up until now you have attempted to correct these errors. You have become concerned that the registrar is increasingly forgetful, vague and periodically abusive to patients and staff. You have unsuccessfully attempted on a number of occasions to raise this issue with the registrar. At 2 a.m. on this particular shift you page the registrar to assist urgently with a multi-vehicle road trauma that has been air-lifted to the Emergency Department. The registrar does not respond and does not attend. After the patients have been assessed and moved to the respective clinical units you locate the registrar who is semi-conscious in a patient bed having consumed a large volume of alcohol. You locate the bottle of alcohol next to the registrar.

- After consulting with your clinical supervisor what action do you think should be taken?

REVIEW QUESTIONS

To ensure that you have identified and understood the key points of this chapter please answer the following questions.

1 Identify the legislation under which you would seek registration as a medical practitioner in Australia.

2 Identify the qualifications you require to apply for general registration as a medical practitioner.

3 Identify and locate the postal and email addresses of the professional board in your state or territory.

4 Identify the activities that a registered medical practitioner may undertake as a function of registration. For example, consider the provisions of your drugs and poisons regulations or Act. What are the legal powers of a medical practitioner in relation to possession and prescribing of narcotics? How is this authority different from that accorded to a registered nurse?

5 List the structure of the National Scheme.

6 What is included in the National Accreditation Scheme?

7 Identify the conduct that would amount to grounds for disciplinary action against a medical practitioner.

8 Identify and describe the conduct that comes under the mandatory notification provisions.

9 Locate the AMA Code of Ethics.

10 Locate the Good Medical Practice: A Code of Conduct for Doctors in Australia. How are the provisions different from or similar to the Code of Ethics?

11 Identify the possible outcomes of a disciplinary action where the charges of sexual misconduct against the medical practitioner have been proven.

Further reading

Bophy, E, 'Does a doctor have a duty to provide information and advice about complementary and alternative medicine?'(2003) JLM 10, 271.

Cummings, F, 'Complementary medicine regulation in Australia', *Current Therapeutics* (2000) 42: 57–61.

Eisenberg, D, Cohen, M, et al, 'Credentialing Complementary and Alternative Medicine Providers', *Ann Intern Med* (2002) 137 (12): 965–973.

Kerrridge, I, Lowe, M, McPhee, J, *Ethics and Law for Health Professionals*, 2nd edn, The Federation Press, Sydney 2005.

Lewith, G, Bensoussan, A, 'Complementary and alternative medicine with a difference', *Med J Aust*, (2004) 180: 585–6.

Parker, M, 'The regulation of complementary health: Sacrificing integrity?', *Med J Aust* (2003) 179(6): 316–18.

Walmsley, S, Abadee, A, Zipser, B, *Professional Liability in Australia*, 2nd edn, Lawbook Co, Sydney, 2007.

Weir, M, *Complementary Medicine: Ethics and Law*, Prometheus Publication, Brisbane, 2007.

Endnotes

1 National Registration and Accreditation Scheme, application guide for National Boards for health professionals.

2 Council of Australian Governments (COAG) *Intergovernmental Agreement for National Registration and Accreditation Scheme for Health Professions*. Canberra, 26 March 2008.

3 Council of Australian Governments (COAG) National Registration and Accreditation Scheme, application guide for National Boards for health professionals, COAG, Canberra 2008.

4 Above, n 2.

5 Ibid at 3.

6 Health Practitioner Regulation (Administrative Arrangements) National Law Act 2008 (Qld).

7 Ministerial Statement, 'National registration and accreditation scheme for health professions: Health Ministers outline consultation agreement', Australian Health Ministers' Conference, Canberra, 4 September 2008.

8 All policy papers, calls for submissions and information sheets are available at www.nhwt.gov.au/natreg.asp (accessed 2 June 2009). *Communiqué*, 'Design of new national registration and accreditation scheme' Australian Health Workforce Ministerial Council, Canberra, 8 May 2009, p 1.

9 Australian Health Practitioner Regulation Agency (AHPRA). Online. Available: www.ahpra.gov.au/legislative_framework.php (accessed 29 March 2010).

10 Health Practitioner Regulation (Administrative Arrangements) National Law Act 2008. Online. Available: www.legislation.qld.gov.au/LEGISLATION/CURRENT/H?HealthPracRAA08.pdf (accessed 29 March 2010).

11 Australian Health Practitioner Regulation Agency (AHPRA). Online. Available: www.ahpra.gov.au/legislative_framework.php (accessed 29 March 2010).

12 Australian Health Workforce Ministerial Council, *Communiqué* 8 May 2009, p 2.

13 The diagrammatic representation of the structure of the National Scheme is available at www.ahpra.gov.au/aphra_page.php?page=aboutus (accessed 29 March 2010).

14 The COAG Agreement dated 28 March 2008 can be accessed via www.nhwt.gov.au/natreg.asp (accessed 2 June 2009).

15 A 'health profession standard' is defined in s 8(2) of the Health Practitioner Regulation (Administrative Arrangements) National Law Act 2008 (Qld) as 'a standard or requirement relating to registration, practice, competency, accreditation or continuing professional development with respect to a health professional'.

16 Section 14 Health Practitioner Regulation (Administrative Arrangements) National Law Act 2008 (Qld).

17 Ibid, s 26.

18 Ibid, Part 5.

19 Australian Health Workforce Ministerial Council, *Communiqué* 8 May 2009, p 1.

20 Ibid.

21 Ibid at p 2.

22 National Medical Board. Online. Available: www.medicalboard. gov.au/index.html? (accessed 2 June 2009).

23 Medical Board of Australia AHPRA 'Fifth meeting of the Medical Board of Australia' 24 February 2010. *Communiqué*. Online. Available: www.medicalboard.gov.au/News/The-Work-of-the-Board.aspx (accessed 21 July 2010).

24 Medical Board of Australia AHPRA 'Sixth meeting of the Medical Board of Australia' 24 March 2010. *Communiqué*. Online. Available: www.medicalboard.gov.au/News/The-Work-of-the-Board.aspx (accessed 21 July 2010).

25 Ibid.

26 Explanatory Notes for Part 2 proposed registration under the National Law (4 May 2010). Online. Available: www. medicalboard.gov.au/en/Medical-Registration.aspx (accessed 22 July 2010).

27 Health Practitioner Regulation National Law Act 2009, s 9. The Trans-Tasman Mutual Recognition Act 1997 (Cth) extended the mutual recognition provisions to New Zealand. The Australian Capital Territory, New South Wales, the Northern Territory, Queensland, South Australia and Victoria have now all passed Trans-Tasman Mutual Recognition legislation.

28 Health Practitioner Regulation National Law Act 2009 (Qld) Part 7, Division 1, s 52 Eligibility for general registration.

29 The National Medical Board confirmed in the communiqué dated 24 March 2010 that graduates from medical courses currently accredited with the Australian Medical Council (AMC) would continue to meet the requirements for provisional and general registration after 1 July 2010. In addition, fellows of medical colleges currently accredited with the AMC will also be accepted for specialist registration after 1 July 2010 (www.medicalboard. gov.au/documents/Sixth%20meeting%20of%20the%Medical% 20Board%20of%20Australia%2024%20March%202010pdf).

30 Health Practitioner Regulation National Law Act 2009, s 38.

31 In December 2009 the Chair of the Medical Board of Australia finalised the boards proposal on registration standards and related matters for submission to the Chair of the Australian Health Workforce Ministerial Council for approval (www.medicalboar d.gov.au/documents/Medical%20Proposal.pdf). The registration standards were approved by the Ministerial Council in March 2010 (www.medicalboard.gov.au).

32 Medical Board of Australia. Online. Available: www.medicalboa rd.gov.au/obligations-on-Medical-Practioners.aspx (accessed 22 July 2010).

33 Medical Board of Australia. *Recency of Practice*. Online. Available: www.medicalboard.gov.au/obligations-on-Medical-practitioners.aspx (accessed 22 July 2010).

34 Health Practitioner Regulation National Law Act 2009, s 77.

35 Recognised specialists, qualifications and Australasian specialist medical colleges are set out in Schedule 4 of the Health Insurance Regulations 1975.

36 Health Practitioner National Regulation National Law Act 2009, s 140.

37 Ibid, s 5.

38 Health Practitioner National Regulation National Law Act 2009, s 237.

39 Ibid, s 181.

40 Ibid, s 182.

41 Ibid, s 193.

42 Ibid, s 191.

43 *Qidwai v Brown* [1984] 1 NSWLR 100.

44 Ibid at 105.

45 [2005] QHPT 004.

46 Ibid at 6.

47 (1938) 60 CLR 336.

48 Forbes, J, *Disciplinary Tribunals*, Law Book co, Sydney, 1990 at 56.

49 *Byrne v Kinematograph Renters' Society* [1958] 2 All ER 579.

50 Forbes, J, *The Law of Domestic and Private Tribunals* , Law Book Co, Sydney, 1982 at 143.

51 (1993) 50 CLR 228.

52 Health Practitioner Regulation National Law Act 2009 s, 39.

53 *Good Medical Practice: A Code of Conduct for Doctors in Australia.* Online. Available: www.ahpra.gov.au/Health-professions/Medical/Codes-and-Guidelines.aspx (accessed 22 July 2010).

54 www.medicalboard.gov.au/News/The-work-of-the-Board.aspx (accessed 21 July 2010).

55 Freckleton, I, 'Enforcement of ethics', in Coady, M, Blooh, S (eds) *Codes of Ethics in the Professions*, Melbourne University Press, Melbourne, 1996 at 130.

56 Unreported, NSWCA, B November 1990, BC 9001755.

57 [1958] NZLR 396.

58 Ibid.

59 Refer to the AMA Code of Ethics at http://www.ama.com.au/node/2521(accessed 26 August 2010).

12

Research

LEARNING OBJECTIVES

This chapter aims to introduce you to the legal issues relevant to clinical research. While you are reading this chapter you should focus on:

- understanding the importance of maintaining a standard of research practice which is consistent with the standards as provided by the National Health and Medical Research Council, the Australian Research Council, relevant legislation, policies and guidelines of Institutional Ethics Committees
- understanding the significance of accepted standards of research practice to decisions by courts as to liability in civil actions
- identifying the importance of obtaining a legally valid consent from individuals prior to their participation in research
- identifying the legal obligations in relation to privacy and confidentiality of information obtained or required for the purpose of research.

INTRODUCTION

The law is relevant to clinical research in the same way that it is relevant to clinical practice. Where medical students or medical practitioners are involved in clinical research it is important that they have an understanding of what the law requires, what the law prohibits and what the law provides by way of redress, and/or compensation. In the same way that the law applies to allegations of medical negligence, the failure of the medical practitioner to obtain a legally valid consent or to protect the privacy and confidentiality of a patient's information, so the law also applies to the researcher and the research participants. Though there is very little case law or legislation in Australia that specifically addresses researchers, institutions supporting research, research projects or research participants, the general civil and criminal principles, obligations and requirements imposed under Australian law apply. In addition, institutions, organisations and individuals engaged in research are regulated by national guidelines, policies and codes developed to protect the quality and safety of research practices in Australia. While these guidelines, policies and codes do not have the legal impact of legislation or case law they are very significant pieces of evidence to place before the courts as benchmarks of appropriate and competent research practices. While the majority of clinical experimentation aimed at improving the quality of healthcare services is conducted on both animals and humans, it is research involving human participants that will be the focus of this chapter.

WHAT IS RESEARCH?

The National Health and Medical Research Council (NHMRC), Australian Research Council and Universities Australia have defined research as 'original investigation undertaken to gain knowledge, understanding and insight'.[1] A broader definition is provided by the United Kingdom Research Assessment Exercise, which describes research as:

> That which ... includes work of direct relevance to the needs of commerce, industry and to the public and voluntary sectors; scholarship; the invention and generation of ideas, images performances, artefacts including design, where these lead to new or substantially improved insights; and the use of existing knowledge in experimental development to produce new or substantially improved materials, devices, products and processes, including design and construction.[2]

While these definitions include the elements of gaining new knowledge, gaining and improving insight and improving on existing knowledge, the history of medical research in many countries has been found wanting in terms of compliance with ethical and legal standards. The Nuremberg Tribunal hearings, conducted at the end of World War II, resulted in the formulation of the Nuremberg Code consisting of ten principles that set the standards for ethical medical experimentation.[3] The Declaration of Helsinki, published by the World Medical Association in 1964 (and subsequent versions) was based on this Nuremberg Code and provided the ethical principles and values upon which national[4] and international[5] guidelines and statements for research involving humans were developed and applied. It is of note that despite the recognition by medical researchers of the need for compliance with the legal and ethical obligations and standards there continued to be research studies and clinical trials conducted that resulted in the injury and death of research participants.

Examples of such research include: the National Women's Hospital (Auckland), where women unaware of their diagnosis of cervical cancer were left untreated for the purpose of observation; monitoring of the effects of non-treatment of hepatitis in groups of institutionalised children and the vaccine trials on children in the Melbourne orphanages between the 1940s and 1970s.[6] These experiments demonstrate the potential harm where researchers do not observe and abide by accepted legal and ethical standards. As noted by Rothman and Michels:[7]

> Exactly why codes such as the Nuremberg Code and the Declaration of Helsinki have not prevented unethical research from occurring is unclear. The answer to this question is likely to be multifactorial and may derive from the perceived inevitability of scientific progress, the aura of science, the entrenched power of medical professionals, self interest and a perceived utilitarian belief in the benefits of research.

In Australia, research conducted on humans is regulated by legislation and case law, the *National Statement on Ethical Conduct in Human Research* (National Statement) and the *Australian Code for the Responsible Conduct of Research* (the Code). It is important for medical students to understand that the National Statement and the Code in relation to research involving humans are based on, and directly referable to, ethical principles and values. Though many of the principles and elements addressed within the National Statement and the Code will be shared with the legal requirements, compliance with the legal obligations is not within the ambit of either the National Statement or the Code. This chapter therefore focuses on the legal obligations relevant to research involving humans and the legal parameters in which such research must take place.

LEGISLATION

Legislation prohibiting cruelty to animals exists in all states and territories. In addition, New South Wales has legislation specifically directed to the use of animals for experimentation purposes.[8] The NHMRC's Code of Practice for the Care and Use of Animals for Scientific Purposes is incorporated within the regulations under the legislation in each of the states and territories and is directed to protecting animals involved in experimentation.[9] In relation to experimentation involving human participants, however, there is no legislative equivalent to that which applies to animals.

The legislation regulating human experimentation is a combination of general and specific Acts made at Commonwealth, state and territory levels. The following is an overview of the legislation that applies to research involving humans.

National Health and Medical Research Act

The National Health and Medical Research Council Act 1992 (Cth) establishes the NHMRC in Australia and contains the council's powers, functions and obligations. The NHMRC is an independent statutory entity that, in addition to other activities, provides national guidelines for individual and institutional researchers, research participants, human research ethics committees and those involved in conducting or reviewing research. Under s 3 (1) the object of the Act is:

> to make provision for a national body to pursue activities designed:
>
> a. to raise the standard of individual and public health throughout Australia; and
>
> b. to foster the development of consistent health standards between various States and Territories; and
>
> c. to foster medical research and training and public health research training throughout Australia; and
>
> d. to foster consideration of ethical issues relating to health ...'

To facilitate these objectives, the functions of the NHMRC include inquiring into, issuing guidelines on, and advising the community about:

- matters relating to the improvement of health
- the prevention, diagnosis and treatment of disease
- the provision of healthcare, public health research, medical research
- ethical issues related to health.[10]

In addition to inquiring into these issues and developing and distributing guidelines, it is also part of the function of the NHMRC to advise the community, the Commonwealth, states and territories about these matters and make recommendations to the Minister[11] about expenditure on public health, research and training and medical research and training.

Under s 35 (1) of the National Health and Medical Research Council Act 1992 (Cth) the NHMRC must establish the Australian Research Committee and the Australian Health Ethics Committee. The later entity advises the NHMRC on ethical issues relating to health and works to develop and provide the NHMRC with guidelines for the conduct of medical research involving humans. In 2007 the NHMRC released the *National Statement on Ethical Conduct in Human Research* (National Statement) and the *Australian Code for the Responsible Conduct of Research* (the Code). The National Statement provides guidelines and sets national standards for researchers conducting research on humans, human research ethics committees and other bodies or entities involved in the ethical review of research involving humans. The National Statement emphasises the responsibility of the institution, through which the research is being conducted, to ensure 'quality, safety and ethical acceptability of research that they sponsor or permit to be carried out'.[12] The Code[13] provides a guide for researchers and institutions in 'responsible research practice'. While the Code is written specifically for universities and other public sector research institutions it is also considered a valuable resource document for any organisation engaged in research. The first part of the Code is directed to providing guidance on best practice in research and the second part contains a framework for managing any breaches of the Code or misconduct in research. There are no mandatory provisions in relation to compliance with the National Statement or the Code, however, compliance is a prerequisite for access to research funding.

The NHMRC also has obligations and responsibilities imposed under the Prohibition of Human Cloning for Reproduction and Regulation of Human Embryo Research Amendment Act 2006, the Prohibition of Human Cloning for Reproduction Act 2002 and the Research Involving Human Embryo Act 2002.[14]

The Privacy Act

The Privacy Act 1988 (Cth) protects the privacy of 'personal information'[15] (particularly 'sensitive information' which includes 'health information'),[16] collected or held by the Commonwealth or the private sector. Privacy legislation attempts to balance the interests of the public in having the privacy of their information protected against the interests of the public in having information available. In this context the issue is whether, and how, personal/sensitive information can be legally acquired and made available for the purpose of research. The privacy legislation existing at Commonwealth, state and territory levels establishes privacy principles[17] for the collection, storage, disclosure, access, accuracy, security and use of personal information (refer to Chapter 4, Privacy and confidentiality of patient information). These legislative provisions are applicable to personal/sensitive information collected as part of the research process and are reinforced by the National Statement, the Code and the guidelines which also specifically address the requirements in relation to privacy of participant information. The Federal Privacy Commissioner has given approval to two sets of guidelines (issued by the NHMRC) that must be adhered to in circumstances where researchers are handling health information for research purposes without the consent of the individual to whom the information belongs. The guidelines, which aim to protect the privacy of participant information elicited during medical research are included under ss 95 and 95A of the Privacy Act 1988 (Cth). The privacy and medical research guideline under s 95 sets out the procedure for human research ethics committees and researchers when personal information is disclosed for research purposes from Commonwealth agencies. Section 95A deals with access to health information for medical research where consent cannot be obtained. The guidelines require that the public interest in the research outweighs the public interest in the protection of the privacy.[18]

In addition, legislation in a number of states and territories authorises statutory guidelines similar to those provided by the NHMRC in relation to the disclosure of personal information for the purpose of medical research.[19] It is also common practice for individual researchers, research institutions and those involved in the collection of data to be bound by contractual terms protecting privacy of information as part of their employment contract, funding agreement or research access agreement.

Guardianship legislation

Guardianship legislation in a number of the jurisdictions provides the process by which consent, in relation to participation in medical research of individuals without legal capacity, may be obtained (refer to Chapter 6, Consent). As the legislation differs between the states and territories medical researchers must familiarise themselves with the legal requirements in the jurisdiction in which they are practising.

CLINICAL TRIALS

A clinical trial is that part of a research study which aims to discover whether a particular intervention, based on preliminary data, is actually beneficial. Clinical trials are conducted under two schemes for the purpose of researching therapeutic goods. These schemes are the Clinical Trial Exemption (CTX) Scheme and the Clinical Trial Notification (CTN) Scheme. The schemes are utilised when there is a proposal to introduce a drug or drug product, which is not entered in the Australian Register of Therapeutic Goods. This may include where there is a new drug, or a new formulation for, or new use of, an existing drug, or a new route for an existing drug. All CTX and CTN schemes are legally required to have an Australian sponsor that will be the person, body, or institution which takes overall responsibility for the conduct of a trial. The sponsor therefore is responsible not only for ensuring that the trial complies with any legal obligations but also in assuming liability in the event of injury or damage.

The CTX scheme, which is the process for approval or rejection, requires the Therapeutic Goods Administration to evaluate the data and assess safety issues in relation to the proposed guidelines for usage of the new drug and/or drug product. The Human Research Ethics Committee is then required to consider the proposed clinical trial protocols in light of any information supplied by the Therapeutic Goods Administration and the Australian sponsor. In the CTN trial the Human Research Ethics Committee reviews the data on the new drug/drug product and, after giving approval for the trial, the Australian sponsor notifies the Therapeutic Goods Administration.

Legal issues

The researcher conducting medical/clinical research involving human subjects has an obligation to protect the research participants from harm. The type of harm may include an injury due to the negligent conduct of the researcher, the failure of the researcher to obtain a legally valid consent from the participants, and/or a failure of the researcher to protect the privacy and confidentiality of the participant's information. In addition, in relation to professionals such as medical practitioners, there are professional disciplinary consequences for engaging in research in a way that is indicative of professional misconduct and/or unsatisfactory professional conduct. The following provides some examples of the legal actions that may arise for a medical practitioner engaged in research.

Negligence

A research participant may initiate an action in negligence against the researcher on the grounds that the researcher, researching institution, or ethical review body did something or failed to do something that amounted to a *breach of the duty of care owed to the research participant and, as a result, the participant sustained a damage*. In the same way that a medical practitioner owes a duty of care to their patients (as persons they can reasonably foresee) so the research participant is owed a duty of care by those carrying out, supervising or supporting the research. As previously stated, the determination as to whether there was a breach of that duty would be considered in light of whether the research was conducted in a manner consistent with peer professional opinion as to what was competent, reasonable and accepted research practice. This standard is set in the civil liability legislation in each of the states and territories. The significance of the National Standard, the Code and any relevant guidelines and policies to determinations as to the standard can not be overemphasised (refer to Chapter 5, Negligence).

Trespass to the person

The law requires that before undertaking any medical treatment a legally valid consent is obtained by the medical practitioner from the patient or from their substitute decision-maker. The same expectation applies prior to the inclusion of a participant in a research project or clinical trial. To be legally valid *the consent must be voluntary, cover the specific project or trial, and be informed*. In addition, the participant must have the capacity to give a legally valid consent (refer to Chapter 6, consent).

In relation to the *requirement of voluntariness* it is important that any medical practitioner, or medical student who is in a therapeutic relationship with a patient ensures the patient understands that their participation, or non-participation, in the research will have no impact on their medical treatment. That is, the role of the medical practitioner, as the patient's treating physician, is separate and distinct from their role as researcher. A practical way of dealing with this issue is for the medical practitioner to remain at 'arms length' from the activity of obtaining consent when there is any potential for confusion of roles by the patient. The patient must be clear that there will be neither a benefit nor disadvantage to their voluntary decision as to whether or not they participate in the research project or clinical trial.

The law requires that the consent *covers the specifics of the research project or clinical trial*. Though the research participant has consented to one part of a project or trial that does not mean they have consented to other parts or activities that were not included in the original consent. For example, has the participant consented to the use of their information after the data is collected, have they consented to the use of their human tissue at a later date or for a different study? In relation to biobanks, it has been suggested that there may be, in future, the use of levels of consent such as:[20]

LEVEL 1: limited or specific consent for use in a specific and defined research project

LEVEL 2: qualified consent where the participant gives consent to the initial intervention and wishes to be contacted in the future if there is any extension or substantial variation from the initial project

LEVEL 3: full or unspecified consent which would operate as consent to multiple research purposes into the future.

The law also requires that the researcher *fully and frankly discloses information* to potential research participants prior to obtaining their consent. In the case of *Halushka v University of Saskatchewan*[21] the patient was assured that the experimental drug had been used previously and found to be safe. This information was not correct and, after consenting to participate in the research and taking the drug the patient suffered a cardiac arrest. The court found that as there had not been 'full and frank' disclosure of the facts the researchers were liable for the damage. This decision is consistent with the findings in *Weiss v Solomon*.[22] In this case the court held the researcher and the hospital liable where the participant had not been informed of the risks associated and known about the experimental treatment.

The researcher *must obtain consent from the participant with the capacity to give a legally valid consent or some person or body that has the legal authority to consent on their behalf*. It is clear that all adults (over the age of 18 years) of sound mind have the legal capacity to give consent to participate in a research project or clinical trial.

The situation in relation to *children* is similar to that which applies in obtaining a consent prior to medical treatment. That is, does the child have a level of maturity so as to understand the nature of the research and are they able to voluntarily communicate a preferred choice.[23] This is referred to as 'Gillick competent'. While there is legislation in the Australian Capital Territory,[24] New South Wales,[25] South Australia[26] and Victoria[27] that pertains to a child's capacity to consent to medical treatment the provisions are not applicable to research. It is preferable if the child is of an age to understand the nature of a research project or trial that they are included in any discussion prior to obtaining their consent and any refusal should be considered very seriously. It would appear that where a child lacks capacity their refusal to consent might be overridden by the parent or the legal guardian where their opinion is considered to be in the 'best interest' of the child.

Impaired capacity

When an adult has impaired capacity due to an intellectual disability, mental disorder, acquired brain injury, physical disability or dementia it is imperative that they are assessed in light of whether they, as an individual, are competent in relation to this particular project or trial at this particular time to consent. If they are assessed as being incompetent to give a legally valid consent to participate in the research then consent must be sought from a person or body that has a legal authority to give consent on their behalf. The legislation in each of the jurisdictions identifies the person or entity that may give consent to experimental healthcare or medical research and the process by which this consent may be obtained. As an example, the Victorian Guardianship and Administration Act 1986 sets out the legal process when medical research can be performed on an adult who has no capacity to give consent on their own behalf. The 2006 amendments to this legislation require that the research project, for which purpose the procedure is being performed, must have been approved by the Victorian Human Research Ethics Committee. After this approval has been obtained only a registered medical practitioner or dental practitioner can perform or supervise the medical research procedure on the particular patient under the Act, and only if satisfied that the statutory criteria are met in the case of this particular patient. In New South Wales the Guardianship Tribunal, and in Queensland the Civil and Administrative Tribunal, must approve the clinical research or clinical trial before a person who is incapable of giving consent can participate. Approval of the relevant ethics committee is required prior to the application. The approval of the respective tribunals of the clinical research or trial does not operate as consent to the participation of the particular person. In Western Australia the Guardianship and Administration Act 1990 does not permit a legal guardian or next-of-kin to consent on behalf of an adult who is not competent to consent on their own behalf to participation in research. Participation of such an adult is only permitted if the medical professional considers that participation of the adult is in their 'best interest'. Once again, it can be seen that there are significant differences between the individual states and territories. Medical practitioners and medical students must therefore familiarise themselves with the legal requirements in the jurisdiction in which they are studying or practising.

Professional misconduct

Allegations of professional misconduct may arise in circumstances in which a researcher, regulated with a professional authority, does something or fails to do something which amounts to 'notifiable conduct', 'unsatisfactory professional conduct' or 'professional misconduct'.[28] For example, the allegations of research fraud bought against Dr William McBride before the New South Wales Medical Tribunal in 1989 resulted in an order to have his name removed from the Medical Register.[29]

SCENARIO AND ACTIVITY

This is a literature search and reflective exercise therefore there is no answer provided.

Students are invited to locate information on a study conducted by a medical practitioner in the National Women's Hospital in Auckland New Zealand. This study commenced in 1966 and ran for almost 2 decades. The project was designed to

---

show that carcinoma in situ in the cervix was not a precursor to invasive carcinoma. A judicial inquiry was ordered by the Ministry of Health 'Committee of Inquiry into Allegations Concerning the Treatment of Cervical Cancer at the National Women's Hospital and into Other Related Matters' (the Cartwright Inquiry). This study will be very easy to locate on any research or research ethics database. The following articles may be of assistance in getting started: Heslop, B, 'All about research – looking back at the 1987 Cervical Cancer Inquiry', NZ Med J (2004) August (6); Paul, C, 'Internal and external morality of medicine: lessons from New Zealand' BMJ (2000) February 320 (7233) 499–503.

Consider the legal issues and actions that potentially and actually arise from the conduct of the researcher and the institution.

REVIEW QUESTIONS

To ensure that you have identified and understood the key points of this chapter please answer the following questions.

1 Where on the web would you locate the National Health and Medical Council Act 1992 (Cth)?

2 In the National Statement on Ethical Conduct in Human Research (2007) what are the guidelines in relation to protecting the privacy of participant information, protecting vulnerable groups, obtaining consent from persons with impaired capacity, and obtaining consent from children?

3 Once you have read the Australian Code for the Responsible Conduct of Research identify the process for managing breaches of the Code and research misconduct.

4 Identify the elements in a negligence action and describe how they may be relevant to a research participant who is injured as a result of their participation in a clinical trial.

5 Identify the legislation in your state or territory which empowers a person or body to consent for an adult with no capacity to give a legally valid consent to participate in a clinical trial or research project. What are the requirements under that legislation?

Further reading

Australian Code for Responsible Conduct of Research, 2007. Online. Available: www.nhmrc.gov.au/publications/synopses/ r39syn_summary.html (accessed 22 July 2010).

Bennett, B, Deakin C, 'Registration of clinical trials: challenges for global regulation' (2009) 17 JLM 82.

Chalmers, D, Nicol, D, 'Human genetic research databases and biobanks: towards uniform terminology and Australia Best Practice' (2008) 15 JLM 538.

National Health and Medical Research Council Act, NHMRC, Canberra. Online. Available: www.nhmrc.gov.au (accessed 22 July 2010).

Parker, M, 'Naked regulators: Moral pluralism, deliberative democracy and authoritative regulation of human embryonic stem cell (hESC) research' (2009) 16 JLM 580.

Prohibition of Human Cloning for Reproduction and the Regulation of Human Embryo Research Amendment Act 2006 (Cth).

Endnotes

1 Australian Code for the Responsible Conduct of Research, National Health and Medical Research Council, Australian Research Council and Universities Australia. Australian Government, Canberra, 2007 at 1. Online. Available: www.nh mrc.gov.au/publications/synopses/r39syn.htm (accessed 22 July 2010).

2 Research Assessment Exercise (RAE) 2008 Research Assessment Exercise: Guidance on Submissions, RAE 03/2005. See Appendix B 'Definition of Research for RAE'. Online. Available: www.ra e.ac.uk(accessed 22 July 2010).

3 *British Medical Journal,* 7070(313): 1448, 7 December 1996. Online. Available: www.cisp.org/library/ethics/nuremberg (accessed 22 July 2010).

4 National Statement on Ethical Conduct Involving Humans. Online. Available: www.nhmrc.gov.au/publications/synopses/ e72syn.htm (accessed 22 July 2010).

5 International Ethical Guidelines for Biomedical Research Involving Human Subjects. Online. Available: www.fhi.org/ training/fr/retc/pdf_files/cioms.pdf (accessed July 22 2010).

6 Kerridge, I, Lowe, M, McPhee, J, *Ethics and Law for the Health Professions*, 2nd edn, The Federation Press, Sydney, 2005 at 528.

7   Rothman, K, Michels, K 'The continuing unethical use of placebo controls' (1994) 331 (6) *New England Journal of Medicine* 394–8, in Kerridge, I, Lowe, M, McPhee, J, *Ethics and Law for the Health Professions*, 2nd edn, The Federation Press, Sydney, 2005 at 528.

8   Animal Welfare Act 1992 (ACT); Prevention of Cruelty to Animals Act 1979 (NSW); Animal Research Act 1985 (NSW); Animal Welfare Act (NT); Animal Care and Protection Act 2001 (Qld); Animal Welfare Act 1985 (SA); Animal Welfare Act 1993 (Tas); Prevention of Cruelty to Animals Act 1986 (Vic); Animal Welfare Act 2002 (WA).

9   Australian Code of Practice for the Care and Use of Animals for Scientific Purposes. Online. Available: www.nhmrc.gov.au/ publications/synopses/ea16syn.htm (accessed 22 July 2010).

10 National Health and Medical Research Council Act 1992 (Cth) s 7(1).

11 The National Health and Medical Research Council is responsible to the Minister for Health and Ageing.

12 National Statement on Ethical Conduct in Human Research, National Health and Medical Research Council, Australian Research Council, Australian Vice-Chancellors Committee, Australian Government, 2007.

13 Above, n 1.

14 National Health and Medical Research Council. Online. Available: www.nhmrc.gov.au/about/org/role.htm#b (accessed 22 July 2010).

15 Personal information is defined in s 6 of the Privacy Act 1988 (Cth) to mean, 'information or an opinion (including information or an opinion forming part of a database), whether true or not, and whether recorded in a material form or not, about an individual whose identity is apparent, or can reasonably be ascertained, from the information or opinion'.

16 Sensitive information is defined in s 6 the Privacy Act 1998 (Cth) to mean '(a) information or an opinion about an individual's: racial or ethnic origin, political opinion, membership of a political organisation, religious or philosophical beliefs, membership of professional or trade associations or trade union, sexual preference or criminal record; (b) health information about an individual; (c) genetic information about an individual that is not otherwise health information'.

17 The Information Privacy Principles (IPPs) are set out in s 14 and the National Privacy Principles (NPP) in Schedule 3 of the Privacy Act 1988 (Cth).

18 Privacy Act 1988 (Cth). Online Available: http://www.privacy. gov.au/law/act/research (accessed 22 July 2010).

19 Health Records and Information Privacy Act 2002 (NSW).

20 Chalmers, D, Nicol, D, 'Human genetic research databases and biobanks: towards uniform terminology and Australian best practice' (2008) 15 JLM 538.

21 (1965) 53 DLR 436.

22 [1989] RJQ 731.

23 *Gillick v West Norfolk and Wisbech Area health Association* [1986] AC 112 HL; *Secretary of the Department of Health and Community Services v JWB and SMB* (1992) 175 CLR 218.

24 Medical Treatment Act (ACT).

25 Minors (Property and Contract) Act 1970 (NSW).

26 Consent to Medical Treatment and Palliative Care Act 1995 (SA).

27 Medical Treatment Act 1988 (Vic).

28 As defined under the Health Practitioner Regulation National Law Act 2009.

29 As discussed in Kerridge I, Lowe M, McPhee J, *Ethics and Law for the Health Professionals* (2nd ed), The Federation Press, Sydney 2007, p 537.

Answers to review scenarios and activities

CHAPTER 1

1 An action in negligence.

2 In the Supreme Court exercising its civil jurisdiction. It is likely that this particular case would be before the Supreme Court because of the amount of money a family would be seeking in compensation for the loss of the family's sole financial provider.

3 The Coroner's Court due to the sudden and unexpected death of the patient and the tribunal in your respective state or territory that has the jurisdiction to hear and determine disciplinary proceedings brought against medical practitioners. For example, the Queensland Civil and Administrative Tribunal.

CHAPTER 3

1 The purpose of the medical records is to exchange information and notate and direct patient care for the purpose of facilitating optimal patient outcomes.

2 The information recorded should be accurate, objective, clear, concise and contemporaneous, The records should include the date and time (on a 24-hour clock) and the signature of the writer of the entry should be accompanied by a printed version of their full name. All entries should be legible. The medical practitioner should write only what they have seen first hand. If the medical practitioner is to write what another health professional has told them they saw then the medical practitioner must identify the person who actually saw the event. The medical practitioner must never write for another person in the first person. If the facility is still recording information in a paper-based system each medical record page must have the name and UR number of the patient. The medical practitioner should only use those abbreviations which are approved by the employing facility. A medical practitioner must never write a report in advance. Where an error has been made in a patient's medical records the incorrect error should have a line placed through it and the author write 'Written in error' and date and sign it.

3 Refer to Table 3.1.

CHAPTER 4

The general legal principle is that the psychiatrist would treat as confidential all information disclosed by the patient as part of the medical practitioner–patient therapeutic relationship. However, in this particular circumstance the patient has disclosed information which the medical practitioner is legally obliged to disclose. In all Australian jurisdictions, other than Western Australia, there are mandatory legislative provisions which require a medical practitioner to disclose such information to the respective state or territory government department responsible for the protection of children (e.g. in Queensland the Department of Communities, Child Safety). Even if there is no mandatory reporting obligation, the public interest in disclosure of this type of information overrides the right of the patient to have the information kept confidential. Access the mandatory notification provisions in the legislation in your jurisdiction and familiarise yourself with the wording of the obligation and the protection from civil, criminal, disciplinary action provided to a person who notifies based on a 'reasonable belief' and/ or 'in good faith'.

CHAPTER 5

The following is a general overview of the issues that would be raised in answer to the hypothetical. It is important that you consider the legislation specific to the state or territory in which you are studying.

- The legal action Mr Butter is likely to pursue is a negligence action. Mr Butter is most likely to initiate a civil action in negligence to obtain financial compensation for the physical damage he has sustained.
- Mr Butter may sue the medical practitioner as the professional who undertook the surgery which resulted in the removal of the incorrect kidney. He may sue the registered nurse who failed to ensure the documentation was correct prior to the administration of the anaesthetic. He may also consider suing the hospital for failing to ensure that there was adequate numbers of appropriately trained staff employed to deliver the healthcare services (non-delegable duty of care).
- The elements necessary to succeed in a negligence action are:
  1. the existence of a duty of care
  2. conduct or an omission that amounted to a breach of the duty
  3. damage sustained by the patient
  4. a causal connection between the conduct of the health professional and the damage.

Each of the elements of the action must be proven on the balance of probabilities. The issues therefore are as follows:

1 Is there a duty of care between Mr Butter and the respective defendants?

To successfully sue in negligence a plaintiff (in this case Mr Butter) must prove that he is a member of a class of persons whom the defendants (potentially the medical practitioner, nurse and hospital) could reasonably foresee was likely to be injured by their acts or omissions. This legally recognised relationship, referred to by Lord Aitkin in the case of *Donoghue v Stevenson* as being, at law a 'neighbour', gives rise to a duty of care between citizens and provides the basis upon which the plaintiff can initiate proceedings in negligence. The fact that Mr Butter is a patient within the hospital (considered at law as a corporation) and under the care of the nurse and the medical practitioner goes to the existence of a duty of care between himself and the three potential defendants. It could be agued that, as a patient within the institution, under the care of the defendants, Mr Butter was a person they could reasonably foresee as potentially being injured by their actions or omissions.

2 Has there been a breach of the duty of care?

To prove to the requisite standard that a breach of the duty of care has occurred it must be established that the conduct of the defendants fell below a standard considered as reasonable. The civil liability legislation in your particular state or territory should provide you with a benchmark against which the conduct of the professionals will be considered. As an example, the Queensland Civil Liability Act 2003 specifies the standard of care in relation to a professional. The Act states that a professional does not breach the duty of care in providing a professional service if it is established that the professional acted in a way that was widely accepted by peer professional opinion by a significant number of respected practitioners in the field as competent professional practice. This legislative provision is consistent with the decision in *Bolam's* case in which the court held that in circumstances which involve some special skill or competence the standard was that of the ordinary skilled man exercising and professing to have that special skill. In the case of a health professional, this meant failure to act in accordance with the standard of the reasonable competent health professional at the time. In the case of *Rogers v Whitaker* the High Court of Australia referred to the standard of a person holding themselves out as having that level of skill and knowledge. The legislation makes provision for circumstances in which the court forms the view that the standard stated in the evidence given by the professionals is 'irrational'. The court may then determine the standard of practice against which to consider the conduct of the defendant/s.

The conduct of the nurse and the medical practitioner in the scenario could be, on the evidence, found to fulfil the criteria required to successfully make out a breach to the requisite standard. The questions would be: Have the nurse and/or the medical practitioner conducted themselves in a manner that would be accepted by peer professional opinion of respected practitioners (that is a significant number of their professional peers) as competent professional practice? Would the evidence prove on the balance of probabilities that professional peers of the nurse and/or doctor would not have conducted themselves professionally in the way the defendants have done? The evidence before the court may include the expert evidence of peers, policies and guidelines from the relevant Department of Health, the health facility, and/or the clinical unit. Policies and guidelines from professional colleges and research data is also indicative of competent professional practice.

3   Has the plaintiff sustained damage?

The 'gist' of the negligence action is to shift the loss from the person who sustained the damage to the person who caused the damage. The injury (or damage) is therefore described as the 'gist' of the negligence action. The court will consider whether the plaintiff has sustained a type of damage recognised as compensatable. The courts recognise physical injury, pure economic loss and nervous shock. The theoretical underpinning of compensation is to place the plaintiff in the position they would have been in had they not sustained the injury as far as money is able to. The injury or damage sustained by the plaintiff flows from the removal of the incorrect kidney and the future surgery which will result in the removal of the diseased kidney. The medical, financial and lifestyle damage as quantified will be the basis for an assessment of the amount of the compensation.

4   Is the conduct of the defendant/s causally related to the damage claimed?

The case law imposes the legal obligation on the plaintiff to establish that the damage would not have occurred 'but for' (*Barnett's* case) the actions of the defendants and that the connection between the action and the damage makes common sense (*Lipovac's* case). The civil liability legislation also identifies the requisite causal relationship necessary to establish liability.

As an example, the Civil Liability Act 2003 (Qld) requires that the breach of the duty of care caused particular harm. The Act requires the breach to be the necessary condition of the occurrence of the harm and is appropriate for the scope of the liability. On the facts given in the scenario it is open for the plaintiff to argue that the damage claimed would not have occurred 'but for' the nurse not checking the documents at the time she should have and the medical practitioner not undertaking the surgery without the appropriate documents. If this is held to be the necessary condition for the damage then the causal connection is established.

The hospital, as a corporation, has a non-delegable duty of care to the patients and clients (*Kondis's* case) to provide adequate numbers of appropriately trained staff. On the facts given in the scenario, it is open to the plaintiff to argue that the hospital was in breach of the non-delegable duty to the patients. Should the plaintiff successfully prove negligence on the part of the medical practitioner and/or the nurse, the hospital may be vicariously liable for their negligence. The plaintiff will be required to prove the medical practitioner and/or the nurse were employees of the hospital and their conduct was within the course and scope of their employment. The doctrine of vicarious liability shifts the liability from the employee to the employer.

- The defences to an action in negligence are to rebut the damage; the breach of the duty did not 'cause' the damage claimed. There is also a possibility that the defendants may seek to reduce their liability through arguments directed to the proportion of the their contribution to the total loss claimed. That is, the defendants seek to have the damages apportioned on the basis that the damage occurred as a result of the actions of all or some of the defendants. Each defendant would therefore be liable for the proportion of the damage as determined by the court.

CHAPTER 6

The medical student should recognise that taking blood from a patient is an intervention which requires obtaining a legally valid consent. The consent for this can be obtained verbally. It would not be appropriate to conclude that because the person was an in-patient of the hospital that by implication he/she had consented to the procedure. Nor is the taking of blood, in most circumstances, invasive to the extent that a written consent is required. The student should consider the following.

- Is the patient a child or an adult? If the patient is a child is there legislation which determines at what age they can give a legally valid consent (such as in New South Wales or South Australia).

If there is no legislation in the state or territory in which they are studying is the child old enough to have an understanding of the nature and effect of the procedure? If so, they may be Gillick competent to provide a legally valid consent. If not is there a parent or legal guardian who is able to give consent for the procedure? As the taking of blood is not life threatening the legislation and common law relevant to emergencies and life-threatening situations does not apply.

- If the patient is an adult, do they have the capacity to make decisions about their health care? That is, do they understand the nature and effect of the decision they are being asked to make, are they able to make a decision voluntarily and can they communicate that decision? If not, and it is considered that the patient does not have capacity, is there a substitute decision-maker prescribed by the legislation in the state or territory in which the medical student is studying?

- Is the consent obtained voluntarily, making sure that the patient is not given the impression that there is any duress or coercion? While the medical student must give the patient the requisite information for the patient to make a decision about whether to consent to having the blood taken, the medical student must be mindful not to misrepresent any of that information to the patient.

- The consent obtained must cover the specific procedure of taking the blood and the purpose for which the blood is being taken.

- The medical student must provide the information required by the relevant case law and legislation. As discussed in the text, a defence for an action in trespass to the person requires that the patient has been informed in broad terms of the nature of the procedure. However, from a practical perspective the medical student should provide the information prescribed under the state or territory civil liability legislation which imposes a duty to warn a patient of risk (refer to Chapter 5, Negligence).

CHAPTER 7

As with the requirements of consent, the patient must be sufficiently informed regarding proposed treatment and options. It is also prudent practice to check that the patient is competent. Once the practitioner is satisfied that these aspects have been addressed the common law clearly allows competent patients to refuse treatment. However, discussion with the patient to identify reasons for his refusal can often highlight issues of concern that can be further explained, such that the patient may change his mind and accept what is proposed by the treating team. If the patient's decision remains unchanged then the practitioner would work with this changed circumstance in mind.

The reference to the serious illness should alert the practitioner to consider further discussion at some time, regarding future care and treatment and the desire to identify a substitute decision-maker; for example, in Victoria the appointment of an enduring power of attorney medical treatment. When practitioners know the applicable legal principles and available mechanisms they are well placed to have important conversations with patients and their families to enure plans are made for future treatment. It can save time and allows for everyone involved to be clear regarding who can provide consent or refusal for treatment when the patient is not competent.

CHAPTER 8

This scenario requires identification and consideration of which jurisdiction the issue arises in. In any case, the patient would require mental assessment, preferably by a suitably qualified practitioner such as a psychiatrist, to determine the likelihood of the patient carrying out her threat, and verification of the serious genetic disorder. If the medical evidence and opinion indicate that termination of the pregnancy is preferable for the patient's health, the law of abortion and child destruction should then be considered. These conclusions and treatment considerations should be carefully and fully documented in the patient's file.

In those states and/or territories which hold abortion and child destruction as crimes the medical practitioner would require knowledge of the parameters of the law in relation to both crimes. For example, in Queensland the crimes of abortion and killing an unborn child exist, however the insertion of section 282, 'Surgical and medical treatment', in the legislation suggests that where a health professional is performing in good faith and with reasonable care and skill, either a surgical procedure or medical treatment on a woman or unborn child to preserve the mother's life, then the actions are considered lawful. However, where there is any lack of clarity or apparent overlap of law, legal advice should be sought before proceeding. This compares with the jurisdictions of the Northern Territory and South Australia; both have the offences of child destruction and abortion, however the law permits termination of a pregnancy where a foetus is found to have a serious hereditary disorder. In New South Wales there is no crime of child destruction, however it would be prudent to consider the law of abortion, which states that the medical practitioner must honestly believe on reasonable grounds (hence the need to validate the mental assessment and the genetic disorder) that the termination was necessary to protect the mother from serious danger to herself. These jurisdictions compare to others where abortion has been decriminalised, such as Victoria, where late-term abortion is permitted. The legislation specifies that if the woman is more than 24 weeks pregnant two medical practitioners must believe that the abortion is appropriate.

CHAPTER 10

Eric is admitted as a voluntary patient and the common law of consent applies, whereby adults are presumed to have capacity to consent to treatment. Despite the fact that Eric might be suffering with a mental illness therapy can not be given without his consent, or he is deemed to be an involuntary (scheduled) patient. Clearly, the psychiatrist and associated health practitioners should take the time to provide further explanation of the treatment, however Eric is lawfully able to refuse to participate in the therapy. Eric should be made aware of his rights, including his right to discharge himself. Although the Tasmanian and the Northern Territory mental health legislation specifically state that voluntary patients may discharge themselves at any time, in both jurisdictions a medical practitioner or approved nurse can detain the patient for up to 4–6 hours to enable an assessment to be made to decide if the patient should be admitted as an involuntary patient. Other state mental health units may well mirror this requirement of adequate discharge assessment in policy or guidelines. Patients should be informed if this is the case and all attempts to encourage a patient to remain should be made. Nonetheless, if the patient disagrees and force is required to detain the patient, the practitioners must be able to justify the change of status from voluntary to an involuntary patient.

Another consideration regarding the 'new' therapy proposed by the psychiatrist is knowledge that several aspects of treatment are regulated or specifically banned in many jurisdictions. For example, if the 'new' therapy included deep sleep therapy or insulin coma therapy, they are banned in New South Wales, Queensland, Western Australia and the Northern Territory.

CHAPTER 11

Based on your previous experiences of the registrar's conduct and the particular incident it would be reasonable to say that in the 'course of your practise' you have formed a 'reasonable belief' that the conduct of the registrar amounts to 'notifiable conduct' under s140 of the National Law. There is, therefore, a mandatory obligation upon you to report the medical practitioner to the National Agency. It is important that before you do so you consult with your clinical supervisor and comply with the hospital policies and guidelines not only for the purpose of making such a report to the National Agency, but also in relation to complying with the incident reporting procedures of your employing hospital.

Appendices

Table of cases

Table of statutes

Australian Capital Territory

New South Wales

Northern Territory

Queensland

Western Australia

Guardianship & Administration

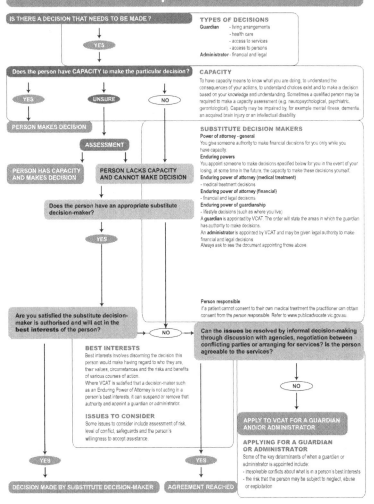

IS THERE A DECISION THAT NEEDS TO BE MADE?

↓
YES
↓

TYPES OF DECISIONS
Guardian — living arrangements
— health care
— access to services
— access to persons
Administrator — financial and legal

Does the person have CAPACITY to make the particular decision?

YES — UNSURE — NO

CAPACITY
To have capacity means to know what you are doing, to understand the consequences of your actions, to understand choices exist and to make a decision based on your knowledge and understanding. Sometimes a qualified person may be required to make a capacity assessment (e.g. neuropsychological, psychiatric, gerontological). Capacity may be impaired by, for example mental illness, dementia, an acquired brain injury or an intellectual disability.

PERSON MAKES DECISION

ASSESSMENT

PERSON HAS CAPACITY AND MAKES DECISION — **PERSON LACKS CAPACITY AND CANNOT MAKE DECISION**

SUBSTITUTE DECISION MAKERS
Power of attorney - general
You give someone authority to make financial decisions for you only while you have capacity.
Enduring powers
You appoint someone to make decisions specified below for you in the event of your losing, at some time in the future, the capacity to make these decisions yourself.
Enduring power of attorney (medical treatment)
- medical treatment decisions
Enduring power of attorney (financial)
- financial and legal decisions
Enduring power of guardianship
- lifestyle decisions (such as where you live)
A **guardian** is appointed by VCAT. The order will state the areas in which the guardian has authority to make decisions.
An **administrator** is appointed by VCAT and may be given legal authority to make financial and legal decisions.
Always ask to see the document appointing those above.

Does the person have an appropriate substitute decision-maker?

↓
YES

Person responsible
If a patient cannot consent to their own medical treatment the practitioner can obtain consent from the *person responsible*. Refer to www.publicadvocate.vic.gov.au.

Are you satisfied the substitute decision-maker is authorised and will act in the best interests of the person?

— NO —

Can the issues be resolved by informal decision-making through discussion with agencies, negotiation between conflicting parties or arranging for services? Is the person agreeable to the services?

BEST INTERESTS
Best interests involves discerning the decision this person would make having regard to who they are, their values, circumstances and the risks and benefits of various courses of action.
Where VCAT is satisfied that a decision-maker such as an Enduring Power of Attorney is not acting in a person's best interests, it can suspend or remove that authority and appoint a guardian or administrator.

ISSUES TO CONSIDER
Some issues to consider include assessment of risk, level of conflict, safeguards and the person's willingness to accept assistance.

↓
NO
↓

APPLY TO VCAT FOR A GUARDIAN AND/OR ADMINISTRATOR

APPLYING FOR A GUARDIAN OR ADMINISTRATOR
Some of the key determinants of when a guardian or administrator is appointed include:
- irresolvable conflicts about what is in a person's best interests
- the risk that the person may be subject to neglect, abuse or exploitation

YES
↓
DECISION MADE BY SUBSTITUTE DECISION-MAKER

YES
↓
AGREEMENT REACHED

OFFICE OF THE PUBLIC ADVOCATE

For more information on medical consent, refusal of medical treatment, powers of attorney and guardianship see our website www.publicadvocate.vic.gov.au or contact our advice service 1300 309 337.

Mar 2007

Glossary

Act/statute/legislation: laws as passed by the parliament through the parliamentary process. This may be the state or territory parliament or the Commonwealth parliament.

Autonomy: the right to self-determination, to make decisions in your own right, independent of others.

Best interests: this is the test used by substitute decision-makers as the basis for decisions about what health intervention and/or other intervention they will consent to on behalf of a person who lacks capacity to make their own decisions. The substitute decision-maker must make an assessment as to what is in the best interests of the person who is incompetent to make their own decision.

Beyond reasonable doubt: the standard of proof that applies in a criminal case. The accused is innocent unless the prosecution can prove the elements of the particular crime 'beyond reasonable doubt'. That is, there is no reasonable doubt that the evidence before the court proves the elements of the offence.

By-law: a rule made by a local authority for the regulation of local government affairs.

Common law: this term can have a number of meanings. It may refer to a legal system which is based on judge-made law, as in Australia, which is a common law country. Similarly, it may refer to the rules of law that are developed by the courts as opposed to those which are created by parliament (Acts).

Defendant: in a civil action the person against whom the action is being brought.

Equity: this part of the law was administered in England by the Lord Chancellor and later the Court of Chancery as distinct from the court of common law. The Chancellor was able to deal with the cases on a flexible basis focused on the fair result rather than the rigid principles of the law.

Fiduciary: comes from the Latin *fiducia* meaning trust. In the context of the provision of healthcare services it refers to a person, usually the health professional, who through their position of trust with respect to the patients and clients is obliged to act solely and primarily for the benefit of those persons.

Guardian: a person appointed as authorised under legislation and/or by a guardianship board and/or court to make decisions on behalf of a person who lacks capacity.

Injunctive relief: an order from the court addressed to either prohibiting or compelling an activity. The court will order injunctive relief only if it is considered just and convenient to do so.

Jurisdiction: the power of a court to hear a matter and make an order and the territorial limits within which the law operates.

On the balance of probabilities: the standard of proof that applies in a civil matter. It is a lower standard of proof than that which operates in a criminal case. The plaintiff must prove their case on the balance of probabilities. That is, more probably than not the evidence of the plaintiff proves the elements of the action.

Ordinance: another term for a regulation which has the authority to dictate conduct or management.

Plaintiff: in a civil action the person who is commencing the action.

Tort: a French word for harm or wrong. The word refers to a wrongful act or omission for which damages can be obtained through a civil action.

Index

abortion 202
    Australian context 203–5
    child destruction 206–7
    decriminalisation 206
    early English law 202
    late-term 207
    rights of the father 206
    wrongful conception/birth/life 207–9
access to patient information 77–9
Acts of Parliament 3–4
    passing 5–6
    see also law
Acts *see* statutes
ADR *see* Alternate Dispute Resolution
advance care directives 180
adversarial legal system 21
adverse events 28
    see also safety and quality in health
AI *see* artificial insemination
Alternate Dispute Resolution (ADR) 22
alternative actions to negligence 131–2
    see also negligence litigation
American Society of Hospital Pharmacists 226
APAC *see* Australian Pharmaceutical Advisory Council
apologies 123–4
    see also negligence litigation
appellate jurisdiction 11–12
    see also court hierarchy
ARTG *see* Australian Register of Therapeutic Goods
artificial insemination (AI) 210
    see also reproductive technology
assault 145–6
    see also consent
'at the time' of the incident 110
Attorney-General's role in regulations 7
Australia's Health Workforce 252
Australian Association of Cancer Registries (AACR) 29
Australian Capital Territory legislation
    abortion 206
    good Samaritan 99
    human rights 45
    intellectual impairment and consent 154

medical power of attorney 184–5
mental health 236
negligence apologies 125
poisons 222
prescribing 225
privacy law 76
psychosurgery 241
retention of medical records 60
standard of care for professionals 105
Australian Code for the Responsible Conduct of Research 281–2
Australian Institute of Health and Welfare 28–9
Australian legal system 2, 21–2
    see also law
Australian legislation website 7, 19
Australian Medical Association *Code of Ethics* 66
Australian Pharmaceutical Advisory Council (APAC) 218
Australian Register of Therapeutic Goods (ARTG) 218
authority of parent or guardian 163–4
    see also consent from child/minor; intellectual impairment and consent legislation
autonomy 144–5, 166, 188

battery 146
    see also consent; trespass to the person
Bills 4–6
birth certificates 58
breach of confidentiality 69–71
    disciplinary action 71–2
    exceptions to obligations 72–4
    see also privacy and confidentiality
breach of duty of care 100–1
    see also duty of care; negligence litigation elements
British law 2, 10

CAM *see* complimentary and alternative medicine
cancer registration 29
case references 16–17
catchwords in law reports 17

11140988R00198

Printed in Germany
by Amazon Distribution
GmbH, Leipzig